#100for1

#100for1

A SHOESHINING EXPERIENCE

J. L. ADAMS

authorHOUSE®

AuthorHouse™ LLC
1663 Liberty Drive
Bloomington, IN 47403
www.authorhouse.com
Phone: 1-800-839-8640

Published by AuthorHouse   08/16/2013

ISBN: 978-1-4918-0922-8 (sc)
ISBN: 978-1-4918-0921-1 (hc)
ISBN: 978-1-4918-0920-4 (e)

Library of Congress Control Number: 2013914716

100 ANSWERS FOR THE 1 QUESTION

WILL YOU MARRY ME?
BY. JL. ADAMS

ACKNOWLEDGEMENT

FIRST, I WOULD like to thank God for the health and strength that he's blessed me with throughout my life, especially while I was doing this project.

Next, I would like to thank my parents for all that they've done for me, especially my angel mother for those little prayers that she would say for me and my other siblings on a daily basis.

I would also like to give a heartwarming thanks to the entire aShine&Co management team, especially Kevin Touhy and Kealani Lada for giving me a chance to follow my dreams and be me.

Thanks to Joseph Johnson for believing in this project and all of the advice he has given to me throughout the time that we've known each other.

Thanks to all of my friends and co-workers for keeping me level-headed while being at work. I really appreciate you guys, and lastly to everyone who has contributed to this project, in one way or the other, Thank You.

"All that I am, or hope to be, I owe to my angel mother"
—Abraham Lincoln

100For1

INTRODUCTION

I WAS BORN and raised in Georgetown, Guyana, a small country that's located in South America. Guyana is known throughout the world for its many natural resources and the infamous Jonestown tragedy that happened some decades back.

Growing up in Georgetown in an extended family—where 90% of my family members were females and mostly mothers—taught me a valuable life lesson: To honor family, and to never mistreat women, it also embedded the love that I have for kids today within heart, because whenever the female's in my family weren't in school studying they were on the hospital bed delivering another bundle of joy, which I would always love, since I loved taking the newborn for early morning walks, and seeing that priceless smile on their faces, which would always melt my heart.

For many years, I watched the women in my family raise their kids alone, and do whatever was necessary to ensure that we were always comfortable and well fed. Because of this, my perception of how romantic relationships and parenting worked was a bit skewed: The men would help to make the babies, but weren't there to help raise the babies, leaving the women to support the family.

Since there weren't any laws in Guyana that required fathers to pay child support, the men did whatever they wanted with whomever they wanted. As a victim of that kind of lifestyle myself, I find it a shameful disgrace to men everywhere. Was my mother the only the single parent? No, not by a long shot; my aunts, some of my cousins and even some of my friends' mothers were single parents. Around the age of seven, I assumed that being a single parent was a cultural norm, and that getting married and having a family were not necessarily a packaged deal. I still remember the first wedding reception that I ever went to.

At that time, it just seemed like a big party with close family and friends, all dressed up celebrating something called marriage. At seven years old, all I was interested in was playing with my cousins that I never saw outside of major family functions. Other than that, it was definitely all about eating and drinking endless sodas. I really didn't care much about, or understand the main point of the celebration.

I didn't recall hearing the words marriage or wedding again, until I was ten years old. I was in primary school and we were having our annual sporting event when I witnessed my teacher showing her blinged-out wedding ring to a classmate's mother. I heard her telling the parent how great it was to be married and how happy she was. After that, I was able to extract a more in-depth understanding about marriage and what it stands for by asking my older family members and teachers numerous questions about the topic, from both a cultural and a religious perspective. I recall my high school friend, Jennifer, who was just fourteen years old, one day telling us in class that she was quitting school because she was getting married. It seemed like a joke at first, especially when she said that she had never met her soon-to-be husband, only her parents had. I also recall my cousin getting married because she was pregnant, for the third time, and she told her new boyfriend that she was going to have an abortion if he didn't marry her. So they got married.

Cultural and religious beliefs played a major role in getting married back then, and they still do, even today. From arranged marriages, like what Jennifer's parents believed in, or getting married because of the kids, or because you're are in love, the question is always there: Will the marriage last? Sometimes they do, even if people stay together because they don't want to negatively affect their kids, or because they don't want to be a disgrace within their religion, which I think are valid reasons to put up with someone else's bullshit for the rest of your life. However, to some, "Until death do us part," seems to have no meaning.

Although I had knowledge of what marriage was about, I still had never experienced it myself. Was it really possible to understand marriage without getting married? Yes it was, and the experience became very possible, and very real, when I moved to America to live with my dad and his wife. My dad and his wife had two kids together, and had been with each other for almost two decades and very much in love the whole time. I've seen my dad and his wife argue plenty over the years that I'd lived with them, but they never allowed it to get out of control where they would even think to split up and throw their marriage down the drain. The thing I liked most about them was the fact that they always worked together, whether it was business, the kids, the house, or anything that would benefit either of them. They always put any issues that were between them aside and together dealt with whatever they had to deal with to get the best outcome. I thought that was very mature of them, and that's why I thought that marriage was a beautiful thing, not knowing there was a lot more to marriage than what I had observed between my dad and his wife.

And then it happened: I got my heart broken, or should I say I broke my own heart? After four sweet years of being in love with the person I thought was going to kiss me on that joyful day after saying "I Do," the person that I wanted to not only be my wife but also the mother of my children, the person that my mom fell in love with and also the person I wanted to die loving, broke up with me. It was so painful, and I had no clue on how to deal with it since this was my first time in such a situation. How was this possible? How could everything just go down the drain like a piece of waste; weren't we in love with each other? Didn't we had lifelong plans with each other?

I always tried my best to keep her happy whether it was financially, emotionally or sexually. Although I was verbally abusive to her at times, my actions would always reassured her of my love. Yet, though I was in love with her, I had been cheating on her constantly for the past four years, did she find out? Even though, I cheated, I was never unfaithful to what we shared, I was still going to fulfill all the promises that I had made to her. I was going to marry her and not only make her the mother of my two kids, but also my lifelong soul mate whom I was going to die loving, and would have died for. Was I wrong for exploring my sexual curiosities, although I was never going to allow my emotions to get involved?

Was this really happening? Did she really mean what she said about leaving me if I didn't find a better job after I graduated college? My shoe-shining gig embarrassed her around her friends, she complained to me numerous times. How could someone not want to be with you because you caught them lying? The cause of this particular problem wasn't my fault it was hers, she's was the one who got caught lying, so why does she want to leave me? Why? Questions upon questions raced through my head. Suicidal thoughts, moving away, isolating myself form the outside world. I took a vacation and isolated myself but it did not help; the memories kept rushing through my mind every second of every day. What was next?

She clearly stated that she didn't want to work out our problems even when I was at my worst: begging like a dog and making proposals on what I will do different this time around. I even asked her to marry me, but she kept saying she's over us. Why was she acting like this, how could she be so ungrateful to what we had, why is she acting as if we're at that age where we can't correct our mistakes? Damn, we're still in our early 20's, so what now? Should I do the unthinkable? Could I do it?

What was going to be the headlines in tomorrow's newspaper? "Man commits suicide after his girlfriend of four years decided that she was tired of his ass and was moving on with her life without him" What would Greg, Ian and Jermaine think of me when they received the news? Would they still consider me as a loyal friend? How would Lashaun, Ahkeem and Nikkel have felt, would they be disappointed in their older brother? Would anybody have try to see that it's only "Who feels it, knows it" I would have definitely broke not only my families' or friends' hearts, but the heart of my angel mother. But I wasn't selfish enough to commit suicide and besides, she wasn't worth it. I thought to myself, anyone who is willing to give up on you shouldn't even be in your life in the first place.

I remember praying every day about getting over her; I remembered talking to my friends in our group chat with tears in my eyes about the situation. Thank God I have supportive friends who never judged me but always try to cheer me up on my down days, I also remember talking to my mom on the phone while crying like a little baby for many nights, trying to get comfort, trying to find answers, trying to get over this miserable feeling since the bar wasn't helping. While the bottles of vodka I drank on a daily basis would put me to sleep at night, it made me sick the next day, which was bad for work. Instead of looking for customers to give them a shoeshine, I would be at the back sleeping or in the bathroom vomiting and therefore I'd lose a lot of money.

I have been a Shoe Shiner for over sixteen months. I really love my job for numerous reasons. I get to take home cash every day, manage myself, and meet different people from all over the world, including celebrities, on a daily basis being located in a very diverse terminal in JFK. Most of all, I loved the knowledge I took home every day from my one-on-one conversations with my customers; it was priceless, as 97% of my customers were successful people. That opportunity came as a gift and as a curse, a curse because a lot of times I would see families travelling together all jolly and having fun, looking like they were the happiest people in the world. That would always hurt me, since that was the kind of life I wanted but didn't have, but as a strong believer of faith, I didn't think it was never going to happen. So, I began to prepare myself for my next relationship.

I did not want to make the same mistakes that I had made in the previous one, whether it's cheating, lying, arguing etc. I was going to do whatever it took to make my next girlfriend the luckiest girl in the world and that was to make full use of my gift as a shoe shiner to get the necessary knowledge that I needed, from people who had years of experience about love, marriage and relationships. I began asking my customers numerous questions about those topics and would always get fascinating answers, which unfortunately I used to forget at the end of my shift, so I decided that I was going to get a pen and a pad, and every time I would finish talking to a customer, I would quickly scribble down the important ideas that they would tell me. The advice that I got on a daily basis certainly helped me in many ways to move forward and try to love again. One day I was talking to a customer about my situation and all the crazy stuff that people say about marriages and relationships and she said "You should write a book and share some of your knowledge with the world," and that's how I came up with the idea to write: *One Hundred Answers For The One Question, Will You Marry Me?*

P.S. I'm just the messenger

God-First **Mentality** Responsibilities *r*

b Appreciates Willing
feeling grief **Fulltime-Job** *r*
e
d **Attention** GIVE&TAKE Patience *g*
r sensitivity The-One upsides **ring** *r*
o **Time** HONESTY *e*
o ACCEPT
m ILoveYou **strength** **ENDURE** *t*
happy **decision**

Stability Leverage successful COMMITMENT
k **100%Sure** Positive sense-of-humor
i s
d **foundation** t **Identify** Serious-Step Faith
s
choice r DISTRACTION *opportunity* Team
s e complicated
Fights *formula* s **Believe**
t
a **Pregnants** **Covenant** *Big-reward*
g **Communication** *Effort*
e **religion** **Sacrifice** Longterm-Goals Spirit **SEX**

peace parameters Benefits *Family*
Listens attitude **respect**
Belief **Do-More** preference
Dedication ACCOMPLISH relationship Aware
Institution *Cheating* compromise
Think *Courting*
Kind good-life **Partnership** Honeymoon
problems Boredom **Good&Bad** Divorce
expectations compassionate *Ready* Constant-Work **CULTURE**
beautiful personality *apologize* tolerance
Headaches Choose-your-battles Hard&Painful Fix-It
bestfriends
companionship **WantsvsNeeds**

IDENTIFY

"I'LL GIVE YOU the bulletproof, ok?" I said as I folded up my polishing cloth. "Where you heading to?" I asked the gentleman that climbed into my shoeshine chair. Since I was one of the resident shoe shiners in JFK international Airport at terminal 5, I loved hearing what far-off destinations my customers were traveling to.

"Dominican Republic." He answered.

"Dominican Republic? You live there?" I asked him with noted impression.

"No, going to visit my mother. She's kind of ill," He replied.

"Are you traveling alone?" I asked next, as I began to clean his shoes.

His quick response was, "Yes."

"So where's your family?" I asked.

He hesitated a bit and stammered the first words of his sentence, "Ah my, um, my two brothers and my nephews; they're on another flight."

"What about the wife, and kids?" I smiled and said.

"Don't have a wife," he said, as he relaxed into the chair.

"You don't have a wife?" I was shocked by my own boldness.

"Divorce." He replied matter-of-factly.

"Why? Marriage is a beautiful thing." I proclaimed.

"Oh you know, shit happens so . . ." He trailed off as if the answer were universal and didn't need to be spoken, then concluded, "Shit happens."

1

"Damn man. How long were you married for?" I asked him.

"Thirty years," he said, this time glancing down the terminal as if his ex were nearby. Then he continued, "Then I remarried somebody else; that lasted for four years. Now, I'm single. It's not 'til death do you part,' it's 'til someone starts doing something wrong,' then it's 'Fuck you and I'm out.'"

I laughed at his honesty, then asked, "What do you do for thirty years to make it last, like, what do you do?"

"Nothing, you just ignore the shit outta them." He advised me as I laughed more robustly and questioned him, "To make it last?"

He chuckled too, and then added, "It's like with anything else in life, my dude."

"Pardon?" I wanted to know exactly what he meant.

"It's like with anything else in life: If you start paying too much attention to everything that's going on around you, you go fucking crazy. So you just got to look at it, observe and respect it, and keep it moving."

"Keep it moving?" I couldn't tell if this was the reason or the goal.

"Because you know, you aren't here for eternity, that's bullshit," he added, as I agreed with him. He then went on to say, "So you make the best of it, you learn, you identify yourself, and you live. I don't bother you; you don't bother me. If you fuck with me, all hell is going to break loose."

I nodded my head in agreement, still chuckling. "So are you still friends with your ex-wives?"

"Yeah." He smiled and responded.

"It's a better relationship now?" I went on to ask, as I applied the last layer of polish to his shoes.

"Yea, I go out with them, I take, well, with the kids. I take them out . . . I go out with them and the kids when there's a special occasion and stuff like that. It's a little bit better, not impossible."

"Oh, okay. That's nice." I commended him as I buffed his worn shoes.

"And my last wife, we have a good relationship. We go out, we talk on the phone, and it's like a good friendship with like no problems."

I then smiled and said, "I think marriage is a beautiful thing."

"It is, it is, but you have to, you know, the thing is, if you're doing good, and you got a job and everybody is working, everybody is making money, you know, everybody is happy, no problem, somebody doesn't start working and staying home and stuff like that, soon they start with the shit and trust me . . ." He trailed off like the end to this sentence was apparent.

"So that's one of the major problems, huh?" I asked.

"Money. They'll stay with you while they can use you and then after that's gone . . . You get married, this is my motto: You get married hoping that your wife never changes and she gets married hoping that she can change you into the man she wants."

"Wow," I am somewhat speechless, never having heard that theory before.

"Analyze it, and tell me it's not true. First of all, they eliminate your friends." He said.

"Yup!" I agree, more to keep him on his roll.

He continues, "That's gone. You used to go out, that's gone. You used to go out whenever you felt like it, but no more. So, what is the deal, are you married for love or are you married for changes? What the fuck?"

"I know, that makes sense," I nod.

"I'm not saying it's a bad thing, but some of us needs some, some wisdom." He advise me, as I smile and say, "Yeah."

He shakes his pant legs down and changes the subject; "I almost didn't make it today. My brother had, luckily I gave the keys to my brothers and they got into my house and woke me up. Otherwise, I would a still be sleeping."

"How long are you going to be out there?" I looked up at him and asked.

"Till Friday morning." He said.

"Well, I hope that your mom gets better." I said as I gave him the thumbs up signaling that he is all polished and ready to settle up.

"Yeah, we're going to keep her out there for at least three months and see what happens after that." He said, then looked down at his shoes and said, "That's very good, looks great," as he reached into his pocket for his wallet.

3

"Thank you, thank you for the business." I tell him as he pays me.

Before walking off he said, "Be very observant with their behavior and any sudden changes."

READY

I HAD A bad habit, a really bad one, whenever I would work the morning shift which started at 6 am and finished at 1:30 pm. I really don't know how it happened, but I would never, ever come into work with the intention of going right to work, meaning that if a customer was already at the stand waiting for me to open to get a shine, I would be kind of upset at that customer. I would never show it, but it meant that I didn't get a chance to take my morning stroll across the terminal to get my morning treats, which were mints, a newspaper, hot chocolate or oatmeal. I also liked to go to the restroom to make sure my face was OK and my hair was looking good. Only after doing all of that was I ready to begin my day.

"You need a couple more minutes?" My next customer asked me as I was setting up the stand that morning, while listening to music from my cellphone.

"Yeah, just give me two more minutes," I replied, as I continued to take out my supplies. I then took out the cushions for the chairs, placed them on it and offered him to take a seat.

"Thank you," he said as he climbed the stand and got seated. I then placed the footrest up and immediately attended to him.

"Which of our shines would you like to have?" I asked as I stood and looked up at him.

"Oh, I'll just take the basic" was his response as I nodded my head and began to wrap the balm rag around my wrist and began cleaning his shoes.

"Can you do a quick one? My flights leaves in less than ten minutes." He requested.

"Of course, we're going to be finished way before that" I assured him, as I began to brush the balm off of his shoes. "Where are you heading today?"

"Ah, DC," he replied.

"You live there?"

"No I go there every week for business, I live right here in New York" he added, then went on to asked, "What about you?"

"I'm from Guyana, but I moved here four years ago," I replied, as I began to clean the soles of his shoes. "How long are you going to be out in DC?"

"Just a week. I go out there every week and come back on Thursdays and spend the weekends here," he stated.

"Oh that's not so bad," I assured him, as I looked up at him then asked, "Are you married?"

He then began to laugh and then said, "No," as he continued laughing.

"Why are you laughing? What's funny?" I asked him since I clearly didn't get the joke.

He continued to laugh and said, "I'm not ready for marriage yet."

We both laughed aloud. I really didn't know why he was laughing, but I thought that it was funny that he said he wasn't ready for marriage and looked as if he was in his late forties, so I kept the questions rolling, asking, "Did you have a bad experience?"

"No, but ah, you know, just not ready, got to find that right person first," he said as he quickly glanced at his watch.

"Do you think marriage has the same value that it had twenty, thirty years ago?"

"Society wise, no. I guess for me it does," he stated.

"Ok, why is that?" I then asked, since I wanted him to be more specific.

"My grandparents were married since they were seventeen or eighteen, something like that, and now they're like seventy-something, and they've never lost love for each other."

"Ok, did they argue a lot?" I quickly asked him.

"They might have," he said, then added, "I stayed with them a lot, but you know what, my parents never saw them arguing and neither did I."

"Ok, so therefore you would get married?" I asked him with a smirk on my face.

"I would do it, if I find the right person, but ah, I haven't found the right person. If she came in my life right now, I still would have to think about it, and I do envy my grandfather for finding that right person, you know, 'because I have a friend who's been with his girl for like, ah, seven years. Since in college and he still loves her like he met her yesterday, so you know, if you find somebody like that, It's definitely worth it for you, but I haven't found that person for me. "How about yourself, are you married?"

I continued to brush the polish into his shoes and said, "No I'm not married, but I just like to hear what people have to say about marriage, because it's something that I'm thinking about."

He then smiled and said "Man, I feel if it's the right person, you should do it."

"Yeah but, you know, I meet a lot of people every day and the stuff most people say about marriage . . . like at first it can seem like it's the right person, or it could even seem like it's not the right person and then 10 years after being married it could be the right person. Different people, different opinions."

"I hear you. Well, I guess the problem is you've got to meet the right person," he said.

"Yeah, but the big question is: How do you know if it's the right person because people change over time?"

"Ah, you got to go out there and search, but I think the right person will come along when the time is right. But, maybe when she does come along, you won't be ready yet," he said, then added, "then that's another story," We both laughed aloud.

"Life is unfair" I joked as we continued to laugh.

"Yes it is." He agreed.

"Thank you," I said to him after giving him the thumbs up, signaling that his shine was completed.

"Enjoy. What's your name?" he asked as he stepped down from the stand and paid me.

"It's Lancelot" I responded.

"I'm Jamie. Nice meeting you."

"Nice meeting you, too" I replied, as he took off.

3

COMMUNICATION

"How are you today?" my new customer greeted me, as she interrupts me from reading my newspaper.

"I'm good, how are you?"

"Good."

"Okay, how much time do you have?" I asked her.

"I only have about fifteen minutes."

"Oh, we're going to be finished long before that. Where are you heading to today?" I asked, to get the ball rolling.

"Back home to St. Marten," she said with a broad smile on her face, I then asked her to place her feet on the footrest.

"Oh, sorry," she said, as she put her boots onto the footrest.

"That's alright." I reassured her, then went right into asking her, "Could I ask you a question?"

As she smiled, she said, "Sure, why not?"

I asked her, "What is your take on marriage?"

"Ah." she said suspiciously.

"Like getting married and staying married. I'm try to get some information about marriage. Are you married, by the way?"

"No I am not. I have a boyfriend and we have two children together. A wedding is very expensive. Plus, my sister just got married over the summer and they're already having issues. So I think things were best, and they were happier, before they got married."

"Damn," I said, surprised.

"My boyfriend and I talked about it, and the only reason that it would be of any benefit to us, is that if he got sick or something like that, I would be able to make decisions, but other than that . . . and the divorce rate is so high." She stared me in the eyes.

"Yeah, it makes you think, right?" I replied immediately.

"Yeah, all that planning and money. Why, are you planning on getting engaged?" She asked.

"No, but I think marriage is a beautiful thing, and I want to take it seriously. I want to know what I'm getting into," I said as I stopped polishing her shoes and looked up at her.

"But I think, you know what? I think that a lot of people don't think about it. They just do it, even though they say these things to the person in front of all these people that are there, witnessing."

"Yeah, in front of a church and all of that, that's what I'm saying. I'm not going to go in front of an altar, in front of a priest and say, "Till death do us part" and then make a mistake, and then you're going to want to leave me and all that. I want to take it seriously," I assured her.

"Yeah, because a lot of people just want a big party," she quipped, as we both laughed.

"They do."

"A big reception."

"Hmm-hmm." She murmured and we laughed some more.

"Instead of actually thinking about what it means, my sister, who lives in Indiana, she called my house this Sunday and she's like 'Maybe I should just get a divorce,' and I'm like, 'Simone, you guys just got married, you said these things, this is for life.'"

"For life, till death do we part," I added.

"And she's thirty-eight years old and it's her first marriage, so that's why I'm like, yeah its hard work and that's part of it, and it's not easy. If It was easy, then people would have been married like they used to be; for fifty years."

I nodded.

"And you could move on like that." She continues.

"Yeah, that's the sad part of it, the divorce. It's even harder to get a divorce than it is to get married." I stated.

"Yeah, you have to decide if that's what you truly, truly want," she said.

"Yeah definitely." I agreed.

"No, I mean if that's what you truly want, then you're going to make sure when you say that, then you're not going to take—" Then she stopped and looked at me and said, "You even asking me this question means that you would do everything that you possibly could to make sure that it won't break up. There are inevitable things, but if you work on them on a daily basis, then it can work," she stated.

"So what is she saying is the problem, lack of communication or money? What is the problem?" I wanted to know.

"Yea, she's saying lack of communication. They're both very, very stubborn people . . ." she paused then said, "My brother-in-law called last night and he talked to my boyfriend and said that they both took off their wedding rings and this is the second time they've done it and they only got married in July. My boyfriend said to him, 'Listen, you could sit here and fight about it, and be bitter about who's right and who's wrong, or you could just be like, you know what, whoever was wrong doesn't matter and go apologize. Is it worth it to fight for another week about nonsense?'"

"I know, right," I say.

"So that was what he told them. They both were like, 'Well I'm not wrong and I'm not wrong, so I'm not apologizing.' Alright then, you know what? Continue to fight and be idiots. It's easier to apologize, suck it up, and be the bigger person." She said as she moved forward and nodded her head while raising her left hand.

"Yeah, that's true." I agree.

"And I've been the same as well, you know, when you think that you're right, and you're absolutely not," she said.

"Yeah." I agreed with her, as I began putting the final layer of polish on her shoes.

"These looks wonderful." She complimented my work.

"Yea, they were looking pretty rough, scuffed up pretty bad." I said to her, as I continued to work my hands.

"Do you think living together first, before getting married, would be a good idea?" I asked her very kindly.

"It depends on what your personal beliefs are." She nodded her head and removed her blonde hair from her face, then added, "If your religion says that that's not a good thing to do, yah know . . .

I on the other hand, I'm a completely optimistic person, so that's bull."

We chuckle.

She goes on, "So you definitely get to know somebody a little bit better, but you know what, way back in the days, when people like my grandparents didn't live together before they got married, well, they were married for fifty-five years. And the only reason that they aren't still married is that they both died." She said.

"What do you think?" I asked her, as I was done with her shine.

"Ah, I totally love it," she responded with a big smile on her face as she gazed down on her newly polished shoes.

"You could put the bags down, and then come down." I said to her while stretching my hands to assist her in coming down from the chair.

"Oh." She replied with a sense of surprise.

"And then come, no, I said you could leave the bags, and then come down, 'cause I down want you to fall." I helped her down from the shoeshine throne.

"That's cute," she said, as she took my right hand and came down.

"I'm Katy," she said and placed a ten-dollar bill into my hand.

"I'm Lancelot, nice to meet you Katy, thanks for the business—and the advice," I replied.

"You're welcome," she said as she picked up her bag and began walking towards the food court.

CHEATING

My next customer walked over to the stand as I was making change for a twenty dollar bill to give to my previous customer and said "I'll take a shine" before walking to the side of the stand and placing his bag on one of the chair, then taking a seat in the other one.

"Have a pleasant day," I said to that previous customer as he replied, "You do the same" before grabbing his pulley luggage and walking off. I then turned my attention quickly to the new customer that was already sitting in the chair waiting on me to attend to him.

"How much time do you have, and do you have to get any luggage?" I asked.

"I have all the time in the world. My ride is going to be 20 minutes late, and that's all the luggage I need for this trip" he added as he pointed to his bag that was on the other chair.

"So how's your day going so far?" I asked, as I began wrapping the balm cloth around my hand.

"Perfecto," my new customer replied.

"Did I do your shoes recently?" I asked, since his face look rather familiar.

"You did mine here, probably been a month already. Give me the glass."

"The glass? Ok." I began cleaning his shoes.

"I haven't done them since I got them, I bought these about a year ago and they haven't been polished at all; they need it."

13

"Yeah, they do." I agreed. His shoes were discolored and scuffed up badly.

"So how's the family?" I asked, to get to the marriage questions as soon as I can.

"Ain't seen the family in seven days, been traveling a lot," he said, as he began looking around the terminal.

"How does the family feel about that?"

"We been fighting a lot. Things are real tough when I get home." He frowned.

"But you guys still pull through it, right?" I asked, as I began to cut off the threads from his shoes that were loosening.

"Ah hope so. We were supposed to get married in February."

"Don't worry, it's going to happen, man. Marriage is a beautiful thing," I said as if I had been there and done that before.

"I been there three times bro; I know what it is."

"Three times?" I asked in disbelief.

"Yeah."

"Wow, what was the downfall of the first three?" I asked him as I began applying the first layer of polish to his brown shoes.

"The first two was, ah, immaturity on their side, and drinking." He replied with a very low tone.

"Ok, what about your side?"

"The last one, I was there."

"You were there?" I said as if I didn't understood what he meant, so that he could get more in details.

"Honestly, I was—" he continued to look around the terminal and then added—"drinking." First one was immaturity, second one was cheating and the third one was mental illness."

I stop brushing his shoes and looked up at him for about two seconds, then continued brushing.

"I'm just finalizing, that's all, been there for 15 years, she was bipolar as fuck!"

"What was the longest you've been married for?"

"Fifteen," he said, before adding, "Wait . . . can't be 15, sorry ah, this year is 18 years and we were only together for ten of them."

"What did you do for ten years, to keep the relationship going?"

"Ah when we were together, we would fight, fight, fight all the time, because there was alcohol and bipolar disorder involved. I was going to make sure it worked, even if I had to spend every cent. But the problem was emotionally and drug-related, so I'm real skeptical on this next one. She's a great lady and I got no complaints at all. She's more manly than I am half of the time, but her tomboy gets to her at times. I told her there's too much empathy on this side and not enough on your side." He said.

I laughed. "So you think this is the one?"

"Fucking better be. She's a good lady," he replied aggressively as he raised his left hand and looked at his watch.

"I like your style. You're a man of faith." I say.

"She's good. I got no complaints that I can't put up with and on my side, when I get drawn down on my work, because my work takes a lot from me, so when my works takes me down, I expect to come home and have her there to help me out, to give me comfort. Well she has her own thing going. Shit I'm gone for five, six, seven, days at a time and instead of sitting there and waiting on me, she goes doing her own thing, that's good." He said this in a way as if he was trying to get me to agree with him, so I nodded my head, as I continued to add polish to his shoes.

He then added, "But when I come home I expect her to drop what she's doing and make me the number one point, sometimes that works and sometimes it doesn't, but she's trying and that's all I can say. I'm not saying I'm any fricking pro at it, ah, mean, it's . . ." He trails off and continues, "Finding the right person is a great thing; finding that person you can settle down with, be happy with, be comfortable in your own skin with."

"Be yourself with," I added.

"Be bored with, because when that, in my opinion, when you get married, that's when the boredom starts and you got to be comfortable with that person." He said chuckling.

"Yes." I agree.

"I fucking hate it," he adds.

"Yeah." I said as I nod, since I didn't wanted to add anything to interrupt him.

"I don't want to be bored, I don't want to be complacent, I don't want to be, not in a negative way, but I don't want to be taken for granted. I don't want you to take for granted that I'm here every fricking day of the week, because at that point I'm no longer important." He then trails off again, this time saying, "I love traveling with this airline, I'm one of their top travelers, literally one of their top travelers. I've traveled as much as the pilots do."

"Wow." I replied in shock, since I wasn't sure if that was possible, but didn't question his statement

"How's business?" he asks me.

"It's been going good yah know, the busy season is about to start. The summertime is the drought, with everybody wearing flip-flops and sneakers."

"Kind of hard to polish, toe nails?" he said, and we both laughed.

"It's getting there though, no complaints man. It's going to be better a few weeks from now."

"Yeah when the weather gets cold." He added

"There, good man, what do you think?" I asked him as I was done with his shine.

"They're good for me. Give me eight back." He said as he placed a twenty-dollar bill into my hand before climbing down from the chair.

"Thanks for the business and good luck man." I said to him as I gave him back his change. He then took off.

5

COMPANIONSHIP

"He DEFINITELY NEEDS a shine," I said to myself as I noticed this Asian guy that was walking towards the stand with what seemed to be his wife and his daughter, all the while looking down to his shoe and then looking at me. I didn't wait for him to ask for a shine, after he looked at the stand once more and then looked at his shoes again.

I approached him, "How about a shine sir?" I asked.

"Do you have clear?"

"Yea of course, we have Neutral."

"Hun, I'm going to get a shine, my shoes are looking dirty," he said to the woman that he was with as he looked at the sign and requested a basic shine.

"Ok, just meet us at the gate," she responded as she and the young girl walked off.

"Ok" he said.

"Very well, have a seat," I urged him.

"Thank you" he replied, as he got seated and immediately looked to see what I was doing. I wasted no time with the questions since his attention was on me.

"Is that your wife?" I asked.

"Yeah, my wife, and my daughter." He replied.

"How long you guys been married?"

"Twenty years, you believe it?" He asked me with a smirk on his face?

"I believe it." I chuckled. "I just would've never guessed twenty years."

"A long time, yeah, it's a long time yeah," he repeated as he fixed his shoes on the foot rest.

I then went on with the questions asking him if it's true that you can wake up and just get bored of marriage. "Is that possible?"

"Nah, always exciting, always exciting." He repeated himself again.

"What do you do to keep it always exciting?"

"Tennis," he quickly replied as he held up the tennis racket that was in his hand.

"Tennis?" I asked, as I raised my eyebrow.

"And support her." He added as we both laugh aloud.

"What would you say is the best thing about marriage?"

"The best thing about marriage is companionship, someone to be with. You're not married?"

"No, but I'm, I'm actually thinking about it, so I always try to get as much information as possible on marriage and relationships."

"Yeah . . . go for it." He gives me the green light, and then asks, "How long have you been going out with your girl?"

"I'm single right now, I just got out of a four-year relationship, but I definitely would like to get married one day."

"How old are you?"

"I'm twenty-six years old."

"You're ready!" he assured me and smiled.

I stopped brushing his shoes as if I was shocked at what he said then repeated, "I'm ready?"

"You're ready!" he said once more, this time nodding his head twice.

"But do people really change after getting married? A lot my customers say people change."

"You got to adapt, you got to adapt, nobody, nobody is very similar, so you got to adapt, and I tell my daughter that, you got to adapt. No person is a perfectionist, right?"

"Ok yeah, that's true because everybody wants perfection." I agreed with him, as I fixed his feet on the footrest, since he clearly had a problem with keeping his feet on it.

"It's very difficult to find perfection, very difficult, a lot of younger people are trying to find perfection now. It doesn't matter, you got to adapt, you got to adapt."

I began to buff his shoes off. "You're good." I tell him, signaling the end of his shine.

"Thank you." He said as he reached into his pocket and took out his wallet to pay.

"Thank you, man" I reply, as he climbs down.

6

AWARE

"HOW ABOUT A shine, sir?" I asked a passenger that passed my stand for the fourth time, who seemed rather loss or as if he had time to kill, since he was basically walking around the terminal for the past hour or so.

"No" he quickly replied as he continued to walk slowly, before stopping and looking down at his shoes, then looked back at me and asked, "You can do these, it's skin?" as if he wanted me to say no.

"Of course I can clean exotic leather," I quickly replied.

"You sure?"

"Yeah" I replied, as I nod my head.

"What the heck, let's do it," he said as he walked towards the stand and took a seat.

"Which of the shines would you like to have?"

"What are my options? Oh, it's right there" he said as he stared at the sign. "I'll just take the glass"

"The glass it is, then" I replied.

"Thank you."

I began cleaning his shoes with the leather balm as he got more comfortable in the chair.

"You traveling alone?"

"Yeah." He smiled and give me two thumbs up.

"What was that about?" I asked.

"That's the best way to travel," he said.

"You married?" I then asked, as I applied the first layer of polish to his shoes.

20

"Oh God man, I've been married. First time, twenty years; second time, eight years," he said, shaking his head while smiling.

"You said, 'Oh God,'" was my reply, as I was shocked at his answer, which was as if he were tired of marriage.

"I'm a lifer, buddy." We both laughed then he continued, "You haven't gone down that path yet?"

"Nah, that's what I'm actually thinking about, that's why, yah know, I tend to ask everybody their take on marriage."

"My advice? Skip it, skip all the stressing." He laughed again.

"Skip it?"

"Yeah." He replied rather boldly this time.

"Why?" I asked.

"Life. It's better if you're with them or even living with them, which is really the same. The only difference with marriage is you throw a big party and then there's a wedding. You could still throw a big party without getting married, and then not have to worry about filling out the paperwork of divorce down the line if something goes wrong."

"So what's—ok, there must be some good to it—what's was the best part about being married? You said twenty years the first time and eight the second time."

"Oh I love my wife. She's a great person and all that, and I would if she hadn't been my wife . . . let me explain. Other people have feelings about marriage, and I don't have any feelings about it, and in that situation I don't. But if you like a person, you just do what needs to be done. But let me tell you something, who needs marriage if you got love?"

"That's true, yeah, and that makes a lot of sense. So what did you do for that twenty years, man? What did you do to make it last for twenty years?"

"We were just good friends, that's how it was at the beginning. We were really good friends and we had a lot of really good times together. I'm still very, very close to her, she lives like half a block away, good person."

"And you guys have a better relationship now?"

"No, no, we had a really good time together, but it's kind of the marriage part that wore out."

"Things got boring?" I asked.

"It's just a certain kind of trouble, it was hard to straighten it out, and it didn't have anything to do with the people or anything like that." He said as he fixed his arms on the armrest and I continued working on his shoes.

I then moved on to another question, "Ok, what would you say is like the number one problem within marriage?"

"With marriage? Dealing with your own shit."

"Dealing with your own shit?" I repeated, as I wanted to be clear of what he really meant.

"Yeah, not dealing with your own shit, trying to make the other person deal with it, instead of you dealing with it," he clarified.

"Trying to be dependent?"

"Being unconscious and stupid you know what I mean. So are you thinking about getting married?" He flipped the questioning on me.

"I'm thinking about getting engaged, but everybody keeps saying like people always change, that after you say "I do," it's a different ball game."

"Well that's one reason, why you shouldn't have to say "I do." That means you got to say "I do" every day."

"Yeah," I nod, as we both began to laugh.

"You live with this woman?"

"Nah, there's no woman, I'm single right now. I just got out of a four-year relationship."

"Ah man sorry to hear that. My advice to you is, don't do anything until you've live with her for a couple of years. Seriously, if I were to give you any advice, that's what I would tell you. Don't marry anybody until you've live with them for at least two years, because you're going to know by then. I don't care what anybody says, not your mother, your father, your friends or her. Live with them first, so you'll know what you're in for, so you'll know if you can handle it or if you want it. There's no other way to live . . . to get married to get an interesting life, knowing you have to have kids to have an interesting life, I mean, people have really narrow ideas of what you can do. Anyway, I have tire tracks on my back, so you might want to take anything I say with the grain of salt." He said as we both laughed aloud again.

I asked him about his second marriage.

"Oh that's great, that's still going on, it's great fun. He smiled.

"What are you doing differently this time?"

"What am I doing differently now? I'm a lot more aware of my own stuff. I don't bring it into the relationship, or I try not to. Plus I'm older and it's just like a slow slide downward from here on," he said. "So I mean, you know, you may as well settle in for the short hall, for the sake of the marriage, anyways. I don't have any advice except—the only advice I really have for you—is live with her, live with her for a couple of years, cause that will make a difference. I don't know if she's into that, but then again if she's willing to get married, I'm guessing, she would do anything, whatever it takes," he advised me.

I began to buff his shoes, and as I was finishing them up, he said, "If you give it two years and you guys are still together and it feels like being around that person is restful, go for it, if being around that person makes you feel at ease, you don't feel stressed, you don't feel like you have any problems, and she's not high maintenance—you don't want high maintenance." He smiled.

"No high maintenance?"

He then laughed and added, "No you don't want that; it drives you fucking crazy after a while. Thanks, man."

"Thank you, thanks for the advice and the business." I said to him as he climbed down from the chair.

"No problem bro, just take your time," he advised me.

"I will."

"There you go," he said as he paid me.

"It's always better to get advice from people who've been there." I said to him.

"Yeah, but sometimes people who've been there and done that don't know shit," he replied.

We both laughed, and he took off as I continued to laugh.

DIVORCE

My next customer approached the stand as I was in the cabinet setting up the deposit that Monday morning. He was wearing red corduroy jeans, a blue button-down shirt and a green blazer, and on his feet were discolored brown loafers, with no socks.

"Can I have a shine?" he said as he stood in front of the stand.

"Yes, of course. Take a seat. I'll be right with you," I said quickly before closing up the cabinet and going over to him.

"The glass shine please," he requested, sat, and placed his feet on the footrest.

"The glass it is," I responded as I began to clean his shoes. "This is good leather." I complimented him.

"Thank you. I've had them for over six years, got them resoled maybe once or twice and it's still keeping up with me."

Since he didn't reply with a one-word answer, I took that as sign to hit him with a question.

"Are you traveling alone?" I asked as I brushed the balm off of his shoes.

"Yeah," he replied in a very low tone.

"You left the family at home?"

"No family anymore. I'm divorced," he replied, before turning his attention to rest of the terminal, as if he was not interested in my questions.

Even though it seemed as if he was not interested, I didn't stop there because he seemed as if he had an interesting story to tell and I was determined to hear it, so I went on to my other question, "How long were you married?"

"I was only married for about three-and-a-half years," he stated.

"Was it a bad or a good experience?"

"There's no one way of looking at that. Bad or good? Both, because you always take good out of something, you just have to understand what, you know what I'm saying? Whatever it is I get out of it makes whatever in the future better because I have learned a lot from it. I stayed and raised my stepson from three to ten years old. I raised a kid, I got to be a father for seven years, and that was priceless, since I can't make children of my own."

"Damn, sorry to hear," were the only words I could think of, and thought were necessary at that point of the conversation.

"Overall, I would do it again. You learn a lot from it," he added, but this time with a smile on his face.

"You said you would do it again."

"I think I would do it again, with the right person." he clarified.

"So tell me something, how do you know if it's the right person?" I asked him as I stopped brushing his shoes and looked up at him.

"I don't really know, because it's not like I got married thinking I was going to get a divorce or she really wasn't the right person. I think if you go through enough experiences together, you know. Know what I mean? The more you experience in life, the better you become with anything."

"With the person or experience in general?" I asked.

"Experience in life, but yeah definitely with experience in different relationships, because eventually you become smarter with it. And, you've really got to figure out what you want, because we don't always know what we want; we try to figure it out as we go."

"You're right," I nod and agree with him.

He then continued, "But after you find what you don't want now, you feel kind of like, you know what you want. I think if you meet that person, you wonder if this is happiness. You hope though! I mean a lot of people were married three, four times more than me," he said as he laughed out loud and nodded his head, then added, "I think some people do it as a hobby. Here's what I would say; I would do it one more time, and I would not do it after that."

"So how long had you guys been together before you decided to get married?"

"Probably four years, but she'd already been married before, so for me it was my first." He looked down at his shoes, then went on to say "When I was thirty-five years old, it seemed older, so to me, I might have been settling in a way. As you get older, you look to make decisions differently, so that's what happened. Like I said, she was already married, she got married again already . . . her third marriage and she's only thirty-three years old. That really sucks."

"Wow, she's doing it as a hobby?" I asked, amazed of what he had said.

"Who knows, might be, I'll ask her. I get all the phone calls, I don't know why, but every time there's a problem, I get the call, every time she needs a friend, I get the call. It's kind of funny now," he said as we both laughed out loud, nodding our heads.

"And do you guys have a better relationship now that you're not married?"

"Yes, she can't argue with me anymore, and I'm glad she's someone else's problem and not mine, so that's one way of looking at it," he replied with a little smirk on his face.

"But starting over must be crazy, man?" I asked, and then added, "Like if you were to do it again, with all the same steps, what would you do differently to make it work?"

"Well, I'd definitely take more of the blame. Everybody tells me from the outside you listen to your friends, you listen to your family, and even her family. I don't think it would work no matter what I did, and I don't know because I won't know, unless I would've done it, but I think It would've been tough anyway. I don't think she knew what she was doing, but I think she's still growing up trying to figure it all out, of course she's doing it marriage to marriage looking. If I had to do it again, I probably would have not let a lot of life's problem or stresses affects the time I put into the relationship, like I work too many long hours and this and that, I should have been a little bit more—"

"Lenient to her?" I interrupted.

"I was very lenient, maybe that was the problem. I would give her anything. I'd give, give, and give. I should have been a little bit more strict and more focused on trying to build the relationship into something, for all that there was, but like I said, I don't know if that would have worked. But that's what I would do next time around, you know what I mean, like I would definitely . . . hey listen, if you get into a relationship it's compromise, any relationship, it's compromise. You have to work together. Relationships are tough, even if you have a great one. It's very tough, and the only way it becomes a great one is if you work at it."

"Yeah, you definitely got to work at it."

"Right. I think there's a lot of lessons with it. What about you? No marriages, huh?" he asked with a smile on his face.

"Not yet, but that's why I'm asking you these questions, I'm actually interested in getting married sometime, but not now."

"How old are you?"

"I'm twenty-five years old." I said as I began to buff his right shoe, getting ready to finish with his shine.

"Well you're still on the young side, so just take your time. Don't rush it," he advised me.

"Is there anything you should look for to know if that person is the right person?" I then asked, as I moved to buff his left shoe.

"I think you know what, I think there is. It depends, but you don't always see it right away, so I think several things happen. Either one of you is not in it, and whether it's an argument or whether if someone strays away . . . Sometimes people find out that, sometimes a man or a woman realizes that the person was the one, after they kind of strayed away a little bit. Everybody thinks experience is freedom, all humans do, you know. Few of us figure it out earlier than others, you know what I mean, we find out the grass isn't greener on the other side, it just uses a different border, you know what I mean?"

"Yeah" I said as I picked up the toothbrush and began cleaning the crease of his shoe sole, although I was finish with his shine. Since I had no customers waiting and his conversation was interesting, I figured I'd just stall him and chat a little more, so that's what I did.

He then added, "To me, today marriage has become something like, marriage has become more like a thing to do. It doesn't really hold up the same value it used to, and it's sad. Maybe it's old school that way, but the problem is people getting into it. A lot of people do it because of the fact that they could just get out if it doesn't work out. But I think there are different ways. I think it's what you make of it; I think it's the conversations you have in a relationship," he stated as he moved forward and said "Hey listen, the number one thing is communication, over anything and about all things, because without that, everything goes to waste and everything becomes a matter of opinion, rather than actually talking about it. I think communication makes a difference. Because I was a communicator and she wasn't, it really made a difference, so a lot of nights I had to sleep on the couch." He joked and we both laughed. He then continued, "Yeah and sometimes you know when it's just the feelings, that when you ask yourself, can you be without that person for the rest of your life? Sometimes you don't know, if you don't know your own life. A lot of mistakes people make happen because they don't straighten themselves out first. If you're not happy with yourself and you're not at a certain place in your own life, it's going to be very difficult for you to stay in any relationship. I don't care what anybody says."

"Yeah," I said as I nodded and began wiping his shoes with the buff rag.

"So I've seen people go ten years and it looks like they're going to be doomed for disaster, and then boom, they stayed long enough together to make it happen, and it happened."

"It starts to work after ten years?" I asked, in shock.

"Yes. I mean, there's no rum and raisin when you get into it, but I'll give this advice to anybody who really wants to get married: Whether you think about marriage, or you think about, oh, communication is so important, find out about that person inside and out. Have a lot of conversations, get to know them. You should hope to determine one of two things: one is if you're going in different directions; two, is if you guys are matching more and more. Go out and eat dinner with them. People learn things about each other and realize what they can put up with later."

I laughed and told him that his shining was completed. He quickly reached into his pocket and gave me a twenty dollar bill and said, "Keep the change; they look brand new," then concluded by saying "I notice, I should've communicated more with my wife; she had me fooled, with the woman she was. It's all a matter of time, communication is the key. With true communication you can see it all and take your time and think about it. Thanks for the shine."

He then climbed down out of the chair and walked away, as I said "Your welcome and thank you" to him.

8

FOUNDATION

"THANKS FOR YOU patients man." Was how I greeted my next customer, who was sitting in my chair waiting for me, since I had took a bathroom break.

"No worries, its fine," he quickly responded,

"Which of the shines you would like to have?" I asked

"Basic shine" he said, as I raised his feet and place them on the footrest,

I immediately began wrapping the balm cloth around my hand, as he sat and stare at what I was doing, "Where are you heading too today" I ask him.

"Boston" he reply with a rather loud tone, I didn't know what to take from the way he replied, and wasn't interested in the reason he was so happy that he was going to Boston neither so I quickly moved on to the next question. "Are you married?" I went straight for the kill,

"Yep twenty five years, now." He said, while raising his left hand and showing me his wedding band.

"Oh that's nice man, so what do you do to keep it going for twenty-five years?" I asked as I began applying the polish to his tan colored boot

"Ah, sometimes, I don't know, how I did it, but, I guess you know, It has a lot to do with give and take, you have to be willing to accept, that you're wrong at times, you know, be the bigger man." He stated,

"Yea" I agreed, and then went on to my next question, "Is it true, that marriage could get boring at times?"

"Yea, it can."

"So what do you suggest, to do when that boredom steps in?"

"Well, you try to find ways to spice it up, you know, you go away, you try to get out of your environment, you know, try do things differently." He advised me

I then went on to my other question as I began to brush his right side boot. "What do you think is the number one reason, that your marriage has been so successful?"

He smiled, then went on to say "Well, am going to hit it right on the nose, the number one thing is communication by far, you can have everything, everything else, but if you don't have communication, you don't have the foundation."

"I was loving this customer" I said to myself, because his answer were so straight forward and so easy to understand, so I went on to my other question, which was "what about choosing a partner, like, how do you if that person is the right person?"

"Well, earlier on you know, you go for lovely, you go for beauty, and stuff like that, but later on, you know, you go for companionship, and ah, the person that you met, you know, can be a good friend, a good mother, somebody that, you look forward to being around, after all those years of being together.

"Yea that makes sense. I'm planning on getting married, a good day, one good day, not right now, though, because I personally thinks that marriage is a beautiful thing, you know, the love, the kids, the family, the security, the whole nine yards, the happiness, you know?" I said, as I smile and look up at him, as our eyes made direct contact,

"Absolutely, I hear a little accent, where are your from Jamaica?"

"No I'm Guyanese, I'm from Guyana, and you? I replied as I smile, since it was somewhat strange, that because I had an accent, most people automatically thought that I was Jamaican, which never seems to bother me in any way.

"Haiti, I'm Haitian, but I've been here since I was seven years old." He replied

"Is your wife is Haitian too?" I then asked him

31

"Yup, but she came to America when she was two years old, so she's basically American," he added

"You're good," I said to him, as I give him the thumbs up, signaling that I'm finish shining his shoes.

"Thank you chief" he replied, as he steps down from the stand, and pays me, before taking off

"Thank you and have a good day," I responded.

9

HAPPY

As I was putting the last layer of polish on a customer's shoes, I turned around and noticed that a guy was standing near the sign. "Are you waiting on a shine also?" I asked.

He looked at me and said "Yes, I would love to have a shine, but take your time, I'm in no rush."

"You can have a seat. I'll be with you in two minutes. Make yourself comfortable," I urged him, then placed the footrest in front of him as he got seated.

I continued attending to my previous customer, and in less than five minutes, it was the new customer's turn to get a shine.

"Thank for your patience" I immediately complimented him, as I wrapped the balm rag around my hands.

"Patience? Do they make you say that?" He stared me in the eyes, with a rather amused tone in his voice, before going on to say "Let me tell you about patience. If I was sitting here for fifteen minutes, that would have been patience. I just got here. Relax, kid.

"OK," I said, as I looked up at him and smiled. "So which of the shines would you like to have today, sir?"

"I definitely don't need the bulletproof, just make them look good," he requested as he place his hands on his knees.

"Ok, I'll give you the glass," I said to him, as he nodded and his eyes strayed away to the food court. I began working on his shoes.

"So what's with the mask, are you sick or your trying to prevent getting sick?" He questioned me.

"I'm trying to prevent getting sick, since I'm allergic to the lint and fiber that comes out of the rags that I use. Do you want to see me take it off and start sneezing all over you?" I joked.

"No, no," he said, while smiling looking down at me.

I continue to attend to his shoes, placing the first layer of polish on them, then went straight to the questions. "How are you doing so far, sir?" I asked him.

"Good, and yourself?"

"I'm doing well also. I hear an accent there. Where are you from?"

"Australia, I live in Australia," he replied, then went on to say, "I'm on vacation in New York, my last month of vacation."

"How's it going so far?" I asked.

"Good, I'm having lots of fun."

"Are you traveling alone? Oh, by the way, these are some nice shoes."

"Yeah, I am traveling alone and thank you, these are my favorite shoes"

"Can I ask you a question?" I asked him as I began to brush his shoes.

"Sure, why not?" he responded with a smile on his face, as if he knew what my question was.

"Are you married?" Was my gateway question.

"No, and never was," was his quick response, as he shook his head.

"Well, what is your take on marriage?" I then asked him.

"Ah, I don't even know if I could answer that question," he said this time, making little hand gestures.

"Are you against it, or do you think it's a good thing?"

"I think it's a good thing, as long as you are both happy," he said.

"Do you see yourself ever getting married?"

"No, I don't . . . I'd rather have a root canal than get married." He gazed away down the terminal, so I decided not to ask him anymore questions, since his actions seemed rather uninterested in what I had to ask. I continued to work on his shoes, not saying another word until I was done.

I LOVE YOU

"Have a seat sir," I said to my next customer that approached the stand requesting to have a shine. He seemed rather happy and jolly. All he did was smile, until he got seated.

"Which of the shines would you like to have?" I asked him as I place my dust mask over my face and slid on my gloves.

"Oh, I'll take the best one you have. Is that the bulletproof?"

"Yes it is," I quickly responded.

"Go for it, then" he replied, still acting all jolly as he sit leaning forward in the chair.

"I'm with my wife. I'm getting married."

That explains the attitude, I thought to myself.

"You're getting married?" I then ask, as I began to burn the loose threads on his shoes.

"Absolutely."

I began to laugh, as I really have never seen anybody this happy ever. He was acting like a young child, sitting in that chair.

"When are you getting married?" I asked, since I didn't want to be rude and switch the topic and also because I figured that I could definitely get some knowledge from this guy.

"Oh Sunday, in the Bahamas. It's that time, yes, it's that time."

"So tell me something, how do you know when it's that time?" I asked.

"Ah it's just that everything kind of slows down, everything is about that one girl. We've been together over three years now, and she's the one."

"I think marriage is a beautiful thing."

"Important, I mean there's city games and you know, the clubs are so cute, but that doesn't get you anywhere. You don't go anywhere unless you get lucky, but that only happens once every couple of months, it's not every time, unless you're the president or some shit."

I laughed as I asked him another question, "You guys lives together?"

"Yeah, we've been living together six months now," he said as his eyes strayed away to the direction in which his fiancé' was coming from.

As she got closer to the stand, he said to her, "Hi, I miss you, I'm getting my shoes shined."

She just stood there and smiled at him.

"Congrats on the wedding" I said to her, as she stood alongside me. She then look at me, smiled and said "thank you" before telling her fiancé that she's heading to the gate and will see him when he gets there, "OK hun, I love you" he responded, as she walked off.

"You guys are so sweet" I said, as I smiled with him.

"We're Indian, we're Indian" he repeated, and then went on to ask, "You're from the Caribbean?"

"I'm from Guyana actually. Where are you guys from?"

"We're from Long Island, but we work in Manhattan."

"How did you guys met?"

"She works for a TV station, she's a producer, so we meet through the industry."

"Oh," I said.

"It's a destination wedding too. We'll get married on the water, on that Caribbean water . . . When you go down, you got to do it on that Caribbean water, that water is next level." He smiled broadly.

They both looked kind of young to me. "Did you consult anyone before you decided to get married, or did you just get engaged?" I asked him, as I began brushing in the third and final layer of polish into his shoe.

"Strange that you ask that, I mean, I asked my family and everybody was like good with it. I think the only downside is going to clubs and all that, but once you get old that doesn't matter anymore," he replied, this time looking towards his gate.

"Yeah exactly" I agreed before asking "What do you think are going to be the key factors that will make your marriage work?"

"Giving in, just compromising, you know, admitting when you're wrong, stuff like that, because that works for a lot of people" he said.

"So what about her family, are they ok with it?"

"Oh definitely, we're Indian families. It's easy."

I was done with his shine, but felt the need to throw in one more question, which I thought was the most important one of them all, so instead of letting him know that I was done with his shine, I asked him, "One more question: Was it something that you wanted or something that she wanted?"

"Both. It kind of comes together," he answered, as he smiles.

"You're good," I said to him as I gave him the thumbs up and removed the footrest.

He climbed down, still all jolly and happy, paid me, and then took off to his gate.

WANTS VS. NEEDS

"Where are u heading today, sir?" I asked my next customer as he got seated and requested the bulletproof shine.

"Out to LA," he replied as he stared down at me cleaning his shoes.

"LA?" I repeated, since I wasn't clear of what he had said.

"Yea, just got in from Buffalo" he added.

"Oh, what time you getting out there?"

"Ah we take off here at twelve get out there at 3 o'clock, after that I'm done."

"So how's your day going so far?" I asked him as I began to brush off the leather balm from his tan wingtip shoes."

"Pretty good, pretty good." He nodded his head then went on to add, "One flight under the belt, another to go, then we're done."

"That's good, so you get to go home to the family right?" I said with the intention of steering the conversation into the marriage lane.

"What's that?" he asked, leaning forward.

"You getting to go home to the family?" I repeated.

"Ah, not till, tomorrow night, late though," he replied as he lifted his head up and began to look around the terminal.

I then wasted not another second. "Are you married?" I immediately asked him as I began to apply the polish to his shoes.

"I am, I also got one kid, he's eight months old," he added.

"Oh that's cute," I replied as I look up at him and smiled before asking my next question. "So how long have you been married for?"

"A year and a half" he responded calmly.

"Marriage is a beautiful thing" I stated.

"It's the best thing, too" he replied as he nodded his head and gave me that look of certainty.

"It is?" I asked as I looked up at him.

"For me, it is, because when she needs her time alone, I do my trips.

"What the hardest thing to deal with in marriage?" I asked next

"Money. Probably eighty or eighty-five percent of our arguments are about money." He went on to add, "Yeah, just trying to plan and other things, and I'm too lazy." We both then laugh aloud, as he continued, "Yeah, she gives me a list of things to do, but it just takes me couple days to get them done."

"She's the boss?" I asked him with a smirk on my face as I stopped brushing his shoe and looked up at him.

"Oh yeah, she's always the boss. She's efficient; she's organized. That's what she deals with at work, advancing people, so she's used to that and she doesn't want to come home and manage me. She expects me to get it done."

"She's the one, though?" I asked him.

"Oh yeah, it's all good," he replied as he place both of his hands on the arm rest and began cracking his knuckles.

"Yea that's the most important part." I responded as if I could relate to what he said.

He then added, "Because the kids, they suffer a lot of the time. Our free time and time we get to spend together is minimum." He then paused for about three seconds and then went on to "Yeah, I think that I'm going to give her a gift. We live up in Philly. I'm going to get her a one-night hotel thing, a very nice hotel, get like a little spa package, you know, massage and stuff like that. It will be just her and I'll stay home with the baby" he said as he looked at me and smiled.

"Oh that's cute," I assured him.

"A friend recommended it, you know, just give them a day to themselves at a nice place, even if it's only for twenty-four hours. Because all she does now is change diapers, wakes up in the middle of the night to feed, and it's all about the little one. Don't get me wrong, it's great, but we need to be adults too and show each other that we appreciate them. What about you, you're married?"

"No, I like to ask questions about marriage, because it's a thought that's in my head.

"You have a girlfriend?"

"No, I'm single" I replied with a smirk on my face as I continued to polish his shoes, then immediately ask him a question to get back in control. "So how do you know if that person is the right one?

"You know when you know," he said smiling, then added, "It's hard to explain, and it came to me four, five months back when we started dating. I'm 35 years old now and I spent most of my twenties and early thirties single, so you know, sometimes your mature about things, so you know what you want."

"But how do you know if she's the right one? What are some of the signs you should look for as a man?" I then asked him.

"Trust, if you can trust her and she can trust you, because believe me, marriage is not an easy streak. There are a lot of things, especially when you get a family, financial stuff, trying to make time for each other, you have your night out with the boys and she has her night out with the girls, compromising. My dad taught it to me best, he said wants vs. needs, you know, what do you want vs. what do you need?"

"That makes sense."

"Do you want a big screen TV, or do you need a big screen TV, and then you think, is it what you want vs. what you need, so, whether you're going to put that money for the kids college education, or for fixing up the house or stuff like that, you know, my dad ah, he's been married for forty-two years, and my wife's parents have been married for thirty-five years, so that a good sign."

"You guys came from a good background."

"Yeah, my dad says it's all about compromising and working things out. He said he see these people getting divorced, you know after two years, three years, all the way up to . . . I had a good friend of mine, his parents got divorced after thirty-five years of marriage, thirty-five years," he repeated as he looked down at me a shook his head from left to right.

"Is that even possible?" I stopped from shinning and asked in shock, as that was the most unbelievable story I've ever heard.

"Yeah, his dad told him, "I haven't loved your mother for years. We were just waiting for you to get out of college to get a divorce."

"Wow," I said, still stunned at what I was hearing.

He then continued, saying, "That was a shot in the heart, man, well, you know what, I think people give up pretty easily, too easily. You don't just give up, you know. People get thirty to thirty-five years out of marriage, and they want to try new things, and they think the marriage is restricting them from them trying new things. You know what I'm saying. Someone wants to travel, and the other one is like, ah, we've already done travelling, I don't want to travel anymore. So those kinds of things man. You got to work at it, it's not easy, but you know what, like I've said, I think I've found the right one and we plan on having one more kid so we're going to do whatever it takes to make it work, and that will be it."

"Well good luck man," I said to him.

"Thanks. You also want to look at their personality, how they treat other people" he added, then went on to say, "My wife, when she meets new people, she's always engaging. She wants to know where they're from, how there doing, and she loves kids. That's a big plus right there. I remember when we began dating. The first thing she said was she wished she had kids, so from then, I already knew that she was going to be a great mom, you know? She cares about people and just stuff like that."

"I seeing you're talking and holding your wedding band at the same time," I said to him as I smiled and continued to work on his shoes.

"Well, out of all of my friends, I was pretty much the last one to get married."

"How come? Were you waiting to see what it was like with their relationships?" I asked him as I began to apply the final layer of polish to his shoes.

"I don't know, but one of my good friends is celebrating his ten-year anniversary, and they're going to take a trip to Hawaii to celebrate, right around his birthday. But when I visit them, she's definitely the king of the household. I could see that they used to argue a lot about little things. Most of it is about money, like I said. The other thing is, my buddy would rather be hanging out with me than doing something around the house, and I was the single guy and he's going out to have fun with the single guy, you know, on guys' night out and stuff like that, but, hey, compromise man." He stated as he began to climb down the stand since I was finish with his shine.

"So how much do I owe you?" He asked.

"That's nine bucks," I replied as I began to take my gloves off.

"He then paid me and before walking away he said, "It's a big commitment, but go on the trip."

I smiled and said, "Thanks for the business. Have a good day," as he walked off.

12

STRESS

"MY PLANE BOARDS in ten minutes. Can you do these in ten?" my next customer asked as he approached the stand pulling a pulley luggage behind him.

"Of course, man. Step on up and have a seat." I quickly began to take out my supplies as he got seated.

"Where you heading to?"

"Ft. Lauderdale, for business. How you doing, you alright?"

"I'm good man, no complaints," I replied.

"You keeping busy?"

"Not really, the busy season is yet to come. You know in the summer time everybody wears flip flops and sneakers" I told him.

He then began to laugh out loud before adding "That's right, it will be jamming here soon. Another month, and you're going to be good to go."

I smiled and said "Let's hope so."

"So do you work for the airline or you work on your own?" he asked as he began to stare at the sign.

"No, I work for the company that leases this spot from the airline."

"Ok, just give me the basic shine, I don't want them too shiny. I like them a little dull, just clean, you know, and besides, I'm not wearing a suit," he said, and we both laughed.

I then went right into the marriage questions, since we didn't had a lot of time. "So are you married?" I asked him.

"No I'm engaged, but will be getting married next year."

"I just met a woman who's going to Nassau to get married and she's all excited."

"I could only imagine," he replied as he continued smiling, while looking down at me working on his shoes. "You ever been down there?"

"No" I said.

"It's beautiful, boss. I was down there, maybe twenty years ago, and I still remember it. That must have been when I was like fifteen years old" he added.

"Let me ask you something, how do you know when that person is the right one?"

"Ah, listen I'm thirty-six years old; it took a long time," he replied.

"How long have you guys been together? I then asked him as I began to stain his shoe sole.

"Nine months. I guess you know when you don't want to go out to the bar with your friends but rather stay in with her. I prefer to cook dinner with her than run out and be drinking all night trying to find some new girls," he stated.

"Yea that makes sense, I can dig that."

"It takes a long time, but you know, if you got something good, stay with it," he advised me, then continued by saying, "Yeah I'm looking forward to getting married; I'm really excited for it. "Are you married?"

"No, I'm not, I'm only twenty-five years old. It's a thought that's in my head, but it's just a thought," I replied as we both began to laugh aloud.

"Some of my friends were already married at twenty-five years old, but you know, you want to . . . I love running around, I did it for fifteen years in the city, and after a while, you got to leave it and move on, find that right person and settle down," he said, looking directly in my face as I stopped brushing his shoes and looked up at him.

"So do you guys live together?" I then asked.

"Yeah," he replied.

"Was that like a strategy of yours, to live together first?" I asked as I began to brush the polish into his shoes.

"No, I mean when I was with her I knew immediately that she was going to be my wife. I knew right away, so she just moved right in, but I think it's good, you know. More than living with someone, you want to travel with them, go travel somewhere hard, like be on a sailboat on tough waters. I know it sounds crazy, but it's not easy traveling with people. You see if they have any weird shit hiding inside of them because it all comes out, like if they can't handle stress or they can't handle changes in plans or delays, or being at the wrong hotels, you know, stuff like that," he said with a smirk on his face.

"I never thought of that. It makes sense, though."

"Yeah you start to see, weird stuff. You start to see people for who they are once you travel with them, they can't hold it in, because not every place is like America. You've got to find the role that fits you well and it's doesn't always work out so well. I went on sailboat last year with my old girlfriend. We dated for six months and were planning on moving in together. We were on a sailboat in Greece for a week, and the day I got home I broke up with her," he said as we began to laugh aloud, then added, "She actually went home and I when to London for work. I came home from London, she picked me up with my own car, and I broke up with her and drove her home." We continued to laugh as he repeated himself. "She picked me up with my own car. I drove her to Vaginia, broke up with her and went back to my apartment in the city. Trust me man, that's how you know. Go travel with them; pressure brings out a lot."

"You get to see their true colors?" I asked.

"Absolutely, and sometimes they're ugly, so you want to know man. The worst thing that you can do is wait till you get married and then try to find out," he replied, as I nod in agreement. He then added, "A lot of my friends found out the hard way, now they're f—and now they're stuck."

"But what would you say is the key factor to keep the relationship together, to keep it going?" I asked him.

"You know, that's a good question. I mean, right now were trying to figure out things to do together, because I work all day, I travel a lot, and we only hang out for like three hours a night when I get home. Watching TV is not enough, that doesn't do it," he explained.

"Ok" I nodded as I began to buff his shoes off.

"You got to figure out something that you have in common, something that you can do together. Like, I've never cooked before in my life, but we just started cooking together. She likes cooking, but she's just not good at it," he said as we both laughed aloud. He then went on to add "We got to work, we just got to work on it, hey, and that's why there're food channels, food books . . . the internet comes in also, so we will figure out a way. You got to do things together, cause otherwise you're just getting together to go to sleep, you know, and that's not enough to make a relationship last."

"That's so true. Anyway, congrats and good luck on your wedding," I said to him as I gave him the thumbs up, signaling that his shine was completed.

"Thank you very much. I really appreciate it and nice job by the way," he said as he paid. "See you here again sometime."

"Of course, man. I'll be right here"

13

POSITIVE

"ARE YOU OPEN?"

"Yes I am," I responded to my next customer, who approached me at the stand for a shine while I was sitting, playing with my cell phone.

"Ok, I'll take a glass shine" he added as he began to smile, then took off his shoulder bag and place it in front of the stand. "Is this good here?" he asked, before getting seated.

"Yes it is, make yourself comfortable," I urged him as I began wrapping the balm cloth around my hand to start cleaning his shoes. I then took out my supplies and went straight into cleaning his shoes as he sat and gazed around the terminal. "Where are you heading to today?" I asked.

"Long Beach to see my daughter. She lives in California."

"Ok, are you traveling alone?"

"Yes I am." He turned his focus to what I was doing with his shoe, so I didn't wasted any more questions and went straight for the marriage talk.

"I noticed you're wearing a wedding band, how long have you been married?" I asked.

"Forty-seven years."

"Forty-seven years is a very, very long time" I stressed, then added, "What do you do to make your marriage last that long?

"I don't know, you just keep your mouth shut," he said as we both began to laugh aloud. He then added, "Just keep your mouth shut, that's all. I'm from the old generation and trust me, it works."

I laughed a little more. "Forty-seven years, that's older than my parents are," as I continued to work on his shoes.

"So where do you live?"

"I live right here in Queens" I replied then went right back into asking him another question. "Is it possible for marriage to get boring after being married for so long?"

"Nope," he replied without any hesitation.

"What do you do, to prevent that boredom from striking?"

"What? How does it get boring?" he asked, as if I just gave him the shock of his life.

"I don't know either, but a lot of my customers say that after a couple of years you could fall out of love and it could get boring," I replied as I began to brush in the first layer of polish into his shoes.

"Well, you just have to do stuff that interests you. I play a lot of golf." He then stopped, cleared his throat and continued, "I run a lot of organizations. I have three kids, three nice kids, and now I'm helping to raise some of the grandchildren. Boy I'll tell you, they're beautiful." He smiled. "How old are you?"

"I'm twenty-five," I replied.

"Oh ok. I got married when I was twenty-four years old," he stated as he looked at me and smiled as if he was telling me something else.

I didn't catch on, so I quickly moved to the next question. "I don't know if you remember, but how did you knew for sure that she was the right one?"

"You got to understand that this was years ago. I got married in 1964 and things in 1964 were different. If you wanted to buy a new car, it was just a couple of thousands of dollars, and if you had a job, you could buy one. It was just different, I mean, I was born in 1938 and World War II was just finishing and the economy was growing, new cars were coming out. Television: I remember watching my first TV. I watched TV on a little screen I like this, through a magnifying glass," he said, as he lifted his hands up and made a five-inch distance between them. "My lifetime, I've seen it all, I've seen television, people had to share their telephone with their neighbors, a party line and all that stuff. It was just an interesting and fast-growing economy and everything. Big things started to happen. We even went to the moon and things like that, but nowadays, it's tough for you guys, you guys got it tough. It's serious, job market's tough, cost of living is tough, everything is tough and people don't even want to get married anymore. I don't think, if I knew I was going to get married and it was only going to last two or three years, I would've gotten married, because I wouldn't be involved in it.

"But how can you prevent your marriage from failing within the first two, three years?"

"I don't know, you just got to be positive about it. Are you married?"

"No, I'm not married."

"Do you have a girlfriend?"

"No, I'm single," I replied as I continued working on his shoes.

"I'll tell you this: When you decide to choose a woman, make sure you look for compatibility."

"Compatibility." I repeated since I wanted him to elaborate more on the term.

"Yeah, that's about it. You have to make sure you like the same things," he said and then went silent.

"Ok, you're good, what do you think, man? I asked him as I give him the thumbs up, before removing the footrest for him to climb down since I was done with his shine.

"Ah that's good. The first time I ever had them shined," he replied as he climbed down from the stand and paid me.

"Thanks for the business and the advice," I said to him as he walked off.

"You're welcome, anytime."

14

GRIEF

"How about a shine, sir?" I asked my next customer, who was standing at the sign gazing at it as I was removing the footrest for my previous customer to climb down out of the chair. "It only takes eight minutes" I added, as he hesitated for a bit, before nodding his.

"Ok, I'll take a basic." He walked toward the stand and got seated. "Have a great week" my previous customer said to me."

"Thank you, and same to you." I replied, before attending to my next customer. "How are you doing today, sir?"

"Great, could you use your darkest brown on these please?"

"Ok" I responded as I began to clean his mahogany shoes.

"So where are you heading today, sir?"

"Boston, for a quick meeting, and then back" he responded.

"How's your day going so far? I asked.

"It's good, I can't complain," he said as I stopped cleaning his shoes and rolled his pant legs up.

I then said "You can't complain" and we both smiled.

"What can you complain about, nobody listens," he joked.

"I'm guessing you're not married?" I stated

"No, hell no, hell no" he repeated, as he shook his head from left to right and we laughed some more.

"How come man? Marriage is a beautiful thing," I said to him.

"I don't need that grief" he said, this time with a straight face.

"Wow, it's a grief? You sound like you've been there and done that before," I said since I wanted him to get more into details about why he thought it's a grief.

50

"No, it's just that marriage isn't for me. I'm too set in my ways. I like my own way."

"Are you saying that it just hasn't happened yet or it's never going to happen?"

"No, never, I don't think that can happen, there are too many choices in New York, too many options. Don't get me wrong, it might be a good thing, well for some people, but it all depends on what you want your life to be."

I agreed then asked him if he had any kids, and his reply was the same. "No, no. I think the world has enough kids," he stated, then added, "We have a hard enough time taking care of those kids that are hungry, starving children all over the world and we need to bring more kids in the world? I don't think so, but as I said, a lot of it depends on circumstances. I do love children; I have nieces and nephews that I love to be around."

I said "Ok" before he went on to add, "I think children are incredible blessings, but I think that some people just have kids 'cause they want something that's missing in their life, and I don't think that's always the smart option, especially if they can't afford to have kids. You know, kids are a lot work, a lot of responsibility. You have any kids? He then asked me.

"No, no kids, I'm still a baby man. Look at me, look at my face. I'm only twenty-five years old." I joked with him.

"Yeah, but still you know, I know a lot of people that are twenty-five that have kids. I know people that are twenty-five and have like three, four kids, and mostly because they aren't responsible for their actions when the have too much to drink."

I laughed.

"You know, I don't know, I think that there's a lot of children in the world right now that can use love, and because some people have three, four of them, these kids are not getting the attention and love that they should be getting, but yeah, to have my own children was never a priority, but I love all the children," he stated with a calm tone in his voice, as if he was becoming emotional.

"Ok" I replied again, since I really didn't know what else to say, and also because I wanted him to keep going, and he did.

"But I do think for some people it's the right thing. Where I grew up, you know, you got your girlfriend in high school, and then you married her when you were twenty, then you start having kids at twenty-five, and you know, by the time you were forty-five your kids were off to college, but time has changed," he said then went silent.

"So would you advise anybody to get married, although it's not something that you would want to do?" I asked as I began to buff the polish into his shoes.

"Well, it depends. I mean, it depends on what your life plan is. I don't think people take accountability for their actions as much as they used too anymore. Marriage is not something that should be taking lightly, and it's not something to be done on the wild, if you truly feel that you can spend the rest of your life with someone, and not just when it's fun but when it's also really shitty, and you can take personal responsibility for your life, then yes of course, by all means. I'm not against marriage, I just think that for certain people, it's not the right thing to do. I have friends that get married and they're the biggest players around. They meet a girl in the bar, then she gets pregnant, and they suddenly have to marry her, and I would say that's the dumbest thing I've ever heard. Why do you have to marry her? You don't even know this chick, you met them one night, you had sex with them, and now you're going to marry them? 'Oh it's the right thing to do,' they would say, and then what happens a couple of months later? Then they have a baby, they're unhappy, they're both miserable, because they don't know each other. Now the child is brought up in an environment which is unhealthy and unhappy, which adds difficulty to the child's life."

"Yeah," I nodded and agreed with him.

He then added "Exactly, you know, I mean, it's unfortunate, cause then it becomes a cycle because, children learn what they live, and if children don't have, if you have a good relationship with your parents, and you feel as if you're a good human being, and when I say good human being, I don't mean that you have money and you have this and you have that. Success is and individual goal, it's not a monetary goal, it's about your personal experience, It's about how you're doing with, karma, with the spirit, spiritual Universe, not ah, oh I'm the president of this and this you know, that's all material bullshit, cause we all dies, and you know what happens when you die and I die, you know what's left, the same bag of molecules."

"Yeah, man," I agreed with him, then thanked him for the advice as he stepped down from the stand.

"Well, if you're in love, and if it's real love, then get married," he advised me, as I smiled and nodded my head.

"But if you're just having a good time with somebody, then maybe you need to wait. Thanks for the shine." he said then took off.

"Ok, thanks, and thanks for the business."

15

SENSE OF HUMOR

"DAMN THAT'S A long way up" was what my next customer said to me after he requested to have a basic shine and I told him to take a seat.

"Do you think you can do it? Here, take my hands let me help you up."

"I have knee problems, so we got to take our time." He said to me as he made it up to the first step and was struggling to get up to the other step to sit.

I realize that he wasn't going to make it up to the chair so I recommended that he come back down and take off his shoe and I'll do it like that while he sits in the waiting chair.

"Ok, that's a much better idea. This is what happens when you get old," he smiled and said after getting down back from the first step. He then took off his shoes, gave it to me and took a seat, while I began to work on his shoes.

"So how's your day going so far, sir? I then asked him.

"Very good. I got through security, my flight is on time and now I'm having a shoe shine. It's good" he said while smiling at me. I then noticed that he was wearing a wedding band.

"Are you married? I asked him, as he sat and was looking very closely to what I was doing with his shoes.

"I am, fifty years now," he replied.

Although fifty years was the longest that I've ever heard, I still wasn't surprised at that coming from this particular customer, because he did look as though he was very old, so I just replied by saying, "That's a long time."

"A very long time, yeah," he repeated. As I moved on to another question.

"So what do you do to keep the relationship going strong, after being married for so long?"

"Well, other than the fact that we're in love, we go out a lot, we like to take care of stuff, you know, we try new things to keep it exciting, You have to be a partner, and you have to have a sense of humor," he stated as he continued to pay very close attention to what I was doing with his shoes.

"Yeah, man. I think marriage is a beautiful thing." I began to brush his shoes.

"Yeah it is. Have you haven't been married yet?" he asked.

"No," I quickly responded, then went on to ask "Would you recommend anybody to get married?"

He then began to laugh out aloud before saying "Yeah sure, why not?"

"So is it true that marriage can change people?" I asked him.

"Yes. Actually it's better for that stage in your life. You know it's better, 'cause it makes you settle down and that's good if feels good to be stable, you know?"

I was almost finished shining his shoes so I decided to throw in one more question: "How do you know for sure if that person is the right partner for you?"

He began to laugh, then added "Ah, I don't know, you have to have a sense of what you're really looking for and the things that you're willing to live with. One or two things that you really, really need to have with your partner is similar Interests, if not you're going to have problems. Also you want to live with them before getting married, because you will know what you're in for, and nothing about that person will come as a surprise to you when you get married. Other than that, take the risk, take the risk."

"Excuse me," I said to the customer as I reached over to the cabinet to answer my cell phone, as it was ringing. "Hey mother, no I'm at work. I'll hit you up later when I get home, I have a customer right now," I said, before pressing off my cell phone and placing it back on the cabinet.

"Ok sir, you're good, thanks for the business." I placed his shoes in front of him.

"Thank you," he replied, as he paid me and then took off.

16

PEACE

I APPLIED THE first layer of polish, brushed that into the shoe, applied the second layer, and as I was about to brush that layer into the shoes, he placed the box that he was eating from on the shine box, then picked up another other box, which seemed to be fruits and began to eat once more. He then stopped eating and asked me, "Could you get rid of that line that's in front of the shoes?"

"No, it's already soaked into the leather. When did it happen?" I asked him.

"A day ago," he responded.

"The day before yesterday?"

"No, a few days ago, but I had them shined the day after it happened, and I got salt on them."

"Yeah I noticed, but because of the fact that it's already soaked in and also you had a shine over it, it would be very hard for me to take it out now," I said.

"Ok," he answered in a tone of disappointment.

"But the next time you get salt on your shoes, make sure that whoever is shining them, take off the salt with De-Salter, before applying any polish to the shoes." I advised him, as I reached into the shine box and pulled out a bottle of De-Salter fluid and showed it to him.

"What's that?" He quickly asked.

"Oh, it's a fluid for salt, something like acetone, you applied it on the area of the shoes that the salt is on, and it dissolves the salt within seconds. Where are you heading today?"

"Florida."

"Are you originally from Florida? I hear a little accent."

"No, I'm from the UK" he replied as he fixed his feet on the foot rest.

"How long are you going to be in Florida for?"

"Ah just a few days, then I go to Brazil, from Florida, and then eventually I get back here next week," he stated.

"How the family feels about that?" I asked him since I wanted to steer our conversation in the lane of my preferred topic, which was marriage of course.

"They're in Florida, that's why I'm going down there. I just flew in from the UK this morning" he replied.

"Ok, wife and kids?" I then asked.

"Yup, I have one boy, and my parents are there also" he added, as he continued to stare down at his shoes, as I worked on them.

"That's nice," I said to him as he nodded his head. I then asked him another question.

"How long you been married?"

"Twelve and a half years, good years" he responded, as he smiled broadly.

"It just keep getting better huh?" I asked him as I continued to work on his shoes.

"It does, it does. She's my peace" he repeated as he nodded his head, then decided to ask me a question. "Do you have kids?"

"No, I'm still a baby, man, look at me," I joked as we both began to laugh aloud, before I went on to say "I'm planning on it though."

"Good, that's cool man," he advised me, as he took a quick glance at his wrist watch.

"So, what do you do to keep the relationship going strong after twelve years of being married?" I calmly asked him.

He then began to smile and said "It's more of what she does. All I do is try to be good to her and my little boy, you know, the best I can do.

"Ok, I'm just asking because I hear a lot of stories every day about marriage."

"Yeah I'm sure," he responded.

"So how long have you had these boots?"

"I don't know, a couple of years now, but I don't take care of them the way I should. I only buff them whenever I get the chance to do so."

"Ok, but you really want to take good care of your shoes, especially when you pay a lot for them," I advised him.

"Yea, I know that but I'm so busy," he stated, as I asked him another question to get back on track.

"Tell me something, does marriage ever get boring? A lot people say, it could get boring and you could fall out of love while being married."

"No, it has never gotten boring for me, but I don't know, you have to talk to somebody who's fallen out of love, I guess," he replied and added, "For me, it gets better. I'm not sure I'm equipped to give advice about marriage, but if it helps this is it, just be good to her.

"You're done, what do you think?" I asked as I signaled him that his shine was completed.

"Yeah, I like it, looks good," he replied as he stepped down from the stand and pulled out a twenty dollar bill, gave it to me and requested to have a ten dollar bill back.

"Good job," he complimented me.

"Yeah man, thanks for the business, enjoy." I said to him as he walked off.

APOLOGIZE

"BULLETPROOF AND GLASS, what's the difference between them?" My next customer asked while she stood in front of the stand and stared at the sign.

"We basically adds extra layers of polish to the shoes and that makes the shine last longer and it also protects the leather more" I explained to her, as she then requested the glass shine before taking a seat.

"Where are you heading today" I asked her as I began to clean her shoes.

"Oh, I'm going to Maine. Somebody is getting a really big award, so I'm going out there to support her. She had a lot of trouble, but finally they've recognized good stuff," she said as she flicked her finger nails together.

"So are you traveling alone?"

"Alone, but a lot of us are going to go out there, because she did a lot of good for a lot of people," she added with a smile on her face.

"Ok" I replied, and continued to focus on cleaning her shoes, since I had no idea who she was talking about.

"Are you a native New Yorker?" she then asked.

"No I'm actually, from Guyana. I'm Guyanese. I just moved here four years ago."

"Most of the people that I know from Guyana are Indians" she stated.

"Can I ask you a question?" I asked her and she nodded. "What's your take on marriage?

She hesitated to answer, as if she had to think first to make sure that she wasn't going to give me the wrong answer. "Well, I think that everybody who wants to can."

"Can?" I repeated

"Yeah," she quickly answered.

"What about should?" I then asked her.

"Can, I don't think you should do anything that you know you shouldn't do, because either you change your mind, and then you will realized you shouldn't because you were right in the first place."

I agreed with her, then quickly asked another question, "Are you married?"

"I was, for twenty-seven years."

"That's older than I am," I said to her as she smiled and said "Yeah, I know that," then said to me "What made you ask the question?"

"I would like to get married one day, so I like to get people with experienced opinions," I replied.

"Alright, I'll give you the smartest advice in the book: You're going to be angry at each other sometimes, your feelings are going to be hurt and you're going to know it's the other persons fault and you're going to be lying in bed and your backs are going to be toward each other, and what you really know is you want that person to give you a hug and make it go away. So if you say 'Look, I'm sure we're both feeling the same thing, we're human, dear. I know I could use a hug, so I'm guessing you could, so I'd like to do that, because I want to make it right between us. Do that and the marriage will work." She advised me, as she nodded her head.

"It will work?" I asked her since I wanted her to say more.

"Any time you're lying there mad, knowing they're wrong, knowing you need a hug, knowing you need them, knowing you need an apology," she then paused and stared at the sign. "That's even worse than the basic shine," as we both began to laugh aloud, then requested to have the bulletproof shine instead of the glass shine, as we continued to laugh.

"So you're saying communication is the key?"

"Not only communication, say it: I want to make it right, I want to make up, I want to apologize, but let's start from somewhere. "How's that, is that good for you?" She asked, staring me in my face.

"Yeah that's nice," I replied as I nodded my head and began applying another layer of polish to her shoes, before saying to her, "And one more question, what do you do to make it last that long?"

"You don't let anything that's wrong get too tick, because if it gets tick, you don't even know what you're fighting about anymore, you did this, I did that, you did this, I did that, if it happens, you solve them. Let's say you're, what's the other person's name who you're thinking to marry? What's his or her name?" She asked.

I gave her my mother's name: "Colita."

"Well at the point you say, Colita, is it a good time, I'd like to talk to you seriously, stuff like that you say, cause it gives the person warning, you're not just going to talk about the weather and we're not going to avoid it. They may say babe, I had a killer day today, do you mind if we wait till tomorrow or wait till after dinner? Then you'll say, sure let's sit down, but you give warning, and after you give warning, and you get permission and now it's going to take time, then you have that discussion, that make sense?"

"Yea it do, it certainly does," I nodded.

"Yeah, but don't let the problem get thick, handle it, as close to that day as you can. That might be tonight, that might be Saturday, if that's the time you decide to let both people know what to say and what you want, because, otherwise it's this layer and that layer and that layer and that layer, and you don't even know what the situation is really. You could be mad because that other person likes hard toilet paper and you like soft toilet paper, why do you always get it and it's hard?" she joked as we laugh and then she added "But if it gets thick, your feelings are going to be in it. You don't think of it if you never think of it, so that's the best advice I can give you," she said as I continued to brush the polish into her shoes.

"How old are you?" she asked.

"I'm twenty-five."

"Twenty-five. Don't rush. Whoever is rushing you, don't rush," she advised. "How come you came here, what was your purpose, coming to America?"

"To go back to school, my dad brought me, and I had a chance to go back to school and I did that and just graduated two weeks ago," I explained to her.

"That's good. From where?"

"LaGuardia Community College, here in Queens."

"Oh it's a good school, I know of it," she assured me.

"Yeah, I just got my associate's degree in business management."

"What would you like to do, what do you want to get into?"

"Photography and fashion designing. I already have two websites, a photography site and an apparel site. They're not big as yet, but I'm working to get it there."

"Sometimes it takes noble work for a lot of years," she advised me.

"Yeah, once you're willing to work hard, anything is possible in America. It is still the land of opportunities.

"Yes, no, yes, no, yes, no, yes, no and yes" she joked as we both laughed.

I then added, "They got hundreds of thousands of immigrants coming every year, to start a new life here, so that alone should tell you something about America

"Oh that legend, that's what makes America vital," she stated, then added "And it's a shame that some people are trying end that."

"Yea, shame on them" I agreed with her, then gave her the thumbs up and cautioned her to watch her steps as she climbs down from the stand.

"Thank you," She said as she paid me and walked off.

"Thanks for the business and the advice, enjoy," I replied.

DEDICATION

"I'LL TAKE A shine," my next customer who approached the stand said, as she stopped and stared at the sign.

"Ok, have a seat, make yourself comfortable," I urged her.

"Which one, does it matters where I sit?" she asked as she pointed to the chairs.

"No it doesn't matter, it's your choice. Whichever one you want to sit in, feel free to do so"

She got seated and then said, "Thank you."

"No problem." I began to take out my supplies to begin working on her shoes.

"Do you live in New York?" she asked, as I was beginning to apply the leather balm to her shoes.

"Yeah, I live right here in Queens, in Rosedale," I responded.

"What time do you have to get up to get to work?"

"Ah, ten to five, five o'clock, it's not that bad you know?"

"You probably got more sleep than I did," she stated, as she began to stare around the terminal.

"Probably. I'm a morning person, so it really doesn't matter. I'll just put this over there, ok?" I said to her as I moved her bag from the front of the stand.

"Sure, I'm a morning person too, but this is night where I came from."

"Where did you came from? I quickly asked.

"Colorado."

"How is the weather over there?"

"We just had snow," she replied, as she quickly glanced at the newspaper that was on the shine box.

"Just had snow already? I said since I was shock, because New York was now beginning to get a little chilly and they had already had snow.

"Yup," she replied.

"So how long are you going to be out here for?

"A week. My very old folks live here so I come here pretty often," she said then added, "My father turn ninety today."

"Oh that's nice," I replied as I looked up at her and smiled, then asked her "Are you going to throw him a big party?"

"He doesn't want a big party. Tomorrow we're going to have a small dinner at a restaurant with a few relatives and we can't call it a party, we have to call it a dinner. He's not in the partying mood," she said as we both laugh aloud.

"Can I ask you a question?"

"Sure, why not?" she said as she nodded her head.

"What are your first thoughts when you hear the word marriage, what comes to mind?"

"Marriage, ah, well, hopefully that it's a union of people who have found similar interest in values and service, like how to be and how to live."

"Are you married?" I then asked.

"Ah, no, I'm actually becoming separated right now" she said then began to laugh aloud, then went on to ask me, "Why, you're getting married?"

"No, I'm just thinking about it."

"Well, do you have someone in mind or is it just like a general thought?

"A general thought for now because I'm single."

"Well, what comes to your mind?" she asked.

"That's why I'm trying to get some information about it. I have no clue about what marriage is, but I do think it's a beautiful thing."

"Yeah, you can make it the way you want, and it's not a thing of itself, it's made up of people who embrace it. I was married for seventeen years, and it took a lot of dedication to make it work for seventeen years, you know, but I more think of my parents, who have been together, let's see, I think they're going close to seventy years. They got together when they were pretty young and now my father's ninety today and my mother's eighty-eight, and the last few years have been horrible. My father is in a very bad mood and he's not who he used to be, and my mother still seems to be very dedicated to him. So when my mother is asked, how they live together so long, she jokes a lot about tolerance. But they used to be very affectionate, because they're from the times when you just stick it out and don't leave. I guess I'm not following that . . . but for many, many years I've still seen them very affectionate, and very joyful, and I think the question is how do you keep that joy alive? That's what it comes down to, but if you're thinking about it, it's probably a good idea," she said.

"I hope so."

"Don't hope. You need to be a risk taker, an adventurer. Life is an adventure. There are never any guarantees.

"That's true, just take the risk," I agreed.

"My profession is being a marriage and family therapist, so I see a lot of people in places in their relationship where they have to figure out where they're going, and I think it's really good that people seeks sources of support when they get stuck. That's going to happen; we're humans and then we have to figure out how to get unstuck," she informed me, then added, "Keep your heart open, even to the pain. When pain is there, you don't get stuck. People close their heart and then they can't go anywhere, because their love can't flow."

"Ok, I understand." I began to buff her shoes.

"It's good you wear a mask," she said to me.

"Yea, this is for the fiber and the lint that comes from the cloth. Whenever I buff the shoes, it goes into my nose and I'm allergic so that's why I wear it," I said to her.

"That's a good idea, but is it just the cloth. Can you use a different cloth that's natural?" she then asked.

"No, we have to use this cloth. It's recommended," I assured her.

"Oh, it's good you figured out what you're allergic to and how to prevent it from going up your nose," she added.

"You're good, watch your step," I advised her as her shine was completed.

"It looks great, thank you," she said as she began to step down from the stand.

"You're welcome," I responded.

"They're really old, I love them though, so comfortable," she added as she looked at her shoes and began to smile before walking off.

"Thank you." I waved bye to her.

19

CULTURE

"HOW ABOUT A quick shine, sir?" I asked a passenger who was walking by the stand, rolling his luggage and had his jacket placed over his left arm.

"What's the price for a shine? Oh, I'll just take the basic," he said after looking at the sign, then walked to the stand, placing his jacket on one of the chairs. He seated himself in the other one. I placed my face mask and my gloves on, then immediately put up the footrest for him to place his feet on. I began cleaning the crease of his left shoe sole with the toothbrush and water, then moved to the right shoe. As I was brushing the sole crease, I noticed that the toothbrush went right into the shoe sole, "Holy shit" I said to myself as I looked up at the customer, and realized he was looking down at me also.

"Don't worry about that; I kicked it out last week" he said, then added that he had yet to take it to get repaired.

I smiled, feeling very relieved that it wasn't my fault. "How's your morning going so far? I then asked.

"Oh, fine" he replied.

"Where are you heading today?"

"San Diego," he replied as he gazed around the terminal.

"Do you live there?"

"Oh no, it's my first time going there, for business, just for a couple of days then back."

"These are some nice shoes. I love shell cordovan shoes" I complimented him.

"Yes they are, and they're over ten year's old and I've never had to get them resoled as yet, but I will soon."

"You have the lifetime warranty, on them?" I then asked.

"Yeah, I have the envelope to send them back."

"Yeah that's good, that's what a lot of the shoe companies are doing these days. It's some kind of strategy, to keep their customers. That's good though, the fact that you can send in the shoes and have them resoled and repaired for a fraction of what you would have to pay for new ones." I explained to him as I looked up and noticed that he was wearing a wedding band. "Is that a wedding band?" I asked while pointing to his left hand.

"Ah, yep," he replied.

"So how long have you been married?"

"A long, long time. The day before yesterday, I celebrated my thirty-seven-year anniversary," he said to me, with a smile.

"That's almost as old as my parents are," I stated. "So what do you do for thirty-seven years to keep your marriage going strong?"

"No, no, no," he said quickly. "It depends on your culture; my culture believes in mental stability and family stability. Other cultures like here are more individualistic. Cultural factors are very important."

"Cultural factors?" I repeated, as I stopped brushing him shoes and looked up at him, since I wanted him to elaborate more on the term, and he did.

"Yeah, like the Spanish families here, they tend to have more couples than the white Americans. People from Italy, they stay longer in marriages, and same with Africans. In our place divorce is a very strange situation. Right here it's a very common situation, so the culture is the real corrupt thing when it comes to marriage."

"Where are you from originally?" I then asked, because of his last statement.

"I'm from Cameroon," he responded.

"Oh. Do you have any kids?"

"Yes, I have five children."

"So does marriage ever get boring to you?"

"No, not at all," he quickly responded.

"What do you do to prevent boredom from interfering with your marriage?"

"You have to value how you build yourself and your children and their understanding. We have all of that which you don't have in other cultures.

"Ok, you're all set, man." I gave him the thumbs up signaling his shine was finished.

He then stepped down and asked me, "How much is it?"

"Eight dollars," I said to him as he gave me a ten dollar bill and took off.

GOOD AND BAD

MY NEXT CUSTOMER got seated after requesting to have a shine and immediately began coughing.

Thank god I'm wearing this dusk mask, I thought to myself, as he continued to cough without placing his hand over his mouth. I then reached over to the cabinet and offered him some napkins. "Thank you," he said as he took the napkins and wiped his nose.

"Where are you heading to? I then asked since he had stopped coughing and was just gazing around the terminal.

"West Palm Beach to play some golf, a small vacation."

"That's nice. Are you traveling alone?"

"Best way, keep the family at home," he joked as we both laughed aloud.

"Ok, so how the wife feels about that?"

"She's ok with it, she knows me," he stated, then went on to add, "We've been married for twenty years, so she has no worries."

"Ok, that's nice" I complimented him, before asking him another question, "If you had to do it again, would you?"

"Ah well, you know what they say, if you got a good wife, she's still a woman, are you married?

"No, not as yet." I replied shaking my head from left to right.

He then continued by saying, "They're good to you, but better to themselves."

"It that a good or a bad thing, or a good and a bad thing?" I asked quickly as I continued to work on his shoes.

"It's good and bad. We argue a lot. I've got a wonderful daughter, but generally, it's not about you anymore, it's about them and the children. That's the deal," he said, then asked, "Is it busy this morning?"

"No, it's not that busy on Saturdays, because everybody has already left for vacation and not that many people are traveling, but it could always be worse though, so I'm grateful."

"And what part of the Caribbean are you from?" he asked next.

"I'm From Guyana, I came to America four years ago, in 08."

"I got a lot of Caribbean people working for me, good people" he stated.

"What type of business are you into?"

"I'm in the restaurant business," He replied then began to look down at his shoes.

I then continued to work on his shoes for a bit and as I was about to apply some more polish to his shoes I went ahead and asked him another question, "Ok, so what kind of advice would you give to me—" and before I finished my sentence he began to laugh, so I joined him and we both were laughing, he sitting and I standing in front of him with my polish in my hands, just laughing, before I went on to finish my sentence—"in order to know if it's the right woman and if it's the right time? What do you look for and what did you look for?"

"How old are you?' He asked.

"I'm twenty-five years old," I responded.

"It's not the right time!" He advised me.

"So how do you know if it's the right woman?" I went on to ask him.

"I don't know, nobody knows, it really starts with the right time," he answered, then added "Why should that ease us down? I met a lot of women in life that I could have married, but I just wasn't ready, and then my lady came along and I said 'You can't let this one go, you can't let this one go,' and she turned out to be a good wife. My first wife sucked."

"Pardon?' I said as if I didn't hear what he said the first time, but I heard him very clearly, and needed him to say more.

"This is my second marriage, my first wife sucked," he repeated.

"How long were you married for the first time, and what was the downfall of that marriage?"

He stuttered his first words and then said, "We were married for ten years and she, ah, she just didn't turn out to be the person that I thought she was. She was antisocial, and she only lived for our son, after we had him. She only lived for the kid, she had nothing, no idea about life and all this. You couldn't contradict her, she was right about everything, so finally I just left her. I couldn't deal with it. When I first got married, I was twenty-two years old. You shouldn't get married when you're young. I just think you got to be in your early thirties before you should think about marriage. There are too many women out there, so you're not going be focus on what you should be focusing on, and that's your marriage. When you're young, life's a party, and besides men don't grow up until they're into their thirties," he stated, as I began to smile broadly and asked "Is that's a true statement?" Since I've heard it before.

"Yep, that's the best advice I can give to you, you know, wait until you're ready, because once it's done, it's done. If you're going to make it, make it and last, it's a lot of years to spend with one person."

"Yeah it is" I agreed with him, as I began to buff his shoes. "What you think man?" I asked, finished with his shine.

"Nice" he responded, as he got up and stepped down from the stand.

"Watch your steps, thanks for the business man and good luck on your trip," I said.

"Thanks" he replied. Take care," he said as he walked off.

73

21

GIVE AND TAKE

"WHAT TIME IS your flight?" I asked my next customer, as he got seated and placed his coffee on the shine box.

"At ten o'clock," he quickly replied, looking at his watch.

"Where you heading too?"

"Vegas."

"Vacation, I hope," I said as I began to clean his shoes with the leather balm.

"No, business," he replied, as he shook his head, from left to right.

I then added, "It shouldn't be that bad, after all its Vegas, man."

"Well let's hope so" was his quick response, as he shook his head once again.

Based on his short answers and his body gestures, it seemed he didn't want to talk about his trip, so I immediately switched the topic and gave him a compliment on his shoes.

"This is good leather, how long have you had them?" I asked.

"Two months now, I really like them," he answered, as he looked down at his shoes.

"Ok, so do you have the lifetime warranty on them?"

"I have no idea. I bought them at the department store."

I then pause for about 30 seconds as I continued to attend to his shoes, then went on to ask him a gateway question to my main topics.

"Do you have any kids?"

"Two" he said, as he smiled and nodded his head.

"Are you married?"

"Ah, no divorced, after twenty-three years" he added.

"Wow, how do you let go after 23 years?"

"I have no idea, believe me, but that's the hardest part."

"Letting go?"

"Yeah, but if your spouse doesn't want to be married anymore, then you don't have a choice," he added, as he continued to pay attention to what I was doing with his shoes.

"Yeah. Were they the best days of your life?"

"Absolutely, absolutely," he repeated.

"So I'm guessing that you would do it again?" I then asked.

"No, I don't need to at this age."

"If I were to say that I'm planning on getting married, what kind of advice would you give to me on marriage, since you've been there and done that?"

"Well, you've got to give and take, do whatever to please your other half, it's important."

"Tell me something, how do you know when the right time is or if it's the right person, what do you look for?" I then asked, as I began to brush the first layer of polish into his shoes.

"It's hard for each individual person. I mean, I would have to say the bottom line is you've got to know what's in your heart. If you feel that this is the right person for you, and always remember it's a commitment every single day of your life, every breath is committed and that you've both got to dream as one, you know, there's no I in team. Don't take things for granted. People like to be treated as if they are something special."

"Yeah, that's true."

"So treat that person every day, like they are something special, because you never know."

"I was up to applying the final layer of polish, and decided to throw in one more question before letting this customer go, so I immediately asked him. "After coming out of a twenty-three year marriage, would you tell your kids to get married?"

"Of course I would. I can't let my bad experience mess up someone else's life," he replied before saying, "Those look perfect, better than when I bought them."

"You like?" I then asked as I remove the footrest.

"Of course. I love it, who doesn't like nice shiny shoes?" He replied as he climbed down from the stand, smiling.

"Thanks for the business and the advice, sir," I said to him as he paid me.

"No problem, anything," he responded, then took off.

LONG TERM GOALS

"How you been, man?" My next customer asked me as he climbed the stand and got seated.

"Awesome, and yourself?" I responded as I quickly slipped my gloves and my dust mask on.

"I'm great, no complaints on this side, just one last trip back to Austin and I'm done for the day, until tomorrow.

"Is that where you're stationed now?" I asked.

"Yeah, I mean, I'll come back soon, but its better flying for me, based on my seniority."

"Do you get to do a lot of international flights?"

"Not really, but a lot of stuff out of San Juan," he said as he smiled. "San Juan girls, they're horrible, but in a good way." We both laughed.

Yes, he's heading in the right direction, I thought to myself, as I went on to ask another question, this time relating to his last statement. "I'm sure you've experienced every category of women, which was the best. I'm talking about personality wise, and attitude wise, that you've had?"

"I have a physical type I like, which is like size four, dark hair, with a ponytail in an athletic kind of a way, but then I get bored of them, unless they've got like a brain or personality. Don't get me wrong, no one's stupid, I don't know how to say it, but you've got to have a woman you can talk to, one that amuses you," he said as he leaned forward and added, "that challenges you, that knows when to support you.

"That knows when to shut up, right?" I added. More laughter.

I then went on to ask another question. "What do you think about marriage? Are you married, by the way?"

"I used to be married. If you marry the right woman, and she married the right man, it shouldn't be a problem. I was married for twenty-three years.

"Twenty-three years?" I asked, as I stop brushing his shoes and stood up.

"Yeah, and you know, at the beginning it was awesome. I was just talking to a captain on the plane and he found this girl and he's kind of head over heels, he met her like a month ago, so I'm like 'Ok good for you bro, it's one thing to date someone, and you get those breaks and you don't see them for a couple days and you're like, oh so happy to see them again, but it's totally different when you decide to take that extra step and marry them. Don't get me wrong, the first couple of years are interesting. It's fun initially and then you go, I want a little time off, and that's where you want to go. I don't really want the time off, I just need the space for me to be myself, and then I'll come back and refresh to be us."

I nodded.

"But eventually, if it works out well and mine did for a long, long, very long time, you find that it's a satisfying thing, you don't worry about it, and I didn't worry about it. I mean, it wasn't like, 'Oh my god I got to make her happy or she's going to want to dump me' or stuff like, you know, when you're in high school, it was like, I just want to make her happy. Shit happens, so talk to her, which is the hardest part of it, cause we are men and want to be macho and say 'Oh I'll solve the problem.' No, you got to go to her and say 'Look, here's the problem, here's what I think we should do, what do you think?' And let her be involved, because sometimes they want to be involved and other times they want you to solve it and be the man, and that's when you're really trying to figure out, is this one of these involved thing or should I just kill the spider?"

"Just man up?" I asked.

"Yes, and that's why knowing someone is important."

"So if you had a chance to do it all over again, would you?"

"With the right woman, oh yeah, definitely. It's nice, for a variety of great things. It's nice to know that, ok, I don't have to re-learn, I know what it will be like, I know to expect that you're mad because I didn't take you to a specific restaurant that you didn't tell me you wanted to go to. I took you out to dinner and I took you to this restaurant, which is a nice restaurant, that serves good food, but you're upset because you didn't go to restaurant X, but you didn't tell me that. Why didn't you just say, 'Hey baby, I want to go to this restaurant'? So don't be upset when we don't go to that restaurant, because you didn't tell me. That's why I laugh at stuff like that, then they'll be like, 'You can't laugh at that.' Ah, yeah I kind of can, cause you're not being an adult. I mean, you wanted something but you couldn't tell me. You should've been an adult and said 'I want you to take me to dinner Friday night, I want to go to restaurant X,' and then my job is to say 'I'll pick you up at 7, does that time work? And is there anything else you want to do after dinner?' 'No, no you figure it out, I already picked the restaurant.' So then you go ahead and say, you know, I suck at dancing, so let's go out dancing, because I know you like it, and you just got to deal with the fact that I am going to look stupid, but I'll be your stupid, so you got to deal with it. Simple."

I laughed.

He then added, "That's all, and trust me, she's going to love that. If it's a great woman. I mean, women are awesome, but there are some that are crazy with that awesome."

"Can't live with them, can't live without them," I added as I looked back down and continued working on his shoes. Since I only had to buff his shoes, I decided to ask one last question. "So would you advise anybody to get married?" I asked.

"If it's the right person and you both agree on long-terms goals, that was one of the things that me and my ex-wife . . . we found out that we had different long-term goals. So every year, we would sit down on New Year's Day, to just talk and make our goals to one, two, five, ten, twenty years and then we talked about it and we worked it out. What we found out was, I wanted to save money, to be able to buy a vacation home, and she wanted money to travel, so I go, 'I don't think we could do both right now, on our income, maybe in the future we can, but not right now. So what do we really want to do, because both are completely different; one is saving to buy a big thing and one is spending a lot. What we decided to do was take a vacation, which was all along what she wanted, then try to save and make a decision in 5 years about whether to buy a vacation home. We ended up deciding not to buy a vacation home, but to buy a retirement type of home, then we had issues a couple years later, but at least we had work it out. That's why talking makes sense, it's very important to communicate to know what your partner wants.

"Yea that makes sense," I added as I gave him the thumbs up signaling his shine was completed.

As he got down from the chair, he stood in front of me and said, "But I had a friend of mine, that recently got divorced from a beautiful girl, a nice sweet girl, and he didn't want to break up, but she didn't want children, but he wanted children, and then she decided that she wanted to party more and she wanted to live, so she left him."

"That's crazy," I replied as I gave him back his change, thanked him for the shine, and he took off.

23

CHOOSE YOUR BATTLES

"How about a shine?" I asked my next customer as she slowly walked by the stand.

She then stopped, looked ahead and asked "How long would it take you to do these?" pointing down to her knee-high boots.

"The bulletproof shine takes less than fifteen minutes, so we will be done in less than fifteen minutes, regardless to which shine you choose," I assured her.

"Ok I'll take the basic then" she said as she placed her bags and her soda down on the stand, then took her jacket off and got seated, "Is that in your way?" she asked, as she pointed to her bags, that were on the other chair.

"No, not really" I said, as I began to apply the leather balm to her boots.

"It's not like you could do two at a time." she added, as we both laughed. As I was about to add the first layer of polish to her boots, she looked down at me and asked "Could these take the glass shine?"

"Of course." Was my quick response.

"Ok do that one then. I have to protect them from that snow in Rochester. I heard it's snowing over there."

"You have a pretty smile by the way," I complimented her.

"Thank you, but I'll never know about you, because you're wearing the mask" she replied as we both smiled. I then took off my dust mask and smiled at her.

"Likewise," she said as she continued to smile.

"Thank you, do you live in Rochester?" I then ask.

"No I used to live there then I moved to Texas last year, but I was in New York for a meeting and I thought well, I'm this close, I might as well go see my friends in Rochester."

"So are you traveling alone?"

"No, I'm with a colleague of mine."

I began to brush her boot and asked, "So are you married, or have any kids?"

"I'm married, no kids, but I have two cats."

"Well two cats is responsibility, too," I added.

"Pretty much, how about you?" she asked.

"I'm not married, I'm single and I don't have any kids" I said as I fixed her boot on the footrest, as she began to laugh.

"Why are you laughing?"

"Don't worry you're going to meet the right person one day and all that's going to change," she said as she continue to smile.

"Ok, what's the first step?" I asked.

"You've got to meet the right person."

"What's the second step?"

"I don't know what the second step is. You've got to work on it, not sweat the small stuff, and choose your battles."

"Choose your battles, ok. So how long have you been married?"

"Twenty-five years," she stated as she smiled broadly.

"That's my age, that's nice, I can tell that you have a healthy and joyful marriage, so tell me what did you do for twenty-five years to make it work that long?"

"I don't know, I mean, we have similar interests, we have similar values," she answered as she smiled, then added "we also have outside interests and outside values, you know. We both work pretty hard, and we don't have to spend every minute of the day together. I never thought I was going to get married, at least I wasn't looking to get married, but then I met the right person so we got married, and now I'm surprised it lasted twenty-five years."

"Your boots are set, what do you think?" I asked as I removed the footrest and stretched my right hand out to help her to come down from the stand.

"They look great, you did an excellent job," she replied as she reached for my hand and began to climb down.

"Can I get a five?" she requested.

"Thanks for the business and the advice and good luck. Enjoy your trip."

"Good luck to you, when you find the right person," she said as she walked off.

24

KIDS

"WHERE ARE YOU heading today?" I asked my new customer as he settled in the chair, preparing to get a shine.

"Austin, Texas" he replied as he stared at the sign. "Which of the shines do you recommend to have on these boots?"

"Bulletproof of course. Let's go all the way. Go hard or go home." I said as I smiled at him and he nodded.

"Ah, I'll just take the basic."

As I began to burn the loose threads from his shoes, I noticed his wedding band. It was as if he wanted me to notice it, the way he placed his left arm almost in front of my face as I was working on his boots, so I didn't hesitate to get into the questions. "I like the way you're flaunting your wedding band. How long have you been married?" I asked.

"Twenty-five years, a long time, with two boys, one twenty and one seventeen" he said.

"Oh that's nice, twenty and seventeen, you got some buddies there."

"Yeah, that's true; they're my buddies."

"If you were to give me some advice on marriage, what would it be?"

"Make sure you're really infatuated," he replied.

"Infatuated?"

"Yeah, and that commitment thing, but to me it's not as big anymore, because people say, 'Oh, if it doesn't work, I'll get a divorce and re-married three, four times,' and that really can screw up the kids. How old are you?" he then asked.

"I'm twenty-five years old." I responded as I began to apply the polish on his boots.

"You've still got plenty of time, take your time and find that right person. So where are you from?"

"I'm originally from Guyana. Georgetown, Guyana." I replied.

"Oh, your English is good," he said as he reached into his pocket for his wallet.

"Yeah, we speak English in Guyana. It's the only English speaking country in South America and that's because we were once a British colony," I said to him.

"I didn't realize that."

"Yeah, we were called British Guiana, before 1966, when we gained our independence." I said to him.

"I didn't know that," he replied.

"So how long have you had these boots?"

"About five years."

"Five years, did you ever had them re-soled?" I asked as I began to buff his boots.

"No, I didn't yet, but I have some boots that I've had for 30 years. I've re-soled them many times before."

"That's nice. Ok, you're good," I said.

"Thank you," he said, as he stepped down, paid me and then took off.

BEST-FRIENDS

"This must be the best seat in the house?" my new customer asked.

"Yes it is," I replied as I placed the footrest up for him, then began wrapping the balm rag around my hand. "Which one of our three shines would you like to have: the bulletproof, glass or basic?" I then asked.

"I'll do the bulletproof I guess," he calmly replied.

"Ok, so how's your day going so far?" I asked as I began cleaning his shoes.

"Good, I've been on the road for almost two weeks, and will take two weeks leave from today, then come back through this crazy airport on the 1st, and head straight to New Zealand then come back from New Zealand on the 4th, then I'm done with business travel for the month," he stated.

"I'm looking at your hand, your fingers and I'm kind of confused, is it a wedding band?"

"Oh, my partner and I, and lot of gay couples, do the right hand," he replied as he lifted his right hand up and made his ring more visible to me.

"I didn't know that, that's interesting."

"It used to be different before all the laws started changing," he then stated.

"So what kind of advice can you give to me about getting married?"

"Male or female?" He asked as he began biting his finger nails.

"It doesn't matter. We're all the same; I'm talking in general," I said.

"In general, hmm, obviously make sure you know who you're getting married to. Hopefully you've been together for a bit. If not, it should be one of those people that as soon as you meet them, there was that spark. My partner and I saw each other once and fell in love with each other, and we've been together for twenty-three years."

"Twenty-three years. Are you guys married?" I asked next.

"No, and that's the one thing with couples, with gay marriage, I mean, we've been together so long, we're set up with the city, and also from a legal standpoint if we travel, should anything happen to either of us, we'd have access, without having to go through a lot of pain and agony. So our plan is, until the federal government, really like, acknowledges it, especially from an inheritance standpoint. Right now, even though we've been together twenty-three years and all of our money is joined, God forbid one of us dies and leaves something. It's all taxable. Anyways, until the federal government does something where we truly have financial legal rights, our income doesn't make any difference, although it's been twenty-three years," he explained as he continued to bite his nails.

"Yeah, that's a long time, man. That's definitely love."

"Yeah, love or tolerance, I'm just saying," he stated as we both laughed.

I then stopped brushing his shoes, stood up and asked him, "Which one do you think it is?" since I wanted him to elaborate more on his last sentence.

"It's all of the above. Listen, we are best friends. I can't say it's always good. It isn't easy. No relationship is—whether it's a friend, or a partner, or a lover, or a husband and wife. It's all about communication and acceptance and unconditional love, and being honest and trusting, and if something does happen, find a way to get through it as a couple, because anyway ok so I'm in the fashion industry," he said and we both laughed at how he just switched up the topic.

"Ok" I nodded, as I began applying the second layer of polish to his shoes.

"A lot of time, my clients are quite challenging to my staffs on supplies. I work for a company in Paris, so I usually bring something to try to ease their day, so that when they're being a pain in the butt or whatever, or if I'm being a pain in the butt, they look at something and go ok, and they either hit it, throw it or touch it." He smiled.

"It's possible for it to get boring, right?" was my next question as I looked at him with a smirk on my face.

"Yeah, of course. There's a different between sex and love, right?"

"Yep," I quickly responded.

He stuttered his first words. "Um, and, with . . . . Ours is a little bit of an interesting situation, because he's HIV positive and he has been since before we met, so sex is one of those things that we have to be very cautious about. When I was young and stupid and before all this craziness happened, it was a lot of crazy sex, but now it's more about intimate respect. We have not necessarily date nights, but we make a lot of time for each other, we cook together. Sorry, I'm just sweating like a pig. I worked out this morning a little bit, so I'm still hot," he said as we both laughed. He then continued where he left off, "So anyway, it gets to a point where it's like . . . I don't know," he then became quiet, as if he didn't know what else to say.

"Yeah you do. You've been in it for twenty-three years, so you definitely know" I quickly said to keep him going on.

"Twenty-three, and it's like a burn on my hand" he joked as we both laugh out loud. He then added, "We have little disagreements here and there, but if you want it to work, communicate, communicate, communicate. If you ever have a disagreement or a fight, you never—I don't care if you have to stay up until darkness when trying to work through it or agree to disagree—don't ever take the conflict in the bedroom. Don't! Don't go to bed where you're like on either side of it. It's about, I hear you, I disagree with you, but I love you and let's go to bed since it's four o'clock in the morning and we have to be up in two hours."

It was time for my last question, since I was almost finished. I stopped from wiping his shoes with the buff rag and looked up at him and asked, "Do you guys have any kids?"

"Oh no, because we don't seem to want to adopt or anything, but years ago we did, but that's a whole other story," he said. He looked down at his shoes and said "Those look fabulous," as he smiled at me. "That's a long drop" he said after he climbed down from the stand.

"Yes it is," I joked.

"What's your name?"

"It's Lancelot," I replied.

"Oh, wow. Here Lancelot, this is for you," he said as I thanked him and he walked off.

26

FULL TIME JOB

"WELCOME BACK, SIR. How have you been?" I greeted my next customer, since I had recognized his face. This was one of my regulars. He would travel out of the terminal at least once every week and would always take a shine, even if his shoes didn't need it. "Take a seat, make yourself comfortable," I then urged him, as he quickly got seated and placed his feet on the footrest. "Ah, I've been good." He replied.

"Where are you heading today?" I immediately asked, since his destination would change every time we would speak to each other.

"Out to Bermuda today, but uh, you got power? I lost power since yesterday," he stated.

"Yeah, I got power back Wednesday, actually," was my quick response as I began to brush the leather balm off his shoes.

"Wednesday?"

"Yeah."

"Oh lucky you, no hot shower?" he asked.

"No hot shower." We laughed. I then went on to ask him which shine he'd prefer to have today.

"Um, let me get the bulletproof," he replied as he stuttered his first word.

"Is that a wedding band?" I asked, noticing that he was wearing a horse-buckle-pattern gold ring on his left ring finger and also because I was already familiar that this particular customer liked to chat, because we would always chat throughout his shines.

"No, it's not" he replied.

"Oh that's cute, did you get it with the shoes?"

"I didn't get it with the shoes, but I bought it in the same store. They don't sell it anymore; it's a horse buckle," he said staring at his ring.

"What karat is it and was it very expensive?"

"I bought it a long time ago and I don't even remember what I paid for it."

"I honestly thought it was a wedding band."

"Ah, it's my wedding band now," he said as he laughed, then added, "I've lost my wedding band about four times so this is the new one." We both laughed.

"So how long have you been married?" I then asked.

"Twenty-seven years," he replied as he turned his focus to the food court, which was straight ahead of the stand.

"Twenty-seven years, damn that's older than me," I informed him.

He laughed. "That's older than you? Now I'm feeling old."

I then moved on with another question, "So what would you say is the key factor, to make it last that long?"

"It's hard, man," he said as he shook his head from left to right before adding, "You've just got to work at it, at all times. It's a full time job. People get married and they think, "Oh, I don't have to work at it anymore, you've got work at it. It's a relationship. Marriage is tough. There are good years and bad years, good weeks and bad weeks, so you've just got to focus on your goals and keep working on it."

"Ok."

"I don't know if I have any wisdom for you, but what I could tell you is that it doesn't come easy for anybody. You've got to work at it," he stressed.

"Do you think that marriage has the same value today that it had twenty years ago?

"No, definitely not. We're an entirely different set of people. Times have changed, marriage and the values are not the same, people change every time, you'll change, she'll change, I did, my wife did," he explained.

"You guys changed for the best, I hope?" I asked, as I began to buff his shoes.

"I don't know, I got so fat and now she's better looking," he joked as we both began to laugh.

"You're good to go, sir," I said, signaling his shine was completed.

"Alright buddy, nice seeing you again," he said as he climbed down from the stand, paid, grab his bag then took off.

"Thanks for the business."

27

OPPORTUNITY

"HOW ABOUT A shine, sir?"

"Can you do navy blue?" the passenger asked, as he stopped in front of the stand and looked down at his shoes.

I quickly reached into my shine box and pulled out the navy polish and replied, "Yes sir, of course I can," as I raised the polish and showed it to him.

"Let's do it," he said and walked over to the stand and took a seat.

"Are we going to go all the way up to the bulletproof today?" I asked him as I began to take my supplies out of the supply box, after putting on my gloves and dust mask.

"No, just the basic."

"Basic shine? Ok, so where are you heading today?" I quickly moved on, as I began to clean his shoes.

"Pittsburgh for work, then back to New York," he added.

"You live here?"

"Yeah I live here, I'm just going to Pittsburgh for work," he said.

"Are you traveling alone, or do you have your family with you?" was my gateway question for him.

"No I'm alone."

"Are you married?" I then asked to be more specific.

"No," was his quick response.

"Do you think that you're ever going to get married?"

"No," was his quick response again, this time laughing out loud. I was determined to hear this guy's story so I stopped brushing his shoes, looked at him and asked, "Why not?"

"I don't believe in marriage" was his answer, as he continue to laugh.

"Why, did you have a bad experience?" I immediately asked.

"No."

"I don't understand. You must have a reason why you don't believe in marriage; there's a reason for everything."

"Yeah, but," he said as he continued to laugh.

"It's like you don't eat a kind of food, why don't you eat this food? Because it gives you an allergic reaction right? There must be a reason," I probed as I began to apply the polish to his shoes.

"Well you don't eat the food because you just don't like it, that's all," he said, this time with a little attitude in his voice.

But that wasn't going to stop me, I was determined to hear the real reason why he was against marriage. So I asked him another question, based on his last response, "So did you taste it before?"

"No," was his quick response again, and we both laughed. "You know how people say, 'I don't like fish,' and the response is 'You haven't tried all fish.'"

"Ok," I replied, "I get it, I thought you just learned from other people's experiences. So is it something that you would never do, or it's just something that isn't in your thought as of now?" I asked.

"That's what I'm saying; I'm never going to say never, the thing is, there's always that opportunity, but right now, no. I'm not like totally against marriage, don't get me wrong, but as of right now, this very moment, it's no. Are you married?" he asked.

"No, I'm not married. I'm still a baby, look at me," I joked with him as I began to brush the polish into his shoe.

"You have a moustache, though," he replied, as we both laughed out loud.

"I'm still a baby, I'll be turning twenty-six years old, in the next two weeks," I said as we continued to laugh." I then continued by saying, "And besides, we men only grow up when we're in our thirties, so I still got a couple more years to go. I'm thinking about it but at the same time, I'm taking my time. I think marriage is a beautiful thing," I said.

"I'm not going to say it's not. I mean, if somebody wants to be committed to somebody, it could be wonderful. Like my aunt that I live with, she had been married for thirty-three years.

"Wow, and you don't want to have something like that?" I asked.

"No."

"What would you say is the key factor, that made her marriage last that long?" I asked, as I began to buff his shoe.

"You know, don't get me wrong, I think any relationship is going to have arguments, and I think that helps. I mean, look at it from a relationship point of view, there's folks that have relationships and all they do is fight, but once in a while, they talk, so that really makes you communicate what you really feel. And mutual interest is another big thing, because ultimately you're going to be spending the rest of your life with that person and you want to be able to do things together, and lastly age. I obviously think age could play a very important role. You could find out that you accept more, like with responsibility, since you're more mature. I just think that, as you gets older, you become more uncomfortable doing the stuff you used to do when you were young," he explained.

"Ok," I said and signaled that his shine was completed.

"Marriage is a good thing," he added as he climbed down from the stand.

"Yes it is," I replied as we both laughed. After I gave him his change, he then stepped closer to me and said "You really want to know the reason why I don't think I will ever get married? Because where I'm from, they don't accept in gay marriage." He then walked off.

"Thanks man,"

28

WILLING

HERE I AM sitting on the stand reading an email on my cell phone, I felt as if someone was looking at me. I looked up and a man was looking right at me, walking towards the stand. He pointed his fingers and said to me, "These are casual shoes, but I'll still take a shine."

"Sure why not, take a seat and make yourself comfortable," I urged him. He was wearing a two-tone shoes that were made from both suede and leather, but just had tiny tracks of suede around them, so they could still be shined.

As I began to take out the supplies, the first other thing I noticed was that his shoes had a lot of stitching that was loose. Since I had no lighter to burn them in, I began to cut them off.

He paid very close attention to what I was doing to his shoes before asking me, "Have you ever been in the Army?"

"No" was my quick response as I continued to cut off the stitching from his shoe.

"We had a nickname for those threads in the Army, "The Irish Pennants," you know, like the Yankees flag," he stated.

"Ok" I responded, without adding anything or asking any questions about what exactly the "Irish Pennants" were since I didn't want to stray away from my preferred topics of discussion, but I did find out what It was later on in the day after looking it up on the internet.

"Oh, by the way which of the shines would you like to have, sir?" I asked as I began to apply the leather balm on his shoes very carefully.

"Basic, shine please," he responded.

"Where are you heading to?"

"Houston, I'm going home" he said then added, "We came in last Thursday, and we got stuck. We were supposed to go back on Monday, now we're going back today. How about you, was your home damaged by the storm?"

"Yeah, just my basement though," I replied.

"You got electricity?"

"Yeah, we just got it back, thank God, because it could've always been worse. You have to give thanks for what you still have. Are you traveling with someone?"

"Oh yeah, I have a partner, he's down there somewhere, at the gate," he replied as he pointed down the terminal. I then asked him, "Are you married?"

"Yep," was his reply as he fixed his feet on the footrest.

"What's your take on marriage?" I asked, as I began to brush his shoes.

"I think it's fine, once the couple is committed, and they're both at a stage in life where they are willing to make that leap to do whatever it takes to make it work."

"So do you think it would be a good idea to move in together before getting married?"

"There are some people who don't believe that, and there are some people who believe it would be good for the marriage. But I'm very skeptical, so I won't move in together before."

"So, can you explain the feelings that you get when you thinks it's the person?" I asked him as I began to wipe his shoes with the buff rag.

"Well, when you have faith, you know. It might sound cheesy, but it's something you feel in your heart, and then you just know. You have that sense of certainty in your heart. It's kind of hard to put into words, but it's a great feeling."

"The feeling of butterflies in your stomach, huh?" I asked him before giving him the thumbs up to signal to him that his shine was done.

"Yeah," he replied as he got up and climbed down from the chair and paid me.

"Well you know what's crazy about that feeling—I've already had that feelings four times before in my stomach," I joked with him as we both stood in front of the stand and laughed. I thanked him for the business and he took off.

29

COMMITMENT

"I'LL TAKE A shine." My next customer approached me as I was sitting in the chair at the side of my stand just gazing around the terminal.

"Sure, step right up. You can put your bags right here," I advised him. He sat after placing his bags on the stand.

"Nice socks, by the way," he complimented me.

"Yea I got a couple of colorful ones too," I replied as I began to clean his shoes.

"Ok," he replied as he smiled and nodded his head.

"Where are you heading today?"

"Texas, for business, then coming back home. What about you, are you a native New Yorker?"

"No, I'm not; I'm originally from Guyana, but have been living here in the U.S. for over four years now. I live right here in Queens. Rosedale," I added, as I grabbed a piece of tissue off of the cabinet and began to wipe my face, as I was sweating a lot. I asked him where he was originally from, because he had a foreign accent.

"Egypt. I mean, my mother is German, so I'm German, too," he replied.

I noticed that he was wearing a wedding band, so I decided to just go ahead and ask him questions about marriage. "So, how long have you been married?" was my first question.

"I've been married now for fifteen years," he said as he looked down at me.

"So what kind of advice can you give me about marriage?" I asked next.

"Marriage is a commitment, and the children come, and it depends on what you feel. If you're committed to look after your kids, you'll work for the marriage. If you just look out for yourself, after a year, you'll leave the marriage and you'll get another one. It's a good feeling to get another one. Having a honeymoon is good," he said and we both laughed.

"Honeymoon after honeymoon, doing a lot of good stuff," I said.

"Yeah the honeymoon is nice. You go overseas, you relax, you enjoy, but that's not life, that's just fantasy. In real life, you have emotions, life can be stressful, you get angry, and you do things you don't normally do. The relationship is easy to break, then you get another one. You get a better one, maybe. But if you don't get relationships, you will get nothing but fantasies, and if you only come together for money or fantasies, that's not right. You're living fast, she's living fast, ya'll not working, ya'll having fun. It's a nice life, right, but that will only last for a short period of time, because today life is different. Once you start having problems, and you get into real business, you're like a bird—you both want to get away. Unless you say, you know, this is from God, you're committed, and this is what I want and work for it."

"Yeah," I quickly agreed with him before moving on to another question, since I was almost finished with his shine. "What would you say is the key factor to rejuvenate the marriage after numerous arguments, disagreements and all of those other things that can affect the marriage?"

"It depends on what your expectations are. If your expectations are just to have a better life with yourself, it won't work. Every day you get older, right? Every day, you are one day older than the day before, right?"

"Yep," I replied.

"So when you're young, you look on stuff different than when you get older. You get stuff, but you lose stuff along the way, and along the way, if you just decide to share your weakness with somebody, if that other person is interested to know about you or to love you, that other person wouldn't leave you, so you have to be committed."

"So I'm guessing if you had a chance to do it again, you would?" I asked.

He then stated, "Marriage happens by itself. You don't think about marriage; if you have to think about marriage, it's fake! When you sit and ponder 'If my life would be better or worse . . .;' 'What am I getting out of this?'; 'What should I do?', then you're thinking it's business. Should I take this seriously or should I be cautious because it looks like it comes with problems? Then it's fake! So you just got to let it happen and get married. After the problems come, you just have to stand with her and be helpful. Then you get children and you try to do what's best for them also. Life goes on without any other option, there's one good option: Should I stay or leave? Because leaving can be a good option."

"You're good, what do you think?" I asked him as I removed the footrest for him to climb down from the stand.

"Thank you," he said, before reaching into his pocket and pulling out a ten dollar bill, giving it to me and saying, "Keep the change."

"Thanks for the business and the advice," I replied.

"Yes, take it easy, don't push for it, but once it happens, go for it!" he advised me as he walked off.

30

BELIEFS

"I'LL TAKE A shine," my next customer said to me as he removed his backpack from his shoulders and placed it at the side of the stand, followed by his pulley luggage.

"Ok, step on up and make yourself comfortable."

He then got seated and placed both of his hands into his jacket pocket while I began to work on his shoes.

"I had the bulletproof the last time, so this time I'll just have the basic shine," he requested.

"Sure man, you definitely still have some protection left on them." I then began to stain the sole of his shoes with the black stain since it was a little discolored.

"How are you?" he then asked me.

"So far so good, and yourself?" I responded.

"Well, it's still early, so, 'So far, so good,' would be the best thing to say, I guess." He said as he smiled and nodded. "You got power back?"

"Yeah I got power back. Are you from New York?"

"Connecticut."

"Oh ok, were you guys affected badly over there?"

"Not really we just lost power for 5 days," he said as he gazed around the terminal.

"So where are you heading today?"

"Orlando for a few days on business. I've just got to figure out how I'm going to get back on Wednesday with this big storm coming," he added.

"Yeah, I heard it supposed to be a snowstorm. Let's just hope it's not a really, really bad one," I said as I began to brush his shoes.

"Yeah, let's hope so," he replied.

"So, are you married?" I asked.

"Nope! Everyone says it's a wise decision not to get married," he responded as he stared at me in my eyes and smiled. I then began to laugh, since I thought what he had said was a joke.

"So are you married?"

"No I'm not, but it's a thought that's in my mind," I responded.

"I guess it's the right thing, with the right person," he then said.

"Ok, so are you saying that you would never get married, or you just haven't found that right person?" I asked as I began to wrap the polish rag around my hand.

"If I found the right person I probably would, but they probably are already married to someone else," he joked.

I then quickly asked him another question since I was already buffing the final layer of polish into his shoes. "Do you think marriage has the same value today that it had twenty, thirty years ago?"

"Nope" he answered, as he shook his head from left to right. "My parents were married fifty-five years, and nowadays that doesn't happen." He then asked, "Where are you originally from?"

"I'm from Guyana." I replied, and asked, "What do you think was your parents' key factor to make their marriage last that long?"

"There's no choice. They don't believe in divorce, and they could've gotten in trouble because they're always working. She works, he works, they've got four kids . . . so, you know, your beliefs have a lot to do with it."

"You're good," I said to him as I urged him to watch his steps while getting down from the stand.

"How did that happen to your hair?" he asked, as he reached for his bags.

"I don't know; I just woke up one day and it was like this," I joked.

"You're lying. It was your girlfriend who did that to you," he said, laughing.

"No, I did it myself. You like it?" I asked him.

"Yeah, it's interesting" he replied as he smiled and walked away.

31

SENSITIVITY

"HOW ARE YOU doing so far?" I asked my next customer as he settled into the chair.

"So far, so good," he replied, as he hiked up his pant legs.

"Where you heading to?" I jumped right in to get this guy's story.

"Fort Lauderdale," he said with a smile.

"You live there?" His short answers didn't deter me.

"No, I live here, in Queens."

I asked him if he was traveling alone, and his response was, "No, with my wife."

"Your wife . . . how long have you been married?" I asked with smile on my face, as I began to stain his scuffed-up shoe sole.

"A long time," he replied as he began laugh a little.

"Long time, how long is that, ten years?" I tried to guess.

He countered my question with his own. "How about you, are you married?"

"No, no. I'm not married, that's why I'm asking you. I ask a lot of my customers. I want to gather as much information as I can before I decide to do it."

"Well, don't live without women," he told me.

"Oh yeah, don't live without women?" I repeated.

"Yes, because you know what? This life only happens once, and women can beautify everything."

"Women can beautify everything?" I asked as I continued to brush his shoes.

"Of course, just think about your mother," he said.

"Yeah, that's true," I agreed.

"Our mothers give us all the love," he continued, then asked me, "You agree?" as I smiled and said, "Yeah," he went on to say, "We have two mothers; one mother gives you life at birth, a life, and the other mother keeps you alive."

"So how long have you been married? How many years?" I tried to get him back on track.

"Well I had, I've had so many women, I'm ashamed to tell you."

"You're ashamed to tell me?" Now I'm laughing. I guess this guy is a player.

"I've been with over six thousand different woman," he confesses.

"Over six thousand?" I questioned, not knowing whether to be disgusted or impressed.

"Over six thousand," he repeated. "If I was careless, I would have over three thousand children. I love women; I can't live life without them. I can't get tired of them."

"Ok, so what do you do to like, to keep the relationship alive, after being married for so long? Because I heard it's possible to just fall out of love while being married." I steered the conversation.

"Let me tell you, sex definitely cannot keep it. Donkeys have sex, horses have sex. Sex cannot keep the relationship. It has to be some kind of high emotional thing of happiness."

I smiled and added, "Commitment?"

"Yes, because you have sensitivity, and when you value the sensitivity of your body, you respect the sensitivity of a woman's body. So when you respect that sensitivity, they come closer to you, so, the best thing to do with a woman is just make her happy. I do everything a woman wants to keep her happy. If you keep saying no, no, no, you keep making excuses, she got to be happy, allowed her to go with the right affection."

"That's true, that's so true. Do you have any kids?" I asked next, as he chuckled and said, "Yeah four, from four different women."

"How many?" I asked to confirm, not hiding my amazement.

"Four, from different women. Each one has a different mother."

"Wow, you're a playboy."

"Yeah, I live my life, because I've got one life," he smiled and said.

"You only live once, right?" I said to him, as he smiled and said, "Yep, yep."

"Ok, you're good man," done polishing his shoe.

"Looks good," he said as he stepped down from the stand.

"Yup, watch your step, there." I advised.

"Very good," he said emphatically.

"You like it?" I asked.

"I love it. They look brand new, good job," he complimented and paid me.

"Nice." I said as I took my gloves off.

"What, you think I'm going to argue with you?" He chuckled, then said," I don't want to make a happy ending ruined."

We both laughed as he took off.

32

THE ONE

"LET ME CLEAN those Doc's up for you man. You guys get a three dollar discount, so you only pay five."

"Really?" my next customer asked, as I tried to sell him a shine.

"Ok, let me eat first," he then added, as he walk to the sitting area and began to eat whatever it was that he had in his bag. After ten minutes, he came over to the stand and took a seat.

"How are you today, sir?" I asked as he got seated.

"Not too bad," he replied, gazing at the sign.

I then began to give him his options of shines. "We have three levels of shines: the bulletproof, the glass and the basics. Each offers more protection to the shoes and a longer lasting shine, and remember, you guys get three dollars off of the original price. So which one would you like to have?"

"Ah, just the basic," he requested, as he fixed his feet on the footrest. I began cleaning his shoes and wasted no time with my first question.

"Where are you heading?"

"Boston for work."

"Raise it up, raise it up please?" I kindly asked him to roll up his pants' bottoms to avoid polish from getting onto them, because I had already put on my gloves.

"No problem" he said, as he reached down and began rolling them up.

"Thank you. So how long are you going to be over in Boston?"

"Just a couple of days, work and then back" he replied, before switching the topic and asking, "Did the airport open again the day after the storm?"

"No, they opened officially on Thursday. It was closed on Monday and Tuesday. They had thirty arriving flights on Wednesday, but nothing was going out."

"Oh," he replied as he began to gaze around the terminal, which I took advantage of and quickly asked another question.

"Are you married?"

"No, are you?" was his response, as if he was waiting on me to ask another question.

"No I'm not," I quickly replied.

"Cheers to that," he said with an unusual smirk on his face.

"So would you ever get married?" I then asked.

"I think so yeah, I'll go for it, it's just got to be the right person," he answered as he continued to gaze around the terminal.

"Ok, but how do you know if it's the right person. What are some signs you would look for?"

"You're asking the wrong person," he said, smiling. "I think as you get older, you appreciate life more. I didn't meet a girl until a while ago, three, four years ago, to be exact."

"Ok, so do you think she's the one?" I calmly asked him.

"Yeah, I think she is, but to be honest, I don't know why I think she's the one."

"You don't know why you think that she's the one, but you think that she's the one," I said as we both began to laugh aloud.

He then went on to say "Yeah, I know, but it's not something that I can put into words, it's more of a feelings thing."

"I had been with my ex-girlfriend for a couple of years, too."

"Ok, what about you, were you feeling anything?" he asked.

"Yeah, I was feeling a lot of stuff, but we're not together anymore."

"Excuse me, I have to take this call" he said, as he took his cellphone out of his pocket and began talking on it. He spent maybe a minute and a half before getting off of it, while I continued to clean his shoes.

"Sorry about that," he said, then went on to say, "But ah, my family has good and long marriages. My great grandparents were married for seventy years, my grandparents fifty, and now my parents are still married for thirty-five years, but her family has had a lot of divorce.

"Ok, so you guys do talk about marriage?" I asked.

"Yeah, but she has to break that divorce curse, and I hope she does it with me" he said, smiling.

"Yes, with you," I agreed, then said "You're all set, thank you man," as I removed the footrest to allow him to step down from the stand.

"Thank you," he said as he paid me and walked off.

33

GOD-FIRST

"THIS IS OSTRICH, right?" I said to my next customer, who came over to the stand and requested to have a shine on his tan boots before getting seated.

"Ah, I don't know, is it?" he asked.

"Yeah it is, I can tell."

"You can?"

"Yes I can," I said as I began to clean his boots with the leather balm. I then went on to ask him "Where did you come from?" since I saw when he was getting off of the jet bridge of an arriving flight.

"Texas."

"So how long are you going to be out here in New York for?"

"Probably a year," he replied, as he stared down at me cleaning his boots.

"Oh you moved here, with your family? I notice you're wearing a ring on your ring finger, are you married?" I asked him.

"Yes," he replied, then asked, "So how you like living in New York?"

"Living in New York is nice, I've been here four years now; it's really nice here." I assured him.

"So where are you from originally, I hear an accent?" he asked.

"I'm from Guyana."

"Guyana?" He repeated, as if that was his first time hearing the word Guyana, so I said "Yeah" while looking up at him, waiting to hear what he was going to say next, but he quickly got off that subject and stated, "This is the first time I've been to New York."

"First time?" I repeated, since I thought that was kind of unusual, coming from someone who was actually living in America, which I later found out wasn't actually. I then added, "Don't worry you'll like it, it's . . . New York is a very, very diverse city

"A lot of pretty women?"

"Yeah, a lot of pretty women," I stressed.

"Really?" he replied with a little smirk on his face, as we both began to laugh aloud.

"And the best part about New York is, whenever you think you saw the prettiest woman, five seconds afterward, you see another woman that's prettier than the last one you saw. But you're a married man; you're not looking anymore."

"Yeah. I'm looking, but I'm not touching. Can't hurt to look," he replied as we both laughed.

"Yep, you're right, so how long have you been married?"

"Thirty-one years," he replied.

"That's a long time," I said, then asked, "So what do you do to make it last for thirty-one years?

"Say yes ma'am and no ma'am" he advised me, as we both laughed aloud, then added, "That's it, nothing else" as we continued to laugh. He then stopped for a few seconds and went on to say, "God has blessed me with a great marriage, a great woman, strength and health. You know, we're committed, no drama."

"That's good, that's really good, so yes ma'am, no ma'am, nothing else, and that's it?" I asked with a smirk on my face, as I began to brush his shoes.

"It all goes along with it. Men like to wear the pants in the relationship, but every now and then you've got to take them off, and it doesn't hurt, to say yes ma'am, no ma'am at times" he joked, as we both laughed some more. He then went on to say, "Tell me something; I heard rent is high in New York."

"Yeah rent is a killer out here."

"So what do you get, what do you pay?"

"For a three bedroom apartment in Queens, the least you might pay is fifteen hundred dollars a month, but in Manhattan, it could be up to three or four thousand for the same space."

"Fifteen hundred a month?" he repeated, as he opened his eyes wide.

"Yeah, and that's in Queens and some parts of Brooklyn. In Manhattan, you pay the bigger dollars," I added.

"How do you feel about the damages of the storm?" he asked.

"It was pretty bad, really bad; a lot of people are still without power," I replied as I continued to brush his shoes, then quickly switched the topic back to talking about marriages. "So what would you say is the key factor to make a marriage work today, since to most people marriage really doesn't have the same value today that it had twenty, thirty years ago?"

"Honestly, mean what you say, and say what you mean. I have four beautiful kids and a lovely wife, so I really try my best to do what's right for their sakes; it's never about me anymore."

"That's nice, so would you advise anybody to get married, to take that risk?" I asked next.

"Yeah, of course. After all those years I got married, I found out all this stuff about God and how you live your life and how you face it. I waited until I was thirty then got married. I won't take anything from my single life, and I won't take anything from my married life, but for a man and a woman to make it without God in their life is highly impossible," he said, then paused for a second, then continued by saying, "God first, family second and job third. My wife and I had made a commitment to God. We've messed up, we've made mistakes, but we always go back to Him and talk to Him. He doesn't talk back to us in words, but if you have good things in your heart and you believe that this is in your heart, then you can do it your way, but I've found out doing it his way has helped me to make my life better."

"Ok, you said, God first, family second, and job third?" I asked.

"Yeah, put Him first and he'll put everything in order like it's supposed to be. He lets you take care of everything the way he wants you to take care of everything. It's not going to be easy, it's going to be the hardest thing you've ever done in your entire life, but some way or the other it works. That's for me! It might not be for you, it might not be for that guy standing right there," he said as he pointed to a passenger that was standing by the restroom, then continued, "But I know for a fact like this right here," he said, then he touched my right hand, and said, "Yep, I know for a fact like that, nobody could ever tell you that I just didn't touch you,

you're going to believe that I touch you till you die, 'cause you know it's true, right?"

"Yeah," I replied as I stopped working on his shoes and gave him my undivided attention. I really wanted to understand what he was saying clearly.

"I know something that God has done in my life that is not an accident, it's not a coincidence, I know it just like you know I that I just touched you, but that's for me and nobody is ever going to tell me any different, just like I can't tell you—or nobody can't tell you—that I just didn't touch you, and I believe that, and I'll believe it till I die."

"That makes a lot of sense." I said, as I began to apply the last layer of polish to his boots.

"There are so many things about life you don't know about. Even though I knew the sun was going to rise this morning, I know I'm going to have to get up, I'm going to have to eat, sleep, I might get a little fuss from my wife, and things are not going to go right, but I'm still trusting you to help me get through all this madness. You don't have to prove yourself to me anymore. I believe in you, but that's for me. I'm not talking for anybody else but me," he said.

I nodded and said, "Ok, you're all set. Thank you, for the business and the advice."

"Thanks, take care," he replied as he took off, after paying me.

34

FAMILY

"How long are you going to be out there for?" I asked my next customer that approached the stand and requested a shine. As he got seated, who said he was heading to Maine.

"Till Friday, it's a quick one," he replied, then asked me, "So how did you deal with Sandy, you got power?"

"Yeah, it came back on a few days after the storm, but it could have always been worse, so you still got to give thanks for what you have.

"Yes, at least you still have hope." he said, as he nodded.

"Yeah exactly, and my life," I agreed, then I immediately asked him, "So where do you live?"

"Ah, out in Long Island."

"Ok, were you affected in any way?" I asked next.

"I just had no power for a few days, so with a three-month-old and a three-and-a-half-year-old, we were force to go to a friend's house that had power, but it could have been worse, like you said. We still had a home to come home to. Everybody is healthy and safe, thank God," he said smiling.

"Thank God," I repeated. "Are you married?" I asked next.

"Yes, almost six years now."

"Ok that's nice, so tell me, what would you say is the hardest factor of marriage?" I asked, as I applied the first layer of polish to his shoes.

"I would say, well, my wife probably won't want me to say it, but with everything that's within and out of the relationship, it's

114

all about having a family. It's not that difficult. I don't think it's that difficult as long as you have communication. Whenever communication breaks down, it can be chaotic. When my wife is at home, I travel. I have to be out of town a lot so, I would probably say that's the most difficult part of it, 'because you get home, and you have to deal with her attitude and whatever else, but the kids makes it easy. When you are mad at times, it's not even about you anymore, it's about what's right for them. Are you married?"

"No I'm not"

"Engaged?"

"Nope."

"Enjoy it, because it's fun, and before you know it, you're married and can't have fun anymore. Going out late, that stops. I had a lot of fun don't get me wrong, but at some point, you get old. I think the longer you wait, the harder it will be. Having somebody, who likes to do everything their way, they're so set in their own ways, those types don't seem like they'll ever understand that somebody else takes priority," he said.

"Do you think that marriage has the same value today that it had fifteen, twenty years ago?" I asked next.

"I would say with certain people it does, but I would also say, with the majority of people, definitely not, because I've seen people look at marriage just as the next step of a relationship, not as, you know, good times, bad times, it's like ok if we're together, since we're married now, and then things don't go the way we want them to, then people move on, so I definitely think that it don't have the same values." He assured me.

"So did you and your wife live together before ya'll got married?"

"Yeah we did, but my father wasn't too happy with that. I talked to him before. I said 'Look, I'm not looking for your approval, I'm looking for your support and he was like, 'Just listen, I give you your thing, you could do whatever, and you know, once you get married and go through the full process then you're going to understand that when things get tough, you have to figure it out and not leave, because things will get tough.' But I do recommend moving in before marriage because that seems to be the biggest issue with people who don't."

"All set," I said to him as I give him the thumbs up, followed by removing the footrest.

"Thank you," he replied.

"Thank you, for the business and the advice," I said to him while I began putting away my supplies.

"No problem, enjoy," he said, as he smiled then walked off.

BEDROOM

MY NEXT CUSTOMER came to the stand while I was standing at the cabinet and requested a shine, on her tan boots. "I'll go get some batteries in the tech store hun," the guy that she was with said to her before walking off. She then got seated. I began to wrap the balm rag around my hand, then placed the footrest up, for her to place her feet on.

"Where are you guys heading to?" I asked her immediately.

"Turks and Caicos, for vacation," she replied with a broad smile on her face as she leaned forward in the chair.

"Are you guys are married?" I asked her next.

"Yes we are. We just celebrated our six-year anniversary," she replied with that same broad smile again.

"Yeah I guess. I should have brought my other boots, they're really bad."

"Don't worry, bring them next time, but these are going to look really good once I'm done with them" I assured her. She nodded her head and began to look in the direction of the tech store.

I then began to apply the polish to her boots and looked up at her and realized that she was looking down at what I was doing, so I took advantage of that and asked another question. "What would you say is the hardest factor of keeping the marriage together, I mean, like what do you guys have to go through the most, like the most complicated thing?"

"Oh the most important thing or the most complicated thing?" she asked, smiling.

"Both," I responded as I continued to clean her boot.

She then laughed and said, "Let's go with the most important thing first," then laughed a little more, and asked me, "You really want to know?" while staring me in the face. "The bedroom, that's the most important thing."

"And what's the most complicated thing?" I then asked.

"Complicated, the daily stuff, like getting mad at each other for completely nothing," she replied, as we both laughed aloud. "It's crazy, but it happens all the time."

"So how do you guys deal with that?"

"How else? The bedroom," she said, and we laughed some more.

"Ok, so how do you know if it's the right person? What are some of the signs that women look for?" I asked.

"No signs—feelings, it has to be something that you feel. If the relationship starts off complicated, it's not going to work. Do you have a girlfriend?" she then asked.

"Yeah I have a couple of girlfriends," I joked.

"Oh," she replied smiling.

"No, I'm actually single."

"Oh, sorry to hear. Where are you from, Jamaica?"

"No, I'm from Guyana" I said.

"Oh, Guyana is like Trinidad right?"

"Yeah, kind of," I replied quickly, since I was almost finished with her boots and wanted to get at least two more answers out of her, before she left. So I then asked, "So is it possible for marriage get boring?"

"It is possible, but you can't allow it to. Otherwise you're going to want out. Whenever it gets boring, nothing seems well, nothing seems like it's moving. Shit becomes, I don't know, just like dull."

"So what are some of the changes a person can look forward too after being married for so long, because I'm sure a lot of stuff changes?"

"Yeah, everything changes; you have a new boss," she added and then began to laugh.

"You have a new boss, or you're the new boss?" I asked her since I wanted to be clear of what she had said.

"You have a new boss. I'm the new boss," she responded and we both laughed aloud again. She then continued by saying, "Believe me, marriage is fun, we're having fun; you just got to keep the right attitude. Nobody should tell you what you should or shouldn't do, and then you get pregnant and it's like scary, stress, this that, but then you get closer. My friend and her husband have been married for fourteen years and it's like they just met each other, they're always hanging out, they're always having fun, they're each other's best friend. You know, you just need a good baby sitter, and when you have a good babysitter, you go out, you party, you keep it alive, you live, and that's all that matters," she assured me, then looked down at her boots and said, "Those look nice" as I was finished shining her boots.

"Yes they do. Take my hands and watch your step," I urged her.

She took my right hand and slowly stepped down from the stand and said, "Oh, thank you."

"Thank you, and enjoy Turks and Caicos," I said to her, as I smile and wave her goodbye.

"We will, thanks" She replied as she walked off.

36

ATTENTION

"ARE YOU OPEN? We'll take a shine" was how I was greeted by my next customers. Two males, both probably in their early thirties, dressed formally. "Yes I am, take a seat," I replied as they both got seated.

"You can do his first, he needs it more," the guy in the right chair said to me as they both began to laugh.

I had already taken out the supplies from the shine box, so I was ready to begin cleaning the first shoes, while the other guy on the right began to focus on his cellphone, I couldn't tell if he was texting or just playing a game, so I continued to focus on what I was doing. I began to apply the leather balm to his shoes, while he watched me do so, before saying, "I think I came the wrong time, to New York, I need to get my ass back to Florida."

"Yeah," I agreed with him then added "We're expecting another storm, so you definitely got to get these bad boys in shape," referring to his shoes.

"Yeah man, I know, but it will probably get messed up again," he stated, as I went on to ask him what shine he would like to have.

"Just the regular one, but what's the difference between the shines?" He asked, as he stared at the sign.

"Extra layers of polish so it will last longer, and if by any chance snow catches it, you can just wipe it off and the shine will still be there," I explained to him.

He changed his mind and requested to have the bulletproof shine instead.

"That's what I'm talking about, it's only right," I said to him, nodding my head.

"You got the mask and everything, you don't fuck around," he said to me smiling.

"Nope, we're professional's. What do you expect? We're the real deal," I assured him as we both began to laugh aloud. "So do guys you live in Florida?"

"Yeah, we do, but we're going to be out here till next Friday." He began gazing around the terminal.

I then went on to ask him. "What is your take on marriage?"

"I think it's important to be with someone, but if you have kids then it's more important, because it ensures stability within the family, but if you don't want kids, well, I don't know," he stated, then went on to add, "but you know what, I think with certain people it doesn't matter if you have kids or not, but that's just with certain individuals."

"So are you married?"

"No!" he quickly responded.

His friend on the right said, "Don't even think about getting married," while staring me in the face and shaking his head from left to right. We all laughed.

"You said don't even think about getting married. Are you married?" I then asked him.

"Been there and done that, twice," he said as he paused and continued to stare at me, then went on to say, "Seven years the first time; four years second time."

"And what did you do to ruin those marriages?" I joked.

"Absolutely nothing. I just got married to two crazy women," he said and we all laughed.

"So would you do it again, if you had another chance?"

"No, I'm too smart for that. My first wife thought that when we got divorced she was going to get the house, you know, and that I'd support her, but I had already put the house in a trust fund, so she couldn't touch it. She was too stupid to know it, and when I divorced her, it was at the beginning of the women's liberation and judges were male. I got an alimony of only child support. I didn't mind supporting the kids, that's fine. I would tell anybody, the one reason you should get married is for the kids."

"For the kids, yeah." His friend on the left agreed, as he continued and said. "That's the only reason to get married, for the kids. If you don't want any kids, forget marriage. What is the point? If you're not planning on having kids or don't want kids, why would you want to get married? Just to pick up a parasite? Because that's all they are."

"Unless they're really rich," his friend on the left added.

The man on the right disagreed and said, "No, no, it's even worse. My brother had a friend who had married a wealthy woman, and the last time he saw us, he said, "You know when you've married for money, when a man marries for money, he earns it." We all laughed and he continued, "His wife was one of the vicious women that made him earn it, every fucking day. It's not worth it marrying for money, not for a man at least, you know, but women do it all the time. Now I tell my sons, 'Look, you want to have kids and it's great, but ah, even for kids I won't really recommend marriage. You know, you could always get your name on the birth certificate just so that they could have your name. I have a girlfriend now, and because we're not married, she has no rights at all," he stated as his friend on the left began to laugh, he then continued by saying, "What can I say, we get along very well."

"You usually do till you get married," the customer on the left stated.

"So at what age did you get married the first time?" I asked the customer on the right.

"I was twenty-one, but that was when you got married, when I was that age. You finish college and you get married, and live. The first two years were ok, but then, once she got pregnant, then she decided that it was her job to whine, with no possibilities of solving any of her problems. All she wanted to do, was whine and whine and whine. Now men, we like to solve problems."

"While women like to create them," the customer on the left added.

The customer on the right continued by saying, "They create them, especially when they want attention."

"My girlfriend does things that she knows she's not allowed to, and says, "I know I'm not allowed to, but I don't care," the customer on the left said.

"There must be some women worth marrying out there, there really must be, but I don't know any," the customer on the right joked.

"Out of all of my married friends, only like a quarter of them are happily married," the customer on the left added and we all laughed.

The customer on the right then said "No seriously, half the people gets divorce and most people that stay married really aren't that happy."

"That's what one of my customers was saying, that everybody he knows, who's ever been married or is still married is happily divorced or miserably married," I said to them as I began to work on the customer on the right shoes, after he requested to have a basic shine, while the customer on the left just sat there and waited.

"I tell my sons, why buy when you can demo, just demo it, and besides marriage wasn't designed for men anyway. You know, daughters should get married, if they find somebody good, cause they really is nothing in it for men."

The customer on the left added, "It's a lose-lose situation for us," before stepping down from the stand in search of a beverage.

The customer on the right then continued, "Yeah, it really is. The worst is for a woman to get pregnant and then nail you. They claim they're on the pill and then they get pregnant on purpose and nail you for paternity. It really works, it happens all the time. A friend of mine, actually one of my best friends, he was trying to push his girlfriend out the door of the apartment, and he couldn't get her out, so a couple months later, she got pregnant, even though she was supposedly on the pill. She destroyed his life. You know there's some states in this country, where if you're marry and are getting a divorce, if your wife gets pregnant by another man, guess who will have to pay child support? You."

"Even though it's not your kid?" I asked. I stop brushing his shoes, since I was shocked of what I was hearing.

"Yeah, there are some states that say if you're still married that you are to be the father and it doesn't matter what the DNA shows. Talk about sick, that shit is sick. Now you've got to take care of some other man's kid till they're eighteen, by law. You know, the only real solution is the man should not be responsible for the child unless he signs that he's responsible, that he wants to be responsible. You know, even when you get married, you should not be responsible for others' kids. This all came from British laws, because first they didn't know who the father was, so they said, 'Ok, whoever is married is the father, sign off.'"

"Ok, you're set," I said.

"Thank you," he said, as he stepped down from the stand and paid for both his and his friend's shine.

37

TIME

"THANKS FOR YOUR patience," I said to my next customer, who was already sitting in the chair, waiting for me to finish my previous customer.

"No problem," he replied as I began to clean his shoes.

"How are you?"

"I'm good, and yourself?"

"I'm doing all right. Which of the shines would you like to have: bulletproof, glass or basic?"

"I don't want them too fancy, so give me glass," he requested.

"Ok. Where are you heading?" I asked him as I began to stain the sole of his shoes, which were scuffed up really bad.

"Into the city. I flew in from Boston. I've got a meeting," he said to me while placing his hands on the arm rest. That was when I noticed that he was wearing a wedding band and asked him, "Is that a wedding band?"

"Yes, it is," he responded.

"How long have you been married?" I asked next.

"Not long, just five years," he replied.

"Is this your first marriage?"

"No, number two my friend, number two," he repeated, before sneezing.

"Do you think that marriage has the same value today that it had twenty, thirty years ago?"

"Well I think people are," he said, paused for a second, and then went on, "well, the divorce rates are up these days. I don't know how much it is, you know, it's funny though, 'cause if you look at—I'm going to be a little political here—but if you look at the states with the highest divorce rates, there are more republicans, and those are people who are supposed to be more religious and stuff, and yet, they still have high divorce rates. For example, if you take how the republicans are against pornography or whatever. The people who are probably most against pornography are the Mormons in Utah, and if you look at which state downloads the most pornography, Utah is number one."

I said "Wow, and they're against it?" and began to laugh, since I was kind of shock of what I just heard.

"True, yeah. They're against it if you do it, but if they do it, then its ok," he stated.

"So tell me, what are you doing differently to make this second marriage work?"

"What is this an interview show?" he asked.

"Yes, it is." We both laughed.

"Well my wife, my new wife's got a thing which says that if you don't love taking care of the kids, you probably don't love taking care of each other, so you got to make sure that you make time for each other, you have your special time together, you make time to be intimate with one another, because before you know it, you might just be focused on the kids and focused on work and you stray away from realizing that your marriage needs both of you to survive, you know?"

"I understand," I replied, nodding my head as I began to buff his shoes. "Is it really true that women change after saying 'I do'?"

"No. I mean, we joke about it a lot, but it's not true," he assured me, then asked, "What's the difference between the basic and the bullet?"

"Extra layers of polish; we add two more layers of polish for the bulletproof shine," I said to him.

"Ok."

"So it makes sense to get the bulletproof at any time," I assured him, then gave him the thumbs up, since I was finished with his shine.

38

RESPECT

As I BEGAN to clean the shoes of the customer that was in my chair, another customer approached the stand and immediately took a seat, then said, "They told me you're the best, you know, they say the guy with the blond patch in his hair."

I laughed. "They weren't lying, I am the best." I replied as we laughed some more. I then continued to clean my previous customer's shoes and was soon finished.

"Thanks for your patience," I greeted him.

"No problem. I should have brought a bag of shoes to stay here all day. These chairs are some comfortable chairs," he said, then requested to have the bulletproof shine.

"Ok," I said, as I fixed his feet on the footrest.

"Make sure you do a good job, because if you don't, I'm leaving these shoes right here," he joked as we both laughed. He then went on to add, "This should be a super polish."

"Yep, a super polish," I agreed.

"I only like super polish. I don't want a polish; I want a super polish," he continued as he laughed aloud.

"If you have a piece, you can check it out when I'm done, to see if it's really bulletproof," I joked, as we laughed some more. I then asked him my gateway question. "Where are you heading?"

"Right here in New York. I just landed," he said, then added, "After this past week, no electricity, no water, it's crazy and the bad shit is that I live in lower Manhattan," shaking his head from left to right.

"Are you guys still without electricity over there?" I asked next, while cleaning the sole of his shoes.

"It came back Saturday," he replied.

"Ok, is that woman your wife, the woman that you were walking with earlier?" I asked, because I could recall seeing him and a woman walking by the stand about fifteen minutes before him coming for the shine.

"Yeah, that's my wife," he said, smiling broadly.

"You're not wearing any wedding band, I noticed," I said to him.

"I took it off, because actually I get a lot of reactions."

"And your wife is ok with it being off?" I then asked.

"Yeah, she could live with it, once I was getting reactions," he stated. "We've been married for twenty-two years, but we've been together for thirty. You're not even thirty years old, are you?"

"No, I just barely passed twenty-five years old. Barely," I stated, as I began to brush his shoes, while he stared at me.

"Look, it's important to be with someone, we humans, we need somebody to be together with, and once you have kids, it's even more important to be married. I mean, you give them a base, a ground, you know? All these Hollywood people who have kids and don't marry, who you thinks feels it the most when they just split? The kids, of course." He raised his left hand and asked me, "So when are you getting married, what's the date, did you set a date?"

I laughed and continued to polish his shoes, then responded, "No, not as yet," while we both smiled at each other.

"So would you advise anyone to take the risk and get married?" I asked next

"Absolutely. It's interesting. All you've got to do is hold the door and pick up the groceries sometimes, and that's it."

"So what would you say is the hardest factor to make any marriage work?"

He then leaned forward in the chair and said, "Listen, respect each other, never go to bed mad at each other, work together as a team. It's like a sport. Look at it as a sport like I do. You don't want to work alone, you got to work in harmony, because marriage is not easy," he assured me, then stopped from speaking, since his wife had walked up to the stand. "I'm getting the super shine today, I'm getting super bulletproof hun," he said to her while smiling.

She then said, "Of course, he's a professional."

"I am," I responded, with a smirk on my face.

"Your shoes looks like glass," she stated, as she pointed down to my shoes.

"Its patent leather," I replied.

"I was brought up in the time, where a proper man never leaves his house with a pair of unpolished shoes. But this generation, I don't know, it's a crazy generation."

"They don't care about anything," the husband agreed, then added, "They don't shave, they don't shower, and they're just disgusting."

"Honey I'll head to the bags," the wife said to him as he nodded and said "Ok," as she walked off.

I then said, "Yeah, it is awful, so you could just imagine what I'm going through right now, knowing some of those people?"

"Yeah, it's crazy, now here you are, proper guy, and you're surrounded by your generation," he joked as we began to laugh aloud. He then added, "I have a cousin your age, I'm like 'Glen, what's the deal? You know a little shave once in a while, or a little shower, clean clothes would help you know.'" We laughed some more, as he continued by saying, "So our place was so bad that we had to leave our apartment and went up to our friends' place uptown. I asked the doorman, I was like, 'I want to get my shoeshine,' and he told me to go down Lexington. The thing is when you go there all they do is spray a little bit of whatever, but they really don't layer the shoes. The key to a good shine is the layers. Keep building and building."

"Yes," I agreed with him as I began to buff his shoes.

"So this is owned by Veterans and women?" he then asked.

"Yeah," I replied.

"Do they take care of you?"

"Yeah, of course, they're the best," I added as I continue to buff his shoes.

"Oh, this looks great. These shoes have never looked like this; this is amazing," he said before stepping down from the stand and placing a twenty-dollar bill into my hands. "That's for you, you're awesome."

"Thank you," I replied, as he took off.

39

BOREDOM

"JUST HAVE A seat sir. I'll be right with you." I said to my next customer, as he approached the stand and requested a shine, while I was preparing the company's deposit that Monday morning.

"Thank you," he replied as he climbed the stand and got seated. I then closed the cabinet and went over to the customer, I then placed the footrest up, put my gloves and my dusk mask on and began to clean his shoes with the leather balm.

"Where are you heading?" I asked him

"Back to West Palm," he responded.

"Oh, ok. Nice tie by the way," I complimented him.

"Thank you, it's an old one, a vintage one, I think this came out in the late eighties" he added, as he began to touch his necktie, then went on to say, "I have all the vintage ties."

"You're a vintage clothing fan?" I asked, as I began to apply the polish to his cordovan wingtips.

"Yeah, its good stuff."

"So how long were you in New York for?" I asked, since he immediately got silent after his last sentence and began gazing around the terminal.

"I arrived on, let's see, Tuesday, for a few business meetings, and was supposed to get home since six this morning, but they canceled the flights," he said, this time fixing his left hand on the chair's arm rest, and that was when I noticed what seemed to be a wedding band on his ring finger, so I complimented him on it.

"That's a nice wedding band, sir. I like that, it's nice. Oh, it spins?"

"Thank you and yeah, it does," he replied as he began to play with his wedding band, rotating it around his finger.

"So how long have you been married for?" I asked.

"Ten years," he quickly responded, with a rather unusual smile on his face.

It was as if he had just got the best news ever, so I stopped polishing his shoes and asked him, "What's funny, share the joke?"

Instead of saying a word, he began to laugh, so now I'm saying to myself, 'What's really going on with this guy?' I asked him again to share the joke, as he laughed some more.

"Ok, I was originally married for ten years and now I've been living with someone for seventeen years."

"I don't understand that," I said to him, since I wasn't clear of what he was trying to tell me.

"No, why?" he asked with a smirk on his face.

"You said that you were originally married, and—

He interrupted me "Married and divorced."

"Oh, ok and divorced. But now you're living with someone and you guys have been living together for seventeen years," I said, as I finally understood, what he had meant. "Single or married?" I quickly asked.

"No, single" he replied, smiling.

"So that's not a wedding band?"

"It's a commitment band, you know, like a promise rings?"

"Ok," I replied with a smile on my face, as I continued to shine his shoes before asking him, "So which is better, which one would you say is better?"

That's when he looked down at me in my face and said, "I'll never married, again. Too much attachment. It's nice to be together because you want to be together, not because of the papers, and then when you do the papers, you're indebted for life, and you know what? To be indebted because you want to be is much nicer, it has a better feeling. You don't feel caged."

"So what would you say changed, in the ten years of marriage?" I asked.

"Boredom. She got boring; she was really boring," he repeated as if he was disgusted even talking about her.

"Boredom really happens?" I asked him, since I wanted him to get into more details about what he said.

"Well I think we were very young at the time, and I grew and she didn't—she stayed the same. The same reason I married her for, I divorced her for."

"What was the reason?"

"Well because she was too conservative and quiet. I couldn't take it. She was terrible in bed. She didn't do the laundry, I had to do my own. So I said 'What the hell?' I woke up one day and was like 'What the hell am I doing here, wasting my life away?' We have two children," he stated.

"Is that good or not so good?" I asked.

"Well, not so good. They're spoiled brats, but you live and you learn. I would never marry again; I would never have children again. I have a dog and my dog now is so nice to me. She's beautiful, she doesn't talk back, she always kisses and loves me, she doesn't ask me for money, and she still has unconditional love for me," he joked. "She's beautiful, her name is Belle, and she's seven months old, as he reached into his pocket, took out his wallet and showed me a picture of a little shih tzu. "She's cute," I said to him as I continued to work on his shoes.

"She's coming to New York next week. I'm bringing her."

"Oh, that's nice." I replied.

"I will have to bring all of her clothes, because it's cold."

"It is cold, so make sure you do."

"Well, I bought her all types of vintage sweaters, so she'll be fine. I'm surprised there are so many flights going out," he said as I gave him the thumbs up "finished" signal and told him to watch his steps as he climbed down from the stand.

"Thank you. I'll be back around Monday, Tuesday, so I'll see you then," he said as he paid me.

"Thank you," I said.

"Take care" he advised as he walked off.

40

FEELINGS

"HOW ABOUT A shine, sir?" I asked the passenger, who was speed-walking past my stand.

"Sure, that's the best suggestion I've heard all day" he replied, as he stopped and walked over to the stand. Since you're wearing such expensive shoes, it's only right that I give you the best shine," I advised him as he got seated.

"Let's do it."

I quickly slid on my gloves, placed my dust mask on, and was about to apply the leather balm on his shoes as he looked down at me and said, "Look out for the socks. Got to keep them clean for the ladies."

I nodded as we both smiled. I then began placing the playing cards around his shoe, on the inside, in order to prevent polish from getting onto his socks.

"What's the bulletproof shine?" he asked, staring at the sign.

"That's the one that you're getting. That's my best shine," I replied as I stood up and looked at him.

"Twelve dollars. You guys should call that the tourist shine," he stated and we laughed.

"Where are you heading to?

"I'm heading to Rochester, New York," he responded.

"Do you live out there in Rochester?" I asked next.

"I live in San Francisco," he stated.

"Ok, that's where we actually are originated from, San Francisco, we have a couple of shops out there," I said to him, as I began to stain his scuffed shoe sole.

He then nodded.

"You seem exhausted," I said to him, since he was looking kind of drowsy.

"I am. I didn't sleep all night last night, so I'm definitely going straight to sleep when I get to Rochester," he assured me.

"You definitely should," I advised him, before saying, "I assume you're traveling alone?"

"Yeah, how long have you been living in New York for?" he then asked.

"Actually, I moved here in '08, so it's been about four and a half years now. April is going to mark five years."

"So how long have you lived in San Fran?"

"Oh I started living there a couple years ago, three, four years ago" he replied.

"Is it very expensive to live over there?" I asked next.

"Really expensive," he said, stressing it.

"Our prices over there are two dollars more than over here."

"Everything is more expensive over there," he stated, as I continued working on his shoes.

"So you have any kids?"

"Two kids. Two girls," he said.

"Are you married?"

"Yeah, twelve years now," he responded.

"I had a customer and he was telling me that it gets boring after a while, is that true, does it really get boring?" I asked.

"No, it never gets boring. It's just different. It definitely never got boring for me," he assured me, then went on to asked me, "So where are you from originally?"

"Georgetown, Guyana," I said and immediately asked him another question. "If you were to give me advice about finding the right person, what would you say to look for?"

"Don't look for anything, just go with your gut. It's a feeling; it's like air. You see how you can feel air but can't touch it? It's something like that. So do you have a girlfriend, are you married?"

"No I'm not married, but it's a thought that's in my mind, so I like to get different people's opinions on the topic. People with experience, preferably," I replied.

"It's a tough thing. You've got to stay working at it. It's never easy. When marriage takes off, you can't just take it for granted. You have to be on it every single day."

As I looked up at him and said "Ok," then began to buff his shoes.

"Is there a smoking area in the terminal or would you have to go back outside?" a female passenger asked me while I was buffing.

"No, you would have to exit out of the terminal to smoke," I replied.

"Oh, damn," she responded, with a rather disappointed tone and body gesture before walking off.

"Ok, you're good," I said to the customer as I removed the footrest and thanked him for the business.

He paid me then thanked me for the shine and took off.

PATIENCE

"WHAT A NIGHT," I said to myself one Sunday morning as I sat on the stand and reflected on how much fun I had clubbing last night. I was still feeling a little tired, since I went straight to work after leaving the club, and the coffee that I had drank when I got there didn't really help much. I could still smell the alcohol in my breath, but wasn't concerned too much about my customers getting the scent since I always wore my dust mask while shining their shoes.

"How about a shine?" I asked my next customer, as he walked slowly towards the stand.

"Yeah," he said as he pointed to me. He then placed his pulley luggage at the side of the stand and quickly took a seat before reaching into his jacket pocket and took out his glasses, put them on, reached for the newspaper and began to read it.

I would always tell my co-worker that whenever a customer comes for a shine and the first thing he or she does was try to get busy, meaning, that they pull out their cell phone, pick up a magazine or newspaper and starts to read or even gets on their computer, it's a sign that they don't want to be bothered.

So I quickly explained the shines to him and he requested to have the basic shine. I began cleaning his shoe.

"How are you?" he asked.

"I'm good, so far, so good," I replied as I continued to clean his shoes.

He placed the newspaper back on the shine box and asked me "What time did you have to get here this morning?"

"Six."

He nodded and said, "Not bad."

I agreed with him and asked a quick question to see how he was going to respond, to determine if he was in a conversational mood or not. "Where are you traveling to?"

"California, to meet up with my wife. She's out there on business, so I'm just going up to meet her for the weekend."

I quickly asked another question, since it clearly seemed as though he wanted to talk after his last answer. "How long have you been married?"

"Seven wonderful years," he replied with a smile.

"Ok, question, is it true that marriage can get boring after a period of time?" I asked.

"Depends on who you're married to."

"So it is true?"

"To be honest, I had one that got boring, just to say this is number two, so hopefully it's right this time," he explained, then asked "How long have you been doing this?"

"A little bit over a year now."

"Yeah, so how's it going?" he asked next.

"Pretty good. I love my job. I get to meet a lot of interesting people and learn a lot every day," I explained to him.

"Yeah, that's certainly something," he agreed and nodded his head.

"If you were to give me some advice on marriage, what would it be?" I asked him, as I began to brush the polish into his shoes.

"Why, are you thinking of getting married?" he asked.

"Yeah, it's a thought that's in my mind, definitely," I assured him.

"Ok, give yourself enough time, spend enough time together before you get married. Trust in your heart that it's a good idea, and just be careful because the glow of the early excitement can overwhelm you and you might make decisions that can affect you in the long run. You see a lot of things that you don't see when you're dating and are on your best behavior and they're on their best behavior, see what I'm saying?" he asked.

"Yeah, but what would you say is the hardest factor to keep the marriage together?"

"Ah, patience, flexibility. Be able to stand and put up with the particular things of your partner that you don't like, just those things, their hard things. You've just got to remember that you get some stuff that you don't like along with all the stuff that you do like, and you can't let that get you too upset."

"Ok," I responded.

"Yeah, man," he added.

"You're good," I said to him as I gave him the thumbs up, signaling his shine was completed.

"I'm done?" he asked, as he stared down at his shoes, then removed his feet off of the footrest.

"Yea, you're good," I repeated as I removed the footrest.

He then stepped down from the stand and handed me a twenty dollar bill and requested to have ten back.

"Ok, here" I said as I handed him a ten dollar bill.

"Thank you very much" he said to me.

"Thanks for the business, sir," I responded.

"No problem" he assured me, then went on to say, "Good luck on that marriage idea, but remember to take your time and follow heart, and you'll be all right."

"Ok, thank you."

42

FIGHTS

MY NEXT CUSTOMER approached the stand with a box in his hand which you would get from purchasing food from the food court in the terminal. I looked at him and he nodded his head to me and then looked at the sign.

"Step on up. Make yourself comfortable," I said to him.

"Which one should I sit in? Do you mind me eating?" he asked.

"Any chair, and of course not, we've all got to eat, right?"

"Yeah, we do," he responded, as he climbed the stand, got seated and immediately opened the box and began to eat what seemed to be pancakes.

"How much time do you need?" he then asked.

"Well the bulletproof, which is our best shine, takes less than fifteen minutes." I assured him, as he leaned forward and began to put his shoe lace into his grey cap toe shoes.

"Ok, I'll have that one," he said before continuing to eat.

"Good choice," I responded and began working on his shoes. After five minutes, he was finished eating and placed the box on the top of the shine box.

"How's your day going?" he asked, looking down at me.

"Good man, no complaints," I said, looking up at him and then back at his shoes, continuing to polish them.

"So are you from around here?" he asked next.

"Yes I am. I live right here in Queens, but I'm originally from Guyana," I said to him as he nodded his head. "What about yourself?"

139

"I'm from LA. That's where I'm heading back to. I live out there."

"How long were you in New York for?" I asked as I began to apply the second layer of polish to his shoes.

"Ah, since Monday. We're here for a conference."

"You said we?" I said to him.

"Yeah, there's like twenty-five of us."

"You all got shoes?" I asked with a smile on my face, as I began to brush polish into his shoes.

"Not all of us, but that would be good business for you right?"

"Yep" I nodded, then went on to say, "I can't help but notice that ring. Is that a wedding band?"

"It is." He quickly replied, as he gazed down at me and his shoes.

"Oh, that's cool, that's different," I said to him since I've never seen a wedding ring like his, which looked like tiny ropes around his finger.

"Thank you," he responded, as he continued to gaze down at his shoes.

"So how long have you been married?" I asked next.

"Fifteen years, a very long time."

As I began adding the final layer of polish to his shoes, I asked "Is it true that marriage can get boring after a period of time?"

"I think so, but if you stay busy, and it depends on who your spouse is—it can get boring and difficult if you don't get along with your spouse—so yeah, it's possible," then went on to say, "But I don't think about that, because I have a good wife; she's a good person."

"So what would you say is the hardest factor of keeping the marriage together to make it work?" I asked next.

"Understanding and communicating. That's what I think," he stated. He then got silent for a few seconds and said, "Oh, yeah, beware of the fights, because there will be plenty of fights, but that's where understanding and communicating comes in, so once you have those, the fights won't affect your marriage."

"So how do you know if it's the right time to settle down?"

"I can't say. I honestly don't know. You've just got to be ready . . . it's all about you," he said.

"You've got to be ready?" I echoed.

"Yeah you know, I don't know what it is, but you'll know, you'll know at that point." He assured me.

"You're good, thanks for the business."

"All set?" he asked.

"Yeah, what do you think?"

"Looks good," he replied.

43

COMPROMISE

"ARE WE GOING to go all the way up to the bulletproof shine today, sir? That's the best one we have to offer, with the most layers of polish," I said to my next customer, who was already sitting in the chair, as I began to take the supplies out of the shine box.

"Basic is fine," he replied as he fixed his shoes on the footrest.

"Basic is it then," I said to him, as I began to clean his shoes with the leather balm, while he sat and stared at what I was doing.

When I was about to apply the polish to his shoes he said, "Funny story. I had a party last summer for my 50th, and we got a pool in the backyard, so by two o'clock in the morning, I was tumbling around and got a little shoved and I went right in the pool," he said as we both laughed aloud. He then continued by adding, "Birthday suit, shoes and everything got messed up, so I said the next trip I take, I'm going to make sure I wear these, because you never do this at home, you know?"

"Yeah, that's true," I agreed.

"It took weeks for them to dry out" he then said, as he nodded his head.

"So where do you live?" I asked next.

"Stanford, Connecticut, not far."

"Fifty years, huh? Are your married?"

"Yeah, my wife is on a different flight," he stated, then added, "Well I'm going on a work trip, so we tried to get on the same flight and it was like double the price. But now we can't sit next to each other and piss each other off," he joked.

142

"So how long have ya'll been married?" I went on to ask.

"Twenty-one miserable years," he said, smiling.

"Is it true that marriage could get boring after a while?"

"Well you know, I mean, I got two girls, so right now, life's nothing but boring for me. I have a fifteen and a fourteen-year-old in high school. They used to be so nice, but now they're so brutal to each other. Boys would just be like whatever, but girls," he said as he shook his head from left to right, "especially now with all of this stuff, you know. My fifteen-year-old, she was at a party last week, she's almost sixteen, and the parents said 'Oh no, there isn't going to be any liquor,' but you know these kids found a way to bring the booze in, so here's my daughter on frigging Facebook, holding a red plastic cup. Now what do you think is in that red cup, eh?"

"I began to laugh at the look on his face as he spoke then said, "Not fruit punch," and laughed some more while brushing his shoes.

"I'm like 'What were you drinking?' 'Oh I swear, I didn't, I didn't.' That's what I mean, you didn't take the picture, but somebody else did," he said.

"Exactly," I agreed, as he went on to say, "And they sent it out for everybody to see, that's the worst part of it, you know, these kids don't realize, they might not be doing it, but somebody else is over there, taking pictures and posting it out there to the internet world and there's a lot of crazy people out there. It's crazy. We didn't have that shit; we used to go out and fucking play in the back yard," he said, as I began to laugh some more, since his facial expression was kind of funny while he was talking. He then continued, "We didn't watch TV or computers or game systems, we played in the fucking backyard. How old are you?" he asked

"I'm twenty-five years old," I replied.

"Don't marry; you're not ready yet," he assured me, as we both laughed. He then went on to say, "I got married when I was twenty-nine."

"That was your first marriage?" I asked next.

"That's it. I worked hard, we started dating when I was twenty-five, and then we got engaged and within a year we got married, so I dated her for about four years," he stated as he nodded his head, then continued, "Nice family. We both have big families, so Sunday dinners are always forty-plus people you know, big bowl of pasta on the table."

"Every Sunday?" I repeated.

"Yeah, every Sunday," he said with a smile.

"Wow, that's nice, that reminds me a lot of where I'm from, Guyana. We do stuff like that. Every Sunday we would have a nice dinner with the family, and it teaches you values, you know. You value relationship, you value family," I said to him.

He nodded and said, "It definitely does."

"So what would you say is the key factor to making marriage work?" I asked him as I began to buff his shoes.

"Communication is great, and you've got to compromise for one another. I'm a big sports fan and my wife doesn't know the first thing about frigging football, you know, but when my Giants are on, on Sundays I'm like eh, you know little things go along way with women. It's not about the jewelry, it's about sometimes holding their hands, bringing them home a bouquet of flowers, but now, it's so different with the girls. When they were little, it was so easy, they would get dolled up, we would packed the bags and we would go to the beach. Now, forget about it. I've got to worry about my kids wearing bikinis," he laughed. I think that the biggest thing is trust, being honest with each other, because once you start lying, it becomes a habit and then that habit can turn into bad things. That's what I try to tell my kids all the time. I know you're lying and the more you lie, the easier it gets," he explained.

"That true, you're all set. Thanks for the business," I said to him, as he stepped down, paid me and walked off.

ACCEPT

"HEY THERE, I'LL take a shine," My next customer said to me as she approached the stand, smiling.

"Of course, have a seat" I responded, with a smile on my face as I pointed to the chair.

She sat and went on to say, "You know what, I went over there to the other location and the sign said to come here," as she smiled.

"Ok," I replied, as I began to wrap the balm cloth around my hand.

She went on, "Now here I am. How are you, though?"

"I'm good, thanks for asking. How are you?" I asked, while smiling at her.

"I'm good myself," she responded, as she nodded her head. I then went on to ask her which of the shines she would like to have, and her response was, "What is the bulletproof?" while staring at the sign.

"That's the one with the most layers of polish, which will last the longest and protects the shoes the most," I explained.

"And it won't rub off on my clothes?" She asked,

"No it won't; it's going to look good, though," I assured her.

"Ok let's go for that," she said, as I continued cleaning her boots, for a few more seconds. As I was about to apply the first layer of polish onto them, I asked her where she was traveling to.

"San Francisco," she quickly replied.

"Oh, San Fran, that's where we originated from, actually," I said to her.

"Oh yeah?" she asked with an amused look on her face.

"Yeah, we have a couple of shops out there still," I said to her, as I continued to work on her boots.

She said, "Ok," then went on to add, "We're New Yorkers, but we're moving out there. We're part-time out here, but most of the time out there."

"You said we?" I asked, with a smile on my face.

"Yeah my husband and I," she responded.

"Ok, how long have you guys been married?" I asked next.

"Twenty-four years and I still can't believe it."

"You can't believe the time that has past, or that it lasted so long?" I asked her, while I stood up and looked at her.

"Both," she quickly replied. We both laughed. She then continued by saying, "Good question. You know the drill, but some days I feel like we've been married for five minutes and other days it's like, wow. My husband is sixty-four years old, but turns nineteen whenever I get angry. He knows how to make me happy."

"So what would you say is the key to making your marriage work for so long, after all the arguments and fights?" I asked next.

"You have to accept whenever you're wrong and show respect for one another, and not confuse being angry with not loving somebody, and that's hard to do. Then you've got to be willing to compromise and be willing to step up to the plate and be the boss sometimes. My husband is not too good at that, but you know, he shows it sometimes and that's ok for me. And oh yeah, you've got to give each other space," she added, as she looked me in the face.

"You've got to give each other space, even when you're married? How do you do that?" I asked, not understanding the concept of giving space.

"Even when you're married, you could take time to do what you like. I don't mean dating other people" she said, as we both laughed, then added, "Unless you're in for that." She smiled.

"So you're saying, find different interests?" I asked.

"Yeah, because you don't have to like all the same things. I'm just saying there should be no reason that I can't like boxing just because you hate it. Also you want to find something that you like together. That can make the relationship more interesting, since you're spending your life together, and don't have kids unless you're ready to be a father," she advised me.

"Don't have kids unless I'm ready to be a father?" I repeated, since I wanted her to be more specific about what she meant.

"Yeah, but it's not something that you can really understand until you become a father," she replied, then added, "You want to have money for bills, money to make decisions, and money for just in case things become critical."

"Do you have any kids?" I asked next.

"I have four kids and nine grandchildren" she replied, as I began to brush the last layer of polish into her boots.

"Do you think that marriage has the same value today that it had twenty years ago?"

"It could, but it all depends. Like, my daughters and their husbands are in relationships where values are very serious and they go to counselors when they're having difficulties and can't resolve it between themselves. They work it out, and I think actually for some reason it's better, because in the past, marriages would stay together because people were in love."

45

THINK

"How about a shine, guys?" I asked two guys not too far from my stand, waiting on their flight to begin boarding.

"You know what? I'll take a shine," one of them said. They both came over to the stand and he got seated while the other guy stood at the side of the stand.

"Where are you guys heading? I asked as I began to stain the sole of his shoes.

"Florida, for business. We'll be back Wednesday," my customer said, then looked down at his feet and added, "Damn my feet are on fire." We all laughed.

"That's why I got loafers, I don't have to worry about that," his friend added, as we all began to laugh some more.

"Either of you guys married?" I asked next.

My customer said, "Yes, I am with two kids," while his friend said, "I'm in between marriages."

"He's in between marriages," my customer said as he and his friend began to laugh, while looking at each other.

"What do you mean, in between?" I asked his friend.

"Getting divorced," he replied.

"So what is your take on marriage?" I asked the friend, as I began to brush my customer's shoes.

"It's a great institution, but once you've done it, it's a lot, and you really have to think about it the second time," he explained.

"What about you?" I looked up at my customer and asked.

"I'm still happily married, so it's good, but if I had to do it all over again, I would," he said, then went on to ask me, "Why, you're contemplating, thinking about popping the question?"

"Yea, kind of. I'm actually thinking about it."

"Good for you," he said to me, then turned to his friend and said, "Man, you were married for a long time. How many years?"

"Twenty-three, twenty-four years, I think," his friend said.

"Twenty-four years . . . How do you let go after twenty-four years?" I asked the friend.

He smiled and said, "You pull through it, the kids grow up, and you say, 'What the hell am I doing here?' and then you leave."

"Twenty-four years, that's a long time," I stated.

"Absolutely. I've been married twenty-three years," my customer said.

"So what would you say is the key factor to make your marriage last that long?"

"You know what, for me it wasn't one," he assured me, then went on to say, "If your relationship is easy now, it's going to continue to be easy, but if you guys are only fighting and parting and it's hard to work out now, it's not going to get any easier. For me, it was like this is easy, this is good." He nodded his head.

I continued to work on his shoes, then said, "You know the divorce rate in New York is like sky-high. It makes you feel like everybody is getting married for the wrong reasons."

"Yeah, I was twenty-six when I met her," my customer said.

"I was twenty-four. I was probably too young," his friend looked at him and said smiling.

"Two years made a big difference," my customer said to his friend.

His friend's reply was, "Absolutely, absolutely."

"So would you do it all over again?" I asked the friend.

"Say that again?" he asked.

"Would you do it all over again if you had another chance to?" I repeated.

"I'd have to think hard, not to say I won't. It's just that, it would be a lot."

My customer said, "When you got married the first time, it should have been like that," while looking at his friend.

"Nah, he's asking if I would do it all over again," the friend said.

"Oh, same route?" my customer asked him.

"Well, I was twenty-four, what the hell did I know about marriage? It just seemed like a really good idea at the time," his friend joked, as we all began to laugh. He then went on to add, "Times have changed, I mean back then, don't forget, that's the other thing. Twenty-five years ago, you know, it was much more prevalent to get married."

"Yeah, because values were different than they are today," I added.

His friend nodded and said, "Absolutely, over twenty-five years, things has changed a lot. How old are you?" he asked me.

"I'm twenty-five years old, one year older than you were when you got married," I replied.

"Yeah, were together four years before we got married, though," he stated.

"Did you guys lived together before y'all got married?" I asked the friend, as I began buffing my customer's shoes.

"Not really. We were engaged and I had a roommate and then my lease was up like couple of months before the wedding, and I said you know, I could get a new lease but we were engaged and instead of getting another place for a couple of months we just ended up getting our own place," he said.

"Ok" I replied, as I give my customer the thumbs up, signaling that his shine was complete

"So veterans and women own this company?" my customer asked as he stepped down from the stand and paid me.

"Yeah," I replied.

"Nice," he said as he took off with his friend.

"Enjoy, guys," I said to them as I began to pack up my supplies.

46

DISTRACTION

"I'll take a basic shine, a quick one though," my next customer said to me as he approached the stand.

"Ok sure, have a seat," I urged him, and began working on his alligator skin boots.

"Are you at this location only?" he asked, as I began to stain his boots' soles.

"No, we have another location in front of the smoothie stand, so we rotate from time to time. Damn, I could see that you were pimping back in your days, retro frames, a gold tooth and all that jewelry," I joked with him.

"A player, I was no pimp. A pimp is someone who takes money from women that work for him. I don't do that. I give money to women, that's what a player does, we give women money, not take money from them. Pimps are bums, stupid people." He said then gave me the thumbs up.

"Where are you heading too?"

"Las Vegas, for a few days. I get back on Wednesday."

"Ok, that's not bad."

"No, it isn't. It's just what me and the wife need."

I smiled and looked up at him, since he had given me a gateway to ask my next question, which was, "Are you traveling with your wife?"

"Yeah, she's in the terminal around here, somewhere," he said, while rotating his right hand in the air.

"So how long have you guys been married?" I asked next.

"Twenty-six years, four kids and I can't forget to mention, eight grandchildren," he said, with a smile.

"That's nice. So what kind of advice can you give to me about marriage?"

"Why, are you thinking about getting married?" he asked.

"Yeah, I am."

"It is, it's just ah," he stuttered his first words, then said, "It has its stresses, especially when you're not communicating."

"Stresses. I like how you added the extra letters."

"Yeah stresses, nothing but stress," he said, smiling, then went on to add, "No, but it's good overall. It's like any relationship. It changes over time, and you just got to keep it going if you want it to work.

"So what's some of the stuff that you go through as a married couple on a daily basis?"

"It kind of turns into one thing, but if you have kids, that can be a distraction, because a lot of times you just focus all your attention on the kids, and then they grow up and move out and it's like you're back with each other, so that's why you have to endure until whatever is done. It took me five years to realize that she was the one."

"Did you guys lived together before y'all decided to get married?" I asked him as I brushed the polish into his boots.

"Yeah, for like the last year, and a lot of people were saying 'Why don't you get married to her?', but I wanted to make sure that she was the one, and I began to feel it, afterward, so I popped the question," he stated, as he began to stare down at his boots.

"You like it?" I asked him, as I began to remove the footrest.

"Yeah, that's for you," he said, as he placed a twenty dollar bill into my hand.

"Thanks, man." Enjoy Vegas, and thanks for the advice." I replied as he took off.

MENTALITY

"WE HAVE THREE levels of shines sir. We have the bulletproof, glass and basic shine. Each offers more protection to the shoes and a longer lasting shine than the next. Which one would you like to have?" I asked my next customer as I began to take out my supplies from the shine box, since he was already sitting in the chair.

"You said there are two levels?" he asked as he began to stare at the sign with the prices.

"No three levels, but bulletproof is the best one. That's the one that will last the longest."

"Ok that's fine. I'll do that one," he said, as he began fixing himself in the chair to be more comfortable.

"Is that a wedding band?" I asked to get the questions rolling.

"This? Yes, it is," was his reply, as he pointed to his ring.

"Ok, so which of the rings would you say is more important to women, the wedding band or the engagement ring?" I asked as I began polishing his shoes.

"Probably the engagement ring, because it's the expensive one. It is also the symbolic one, and it changes their mentality."

"So the wedding band can be simple and not expensive?"

"It all depends on who you're marrying.

I then began to brush his shoes for a couple of seconds, then went on to ask him, "So how long have you been married?"

"Ah, only four years," he replied, as he began to stare down at me working on his shoes.

"I think that marriage is a beautiful thing; I'm actually thinking about getting married one good day," I said to him.

"It is. It's also a big decision, a very big decision."

"Is it really that big of a deal?" I asked next.

"It's a big decision, sure it is. You look at divorce rate. You're more likely to get a divorce than to stay married, so it's a major decision."

"So what would you say is the key factor in making your marriage work?"

"Be level headed. You've got to be into it and to know what it is and what it isn't. It has to be a decision, it can't just be impulsive. You've got to go into it with a clear vision, and to be able to do that, you have to be faithful," he stated.

We both got quiet for a couple of seconds. Then he said, "Patience and flexibility also play an important role in your marriage too, and don't marry anybody crazy," he added as we both began to smile at each other.

"But a lot of people say that people change after you get married," I said to him.

"Not really," he replied, shaking his head from left to right. "I don't think people change like that. I mean people do change, but usually it's just a case of you never saw them for who they were, so people don't change, circumstances do."

"Ok," I quickly responded.

"Yeah, people change, but it's probably because you didn't realize who you're with. I've never, ever been approached by any kind of change," he stated as I gave him the thumbs up, signaling his shine was finished.

"Give me, uh, just four back, thank you," he said

"Thank you," I replied.

"Take it easy," he said as he walked away.

48

BENEFITS

"CAN I WAIT on the chair?" A passenger came up to the stand and asked me as I was polishing my cordovan penny loafers one Thursday morning.

"Yeah, of course," I said to him as he took a seat on the stand.

He then began to stare at what I was doing, so I asked him, "How are you today, sir?"

"I'm fine," he replied as he continued to stare.

"Where are you heading to?"

"San Francisco," he said.

"Oh, that's nice." I then went on to ask, "So how's your morning going so far?

"It's great. I can't complain. I got here two hours early for my flight, thinking that it was going to be a hassle getting through security, but it wasn't, I just came right through, and it was empty. Is it always like this on Thursdays? "He asked.

"It depends. Different days, different luck, I guess," I replied.

"So do you live in New York or San Fran?" I asked next, as I continued to clean my loafers.

"I actually live out there in San Fran. I was just visiting New York, we had a conference out here," he stated, as he continued to watch what I was doing, then said, "This is so much easier. Usually I would take my shoes to a store and then pick them up, and it takes like a day."

"One day to get a shoeshine?" I said as I looked at him.

"Yes, you leave the shoes and then pick them up the next day, but this is much easier," he said.

"Leaving your shoes for one day for just a shine, that doesn't seem serious. I then asked him if he was married.

"Unfortunately, not yet," he replied.

"Not yet?" I asked. "So will you get married one day?"

"I don't know," he said. "It's so stupid."

"I'm actually thinking about it," I said to him, as I placed my loafers onto the cabinet and took a seat since I was finished cleaning them.

"Oh yeah?" he asked, with a rather unusual smirk on his face.

"Yeah, I think marriage is a beautiful thing."

He looked at me, smiled and said "It is?" He burst into laughter.

"Why are you laughing?" I asked next, because I wasn't getting it.

"I have friends who are miserably married," he replied, and we shared a laugh.

"So what do you think of whenever you hear the word marriage?" I asked.

"Well, I just think that it's something we created, us humans. It's a social thing that we created, so that we could have benefits. There're not many benefits of marriage without getting married. I think you could enjoy being with somebody and loving that person with or without getting married, that's what I think," he said with a smile.

"So does your girlfriend talk about marriage?" I asked him next. As he was about to answer, his cellphone rang and he said "I have to go, catch you later, he got up and walked off.

49

RESPONSIBILITIES

"HOW ABOUT A shine ma'am? I asked a passing passenger, who was kind of gazing at the stand as she passed by.

"A quick one, and I'll appreciate it, because my family is waiting on me."

"Sure, have a seat," I said to her as I pointed to the chair, before stretching my right arm out to her to assist her up to the chair.

"Thank you," she said, as she smiled and exhaled deeply.

"Which of our shines would you like to have?" I asked her.

She gazed towards the sign for about ten seconds without saying a word, so I began explaining the difference between the shines to her.

"I'll just take the middle one," she said gently.

"Ok," I replied and began to clean her shoes with the leather balm.

"How are you doing today? She asked me.

"I'm good, and you?" I replied.

"I'm great," she said with a smile on her face, as I began to brush the balm off of her shoes.

"Where are you traveling to? I asked her.

"To Maine. We came down for the weekend, but we're heading back up," she said to me.

"Are you married?" I asked next.

"Yeah, I've been married for eighteen years," she said smiling.

"Eighteen years, that's a long time," I stated as I began brushing in the first layer of polish into her shoes.

"How about you?" she then asked me.

"I'm not married. I'm single, but it's a thought that's in my mind."

"Make sure you're really ready, because it takes work, and do you want to have kids?" she asked, leaning forward in the chair.

"Yeah, of course," I responded.

"Oh ok, that's probably a better way to do it."

I wasn't clear of what she meant, so I asked her "Have kids then get married?"

"No, no, get married first, then have kids. There's a better chance that it will last once kids are involved," she said. "That's hard work also. Kids are a lifetime of responsibilities."

"Yes we are," I joked, and we shared a laugh.

She then asked me where I was living.

"I live right here in Queens but I'm originally from Guyana," I said to her.

"Oh, I see. Any trouble with the storm?" she asked.

"Yeah, our basement got destroyed."

"That sucks."

"Yeah especially since it was with that stinky water, because the sewer got backed up, and the water flooded our basement," I explained.

"Did you have stuff down there?" she then asked.

"Yeah, it wasn't just us though; the entire neighborhood got affected," I said to her, as I continued working on her shoes.

"Did you lose electricity?" she asked.

"Yeah, for a couple of days," I said to her, then asked, "Other than kids, what advice could you offer about making a marriage work?"

"I don't know. I just think that you have to work hard at it and everything is going to be just fine," she assured me. "I like your hair, nice cut."

"Thank you. I wanted it to be as blond as yours originally, but it didn't happen and I got this color."

"Oh wow, I just had a haircut, which took three hours, because she cut off a lot of my hair."

I was finished with her shine, so I asked her what she thought about it, and she replied "Nice," before stepping down.

SPIRIT

"STEP ON UP, sir," was how I greeted my next customer, who approached the stand and requested to have a bulletproof shine.

"Hey how are you?" He asked me as he got seated and placed his feet on the footrest.

"I'm great man, what about you? I replied.

"I'm fine," he responded, as he raised his left hand up and showed me what seemed to be a wedding ring.

"You're married?" I asked

"No, I'm getting married next September," he said with a broad smile on his face.

"Next September. Is this your first marriage?" I asked next, as I began to brush his shoes.

"No crap, are you kidding me? My fifth," he replied.

"Pardon?" I said, since I could not believe what I was hearing.

"This is my fifth marriage," he repeated.

"So that means you would go for the sixth?" We both laughed.

"No, after this, I'm done. You're from Grenada, right?" he asked.

"I'm from Guyana."

"I actually married a girl from Grenada. She was my second wife."

"Really?" I asked.

"Yeah, they can do something to you. The island women," he said as he smiled, broadly.

"What is it about island women that you like?" I asked next.

159

"The food actually is a big part of it, yes."

"So let me ask you something: What kind of advice can you give me about marriage, because you've been there four times already?" I asked.

He smiled and said, "Oh my God, we don't have that long. My flight's in five hours."

We both cracked up.

"I went through a Buddha phase."

"A Buddha phase?" I looked up and asked.

"Seriously," he said.

"What is a Buddha phase?" I asked.

"No food, no drugs, no women, no sex, no masturbation, like nothing. I removed myself from everything. No television, no radio for six months. I'm in this thing and I said, 'You know, my entire life I've been missing God and spirituality in all of my relationships, with my business, my relationship with my kids, everything.' So I'm like this is wack, I'm not doing it right. I got invited to a concert with a buddy of mine, and at 9pm, his cousin gets a phone call from this woman who's now my fiancé, and she said, 'You know, I'm in town for a week and if you guys want to come over for a beer . . . ,' so I tagged along. The moment I saw her I thought 'Wow, this chick is the real deal.' She's actually older than me, which is amazing. I've dated models and shit like that, you know, but this was a big difference because I've never dated anyone that's older than I am, so I personally think that God brought us together. So how do you plan that, how do figure out what you want to do, before doing it? I just think it's destiny, it's more than just faith. You don't believe in faith?" he asked.

"Yeah, I do," I responded, then said him, "So tell me about your past marriages."

"Well my first wife died. My second wife had another guy on the side. The way I found out was—I used to have hair—I went into her gym bag to get some gel. It was like 4 o'clock in the morning, and at the bottom of her gym bag were a whole bunch of love letters from this guy. I woke her up and said, 'I'll be back on the weekend and you better be gone,' and that was it."

"What about the third marriage?" I asked.

"The third one . . . I got sick. We found out that I had Cancer on Thursday. On Friday I got home and she had packed up the kids and left," he said, with a straight face.

"That really happens, I see that in movies," while still in shock of what I had just heard.

"Seriously, she was gone," he said, looking down at me.

"The fourth one?" I asked next.

"Very beautiful. She was white, Indian and had a little bit of Latino in there, too. So hot tempered. She cheated on me twice and I took her back because I loved her, but then the messing around became more constant with her, so I had to let her go," he stated, as I began to apply the final layer of polish to his shoes.

"You know what I like about you? You still believe in the tradition of marriage and you want to be with one person. I admire that about you."

"Yeah, I don't want to mess around. If you have a relationship that's actually endorsed by God, and I mean in a serious way. You shouldn't be messing around on your wife. Guys think that you know, that they can screw around with this other girl on the side, and women do the same thing also, but there's something in our spirit that gets damaged when we go outside of a relationship," he advised me, then added, "I don't want to do that to the girl, or myself."

51

STRENGTH

"I'LL HAVE A shine," he said has he walked toward the shoeshine stand.

"Sure," I replied as I stood up to welcome my next customer, a white male maybe in his late 50's, dressed as if he was going on a vacation.

He was in jeans, a polo T-shirt, and on his feet were my favorite shoes—penny loafers, just as I would wear them, with no socks.

"We have three levels of shines, sir. We have the bulletproof, the glass, and the basic. Each offers more protection than the next, and the shine lasts longer. I said immediately after the customer was seated.

"Basic is fine." He placed his right hand on the chair arm as he tried to get comfortable.

"Basic it is then," I said, as I placed my facemask on and gloves and began to clean his shoes. The first thing I noticed about this customer as I began shining his shoes was the way he held his left hand. It was as if he was advertising his wedding band, so I wasted no time with the questions. He also seemed like the type that was up for a conversation, since his attention was only on me and his shoes. "Where are you heading?"

"Rochester," he replied.

"Business, vacation, or you live there?"

"Couldn't be heading to Rochester for vacation. It's a little too cold," he said, smiling.

"May I ask you a question?"

"Yeah, sure why not?" he said.

"Which of the wedding bands would you say is more important to the woman? The engagement ring or the wedding band itself?"

"That's a good question, that's a really good question," he said as he adjusted his body to get more comfortable in the chair. "Probably the engagement ring," he replied with a tone of uncertainty.

"The engagement?" I asked, surprised.

"Yeah."

"Because of the value and all that right?" I added.

"Probably, yeah, you're asking the wrong person dude. You should ask my wife. Ask the woman," he said, then we both laughed.

"Which one did you put more into?"

"The engagement ring by far. This is not even close, it's not even close. It's not even close," he repeated.

"You said it three times," I replied with a laugh.

"Yep, so you're going to get engaged?" he asked, as he changed his focus on a woman that was passing by the stand.

"Yeah, I'm thinking about marriage, but I'm going to get engaged first for a little while to see what up's, see how that works out."

"Just make sure you get along well, communicate well. It's all about compromising," he advised me.

"Is it true that marriage can get boring? I heard it can get boring after a while."

"Yeah, people lose the strength because they don't want to do stuff, you know. You should have your own outside interests and also like doing stuff together. It's like common sense," he said as he moved his body forward in the chair.

"Yeah," I uttered.

He then went on to say, "Make sure you get along, because it doesn't matter how freaky the sex is. Whenever you have kids, with you being the guy, it's all about the kids."

The terminal intercom came on so I paused until it was over before asking him the next question, "So do you think it's a good idea to like live together before getting married?"

"Live together before?" he repeated.

"Would that be a good idea?"

"I did it, and it was good," he said as he gazed once more at the same woman, before pointing to her and saying, "That's my wife sitting over there."

I turned around and she was looking right at us. "She's beautiful," I said.

"Yes she is," he replied, as he nodded his head and smiled.

"Ok, you're good, thanks for the business and the advice," I said to him as I removed the footrest.

"Thank you," he said as he climbed down from the chair and paid for his shine.

52

ENDURE

IT WAS 8:35 am. Two hours had already passed, and I only had two basic shines looking at my shine log. And besides, my last shine was over 30 minutes ago. I definitely had to get some. I got up and started to do what my other co-workers called hustling. "How about a shine, sir?" "How about a shine, ma'am?" "How about a quick shine sir?" "How about it boss? It only takes 7 minutes." When I saw boots or shoes, even if I thought they didn't needed a shine, I would ask these questions.

"How about a shine, sir?"

"Yeah, sure I could do with a shine," my next customer replied as he walked toward the stand and got seated, as if he was a regular customer and was aware of our operation. His face was not familiar to me at all, but he was definitely dressed up as if he was going to a corporate meeting; his pants were neatly seamed, his shirt was wrinkle-free, and his pair of Grayson's didn't seem to need a shine at all. However, that wasn't important to me. The fact that I got my next customer, was. "Bulletproof shine," he said as he looked at the shoeshine sign with the pricing information.

"Very well," I replied as I rolled his pants bottoms up to avoid polish from getting onto them. I then placed my gloves on and began to clean his shoes. As I began applying the balm to his shoes, he pulled his cell phone out of his jacket pocket and began to talk as if he knew that I was about to start questioning him and he didn't want to be bothered, so I continued working on his shoes.

It seemed as if he was on some kind of a business call, so I didn't pay too much attention to him anymore. I added the first layer of polish, brushed it off, added the second layer, and he was still on his call.

As I began to brush the second layer of polish into his shoes, he hung up his cell phone and placed it on the shine box then immediately said, "Sorry about that."

"No problem." I said, as I got right into the questions. "Where are you heading?"

"St Marten."

"St Marten," I repeated. "Business or Vacation?"

"Vacation?" he said, as he glanced at his cell phone.

"You're traveling alone?"

"Pardon?"

"Are you traveling alone?" I repeated.

"No, my wife is with me."

"Ok, best company huh?"

"Exactly." he smiled.

"I would definitely like to have a wife of my own one day," I said to get the marriage questions rolling.

"It's too expensive," he replied with a straight face.

"It's expensive?" I asked, since I wanted him to get into more details.

"Yeah."

"To get or to maintain?" I asked.

"To maintain. Actually I was very, very blessed. My wife's parents grew up in the depression. Her mother was a child during the depression, so she saves everything, doesn't throw anything away. She goes to the market to buy food, but only buys what we need and makes sure we save what we don't need until we do."

"Very conservative?" I added.

"Very conservative . . . very, very fortunate to have her." he said with a smile on his face.

I then moved onto the next question, "How long have you guys been together, and how long have ya'll been married actually?"

"We've been married forty-nine years. February will be fifty, and we were together five years before that." He glanced at his cell phone again.

"Oh, that's nice."

"So we're an unusual couple," he said.

"Tell me, what I should look out for before getting married?" I quickly asked him.

"With all this infidelity, and people that have big egos, it's tough. You've got to be able to be with somebody who can endure hard times, like when you don't have any money and you have to eat hot dogs. You need to be with somebody who can do that, because you can't just keep spending money if you don't have it. We were out to dinner last night. We were in a restaurant and we hadn't been there in quite a while, and you know . . . How long have you been doing this?" He suddenly changed the topic as if what he was about to say was not interesting.

"Like about two years now."

"So you see all the women traveling, the good-looking women?" he asked with an amused smile on his face.

"Yeah, yeah. I see them every day," I replied.

"You see them every day?"

"Every day." I repeated, as I began to buff his shoes.

"When I started doing business, there were no women. It was all men, there were no women. The one thing we noticed last night is that the women, are, well . . . some of them are very loud, they're very pushy." He then paused for about two seconds, looked at his cell phone, then continued to talk. "And, you know, they're trying to compete. They're trying. They're just loud, and they don't . . . they're not very gracious. They're not . . . they're very aggressive. You can hear it in their voices. You can tell how they walk, how they carry themselves, you know what I mean?"

"Yea, of course," I said, because I wanted him to say more and see where he was heading with this.

"When I look at some of those women, I don't know what kind of wife they would make, so just choose wisely, because most of them are very self-centered," he advised me.

I was finished shining his shoes. "What do you think of the shine?"

"Perfect," he said, climbing down from the chair.

"Give me five back," he said, as he gave me a twenty-dollar bill.

"Thanks." He grabbed his cell phone and walked off.

CHOICE

I BEGAN SETTING up my shoeshine stand that morning, not so happy since it was already 6:20am and I was supposed to be ready for customers at 6:05am at the latest. I continued to set up the stand, while listening to my music and murmuring to myself about how much I disliked airport security at times, like when they always make you late for work for one reason or the other. It was either, "Excuse me sir, you were randomly selected for a search," or there were not enough people on staff to make the long lines go through faster. But I wasn't going to let "airport security" spoil my entire day. I was finished setting up the stand so I placed the "Back in five minutes" sign up and went for my daily treats: a newspaper, change for $50, mints, and hot chocolate (on other days it's oatmeal; I alternate depending on my mood).

I got back to my stand and there was already a customer waiting for me. She looked like she was in her late sixties, white with short, gray hair.

"Are you waiting on a shine?" I asked her.

She smiled and responded, "Yes I am."

"Ok, have a seat, but please watch your step."

She then placed her carry-on luggage at the side of my stand and climbed up and took a seat.

"Put it up," I said to her gently as I placed the footrest up on the stand.

"Thank you," with a smile on her face.

I didn't even get to ask her what shine she was interested in having, neither my signature marriage question, because without hesitation, she began to ask me questions about the newspaper headlines.

"Have you seen those funny headlines in the papers?"

"Yeah," I said, while wrapping the balm rag around my hand to begin cleaning her shoes.

"Yeah, they're hilariously bad." she smiled and said.

I replied, "Yeah," because I really wasn't sure of which headlines she was talking about.

"You know, well, we're all getting screwed. There's no difference," she stated as she picked up the newspaper that was on the shine box, and took a closer look at it.

"It's entertainment," I said while still not knowing which headlines she was talking about.

"It's hilarious," she said, before shaking her head as if she was disgusted by what she had read in the newspaper. She then pointed out the headline that she was talking about to me. It was a story about a famous NFL star who got caught cheating on his wife.

I shook my head and said, "It's crazy how everything comes out in the end."

"Yes, we are all humans."

I nodded my head and continued to work on her shoes.

"It didn't even look like they were really married in their wedding pictures."

I continued to brush her shoes and thought that I'm right on track with this conversation and shouldn't let it slip away from this topic, so I quickly used her last statement to generate my next question.

"What do you do when stuff like that happens, after thirty years of being married?" I asked next.

"You make a choice," she said, as she pointed at me, then went on to say, "Either you stay pissed, you get over it, or you get a divorce."

"Are you married?" I calmly asked her.

She shook her head from left to right and said, "No, and those are the reasons why." We smiled at each other. She then went on to add, "My sisters say I need to lower my standards and just live."

"Settle for less? I don't think anybody should settle for less," I smiled and said to her.

"Yes, that's my motto."

"Yeah, why settle for less?"

She asked if I was married.

"No I'm not married," I smiled and said, as I added more polish to her shoes. She then went on to say, "Don't settle for less," and we both began to laugh aloud.

"I think marriage is a beautiful thing."

She made direct eye contact with me and said, "It's got to be with the right person, though."

"Yeah, but that's another problem. How do you tell if it's the right person?" I asked her, as I began to brush her shoes.

"Well people evolve, you know. Someone thinks they're going to change somebody and that doesn't happen," she stated.

"Oh, a guy actually said that. A lot of men are getting married for love and women are getting married hoping to change their husbands into the guys that they want, is that true?"

"No," she quickly responded. "The one person that can change the guy is himself. You might be able to change one or two things about him, like how he dresses or maybe get him to do the dishes."

"Hanging with his friends?" I added, as I cut her off from finishing her sentence.

She said, "Yeah, and sometimes when your boyfriend wants to watch football, especially on Sundays, you find something that you want to watch, find some kind of soap opera or reality show, find something, there's a lot of girl stuff out there."

I nodded. "My ex-girlfriend always used to get mad at me, because I work from 6am in the morning to 1:30pm in the afternoon, and after work, I would go to chill with her and you know, whenever you leave work and as soon as you see a bed the first thing you want to do is sleep. Well, she would always get mad at me because I would want to sleep, so I'm like 'Are you serious? I've been up since five this morning, I'm supposed to be tired,' but then again, sometimes you just got to look past certain stuff to prevent stupid arguments."

"That's a long day. What type of girlfriend was she?" she asked.

We shared a laugh as I finished buffing her shoes. "You're good. Thank you,"

"Nice, I love it, thank you. I'll be back," she said, before walking off.

54

DECISION

"YES," WAS MY answer immediately, after being asked that question by a potential customer, that had just came off of a flight, who seemed to have a lot of time to kill, cause honestly after taking the first look at his shoes, I realize it wasn't in a bad condition, but who am I to neglect potential business?

"Do I need a shine?" he asked.

"Yeah man, you never know. You always want to be safe when you're in New York. New York weather is unpredictable. Put that right there," I told him generously to place his bag on the shine box as he climb up to the chair.

"Right there?" he asked.

"Yea, yeah," I repeated.

"Oh, I don't want to put it on your phone," he said.

"No, it's good there," I advised him before taking my cellphone off of the box and getting started. "So we have three levels of shines, we have the bulletproof which is our best shine, we have the glass and we have the basic," I explained to him.

"I'm going to do the basic today, because honestly I'm going to replace these very soon." He stated, so I began to work on his shoe. I noticed that he was paying very close attention to what I was doing, so I took advantage of the fact that his attention was on me and began asking him questions.

"How long are you going to be out her in New York?" was my gateway question.

"I fly back out tonight," he replied, as he continued to watch closely to what I was doing on his shoes, then added, "Two meetings and I'm out. I'm here pretty much once or twice a month, though. How long have you lived here?" he asked with a tone of interest.

"Four years now, but I'm originally from Guyana."

"Oh wow, wow," he replied as if he was somewhat amused, then went on with a follow up question, "What part of New York do you live in?"

"I live right here in Queens. Rosedale, ten minutes away from here," I added, then immediately switched back the questioning, since my goal was to get him on the topic of relationships, love and marriage.

"So what about you, where are you from originally?" I asked him.

"Ah, well, I've lived a lot of places. So my first place was Long Island New York, then I went to Florida, started off school there. I went to Seattle. Then I was a talent agent in LA for five years, and now I live in Canada. I've been around," he said then smiled so I smiled back and continued to polish his shoes.

"These have lasted for a very long time, but the bottom of them are bad."

I agreed and said, "Yeah it's a good brand, they will last for a lifetime, but you're probably going to have to re-sole them."

"Well that's what I'm thinking. Do I replace them, or do I just re-sole them?" he asked looking a little puzzled.

"No don't replace it, just get them resoled. The leather is still in good condition. All you have to do is shine them up every now and then, and you're going to be good."

"Yeah, in fact, let's just make it the glass," he said.

I thought to myself, "I've got him. He's comfortable and he's enjoying the conversation." I wasted no time. "Are you traveling alone?"

"Yeah, I like it better like that. My manager worries too much; he worries about everything. I just like going out and doing it by myself," he said, as we both laughed aloud.

"Are you married?"

"Yeah I am. I've been married. It's going to go on to eight years," he said.

"Eight years?" I repeated.

"Yeah, we've been together about eleven and I have a boy from a previous relationship. He's twelve years old and, we just found out that she's five months pregnant, so I went from being the young hip dad, to now being the not-so-young, not-so-hip dad," he said, as we both laughed aloud.

I then congratulated him on his soon to be baby.

"Thanks, what about you?"

"I'm single."

"Single?" he replied as if he was shocked by my answer.

"Yeah, I just got out of a four-year relationship, and besides, I'm still a baby. Looks at me."

"Ah, well I was about to ask, how old are you?" he said next.

"Twenty-five."

"Oh yeah, no rush. I know so many people who rushed to get married, and the person you are when you're in your early twenties is not the person you are when you become thirty. You're really more settled in, you know who you're going to be, and it's just like, for guys there should be no rush. I tell you what, making the wrong decision could have a big negative impact in your life. It's better taking your time and making sure that you make the right decisions, because when you make the right choice like I made, it feels great, but I know so many people who are just miserable because they rushed into something that they shouldn't have," he said, and then went on to asked me if its hard dating in New York.

"No, it's not hard at all. New York is a very diverse city so you can get around. You just have to watch what you're doing and whom you're doing it with," I stated. Now I was two minutes away from finishing his shoes, while he continued to stare and admires my work. I decided to toss in one last question: "Do you think marriage has the same value today that it had twenty, thirty years ago?"

"With the right people. I think overall people are always one foot in and one foot out. A lot of time when things get a little difficult or not the way they want them to be, they're ready to bail. With my wife, we are very dedicated to our marriage, and we're very respectful of each other, so it really works, but a lot of other people . . . I mean, the divorce rate is ridiculous." He leaned back to make himself more comfortable in the chair.

I then smiled and added "It is."

"So is most of your family here, or are they still back in Guyana?" he asked as I began to buff his shoes.

"Most of my dad's family is here, but my mom's side is all back in Guyana. It was my dad that actually brought me to America."

"So do you like the city?"

"Yeah, of course man. New York is a very beautiful place, America overall is a beautiful place, and I'm just grateful to know that America is still the land of opportunities. You can become whatever it is that you want to be in life, you just have to be willing to work hard, and a lot of doors will open for you."

He didn't agree or disagree, but went straight on to complimenting my work since I was almost finish with his shoes, "Damn they look alive again," he said with a cheerful smile on his face.

I removed the footrest and he stepped down from the stand. He then reached into his pocket, pulled out his wallet, gave me a twenty dollar bill and said, "Just give me seven back."

I gave him two singles and a five dollar bill and thanked him for the business before he walked off.

55

RING

"THANKS FOR YOUR patience," I said to my next customer, since he was sitting in the chair waiting on me to get done with another customer's shoes.

I quickly wrapped up the balm rag around my hand and went straight to cleaning his shoes. I didn't even ask him what shine he would prefer to have, since I didn't want to waste any more time. I went straight for the hit and gave him a compliment about his shoes, to observe his reaction to determine whether or not he would be open for a conversation.

"This is very good leather."

"Yeah they are. I don't take enough care of them."

"You should man, especially when you pay a lot of money for them."

"I know, I know," he repeated, nodding his head.

"The least you could do is take care of them, and the leather will last for a lifetime. You're just going to have to re-sole them every couple of years."

"Yep."

I felt as if he was in the mood to talk, because of his body actions and his quick response to my questions, so we continued to chat as I began to stain the sole of his shoe. "Are you traveling alone?"

"No, I'm travelling with my co-workers."

I finally saw my opportunity to get on the marriage track, I thought to myself since I noticed he was wearing a wedding band, so I immediately asked him, "Is that a wedding band?"

"Yes!" he answered excitedly as if he was expecting that question.

"What's your take on marriage, like what kind of advice can you give to me on marriage?" I asked.

"Why, are you thinking about getting married?" he then asked.

"Yeah, I am."

He then leaned back in the chair, placed his left thumb finger on his chin and his index on his cheeks and said, "You don't need to be married to be a committed person. You don't need to, but it says something. It says, I'm with you, I'm with you forever and this ring has only came off twice in eight years. Once in the shower, second time I waved my hand like this and it flew off, but I never took it off. I keep it on at all times, and I don't know, I'm not young, but I'm certainly not old yet, but I know we'll be together till I die, or until she dies—and that's pretty cool."

"You guys are going to die loving each other," I said with a smile on my face.

"Exactly, and you know, we also have a few really good reasons. Three kids: two four and a half year olds and a eight month old," he said as he paused for about three seconds then went on to add, "So yeah, some people I know got married, and I guess it's because we've been dating for a long time, we have to get married. No, that's bullshit. Do it because you want to, do it because you're going to take it seriously and you want to get the most out of it, and the only way you can get the most out of it is if you put a lot into it. It's hard, it's extremely hard. I'm not telling you it's easy, it's definitely not. Seriously, you drive each other crazy, but it's because you're going to be together forever that's why you drive each other crazy. I hate when people say we're going to be fighting about this for fifty-five years. On the good side, we're going to be together for fifty years. So you have to let it go sometimes. I hope that helps," he said as he gazed over to the coffee shop.

"Yeah it did. So would you say it's best to live with that person before you get married?" I asked quickly since I didn't wanted to kill the momentum. This guy was on a roll and I wanted to hear more.

"We did, we lived together for a couple of years, but I think if you're serious about somebody, it doesn't matters because no matter what's going to happen, if it turns out that she snores, she's a slob and doesn't clean the dishes or something, those will be the reasons you're unhappy. So you've just got to see how to work through it. I don't think you have to live together, but we did and it was pretty cool. It wasn't a trial, we weren't testing it out, but it seemed cool, so we moved in with each other."

"You're good," I said to him as I finished shining his shoes and began to pack up my supplies and rags.

"Thank you," he said, as he climbed down from the chair, looked at his shoes with a smile of satisfaction, and gave me a ten dollar bill.

"Thanks for the business and the advice," I said to him, as he walked off.

56

EFFORT

FRIDAY MORNING, 6:21AM. I got back to the stand after setting up, then leaving to get my daily treats—mints, oatmeal an orange, but no newspaper because for some strange reason I never bought papers on Fridays or Saturdays. I stood at the stand and began to eat my oatmeal with 6 packs of regular white sugar, dried fruits and nuts. Yum, tasty. I began to look around the terminal. It's definitely a beautiful sight, airport security, passengers from all over the world, flight attendants and other employees, people from all walks of life, just going about their business, and no one knows what's going on in each other's lives, no one knows. I took another spoonful of oatmeal and before I knew it, my cup was empty. It happened just in the nick of time, because a potential customer approached me.

"How much will it cost to shine these?" he asked.

"Nice shell cordovans," I replied as if I was happy to see his boots, although I was happy to have a customer, I always believed in giving the customer's a compliment first, and then making them aware that you know very much about the shoes that they're wearing. It creates some kind of trust and credibility—in the words of another customer.

"Step on up man. Have a seat," I urged him as he climbed into the chair, "Make yourself comfortable," I also added, has he got seated.

"Thanks man," he replied, then went on to say, "I see you're wearing Docs."

"Yeah, you recognize them?" I said as I began to clean his shoes with the leather balm.

"I like them a lot."

"Yeah, Docs don't come like this, though. I did it myself. They were eight inches and I cut them to a six inches because they used to hurt my ankles and now they fit really well."

"I had a pair of those same red ones a long time ago," he stated.

"I actually have two pairs, this and a black patent leather."

"How do you do that, you scuff up the toes?" he asked pointing to the black shade on my burgundy Docs.

"Yea, scuffed it with acetone to strip the burgundy for the area. Then I stained it with the black stain and polished it." I explained to him.

"That's so cool." He fixed his shoes on the shoe rest properly.

"So where are you heading to?" I asked next, as I cleaned the sole of his shoes.

"Pittsburgh for Thanksgiving," he replied.

I kept the questions rolling in and immediately asked him, "Are you traveling alone?"

His quiet response was, "Yeah."

"So you're not taking the family with you?"

"No, they're coming on Wednesday; they're driving out," he responded.

I popped a gateway question to my main topics, and asked him, "Are you married?" as I focused on his shoes like I had no interest with whatever answer he was going to give to me.

He then looked at me and said, "No, not yet. We live together, though," as he shook his head from left to right.

"Oh, is that like a strategy?" I asked.

"No strategy. I've been with her for six years and we've only have been living together for the past three months."

"I bet now you're getting to know the real her?" I asked, with a smile on my face to avoid him from feeling offended in any way.

"Well, she's getting to know the real me is more like it."

"Really, you're the bad person?" I asked as if I didn't understand what he meant.

"No, I'm a guy, and she has no brothers or no male members in her family so it's difficult on her," he said to me, before asking, "So what about you, are you married?"

I looked up and quickly said, "No."

"Man, please, stay that way."

We both laughed and I asked him his reasons for saying that.

"I don't know. I miss my twenties sometimes, but sooner, you get older you know. My parents have been married for a long time so that changes a lot. I have friends who are going through their second divorce and they're like only thirty years old. I have other friends who've been married for twenty years, so just be careful," he advised me, then switch the topic right back to talking about docs. "My buddy had a pair of Docs, they were steel-toed, and he cut the leather off the steel and polished up the steel under the toes. It was cool, but it took forever . . ." he trailed off, then got back on the marriage track. "How about you, what are your thoughts on marriage?"

"I think marriage is a beautiful thing. I also think once you find the right person and you're willing to make it work, regardless of what may happen, it will work. I meet a lot of people every day, and I hear everything that you could possibly think about when it comes to marriage, so at the end of the day, it's up to the people involved to make it work," I explained to him, as I continued to work on his shoes.

"I know man, it's an effort," he said as if he knew exactly what I was talking about.

"One of my favorite lines that this customer had told me was, 'Who needs marriage when you've got love?' That makes a lot of sense, you know, if you've got love, you really don't need marriage. This other guy told me that he has a friend that only fell in love with his wife till after ten years of them being married, so for the first ten years it was nothing but arguments and fights, then ten years later, that's when they really synced with each other, so you see anything is possible once you're willing to make it work. You've just got to be willing," I said to him.

"Yeah," he said, as if he just wanted me to keep talking.

I continued, "Look at past people's mistakes, look at what people are doing wrong. I am going to take marriage seriously, that's why I'm not rushing into it. That's why I always like to get other people's advice. People who've been there, or people who are heading there."

"How old are you?" he asked as I began to buff his shoes.

"I'm twenty-five years old," I replied, as he smiled and said, "Live your twenties man. Don't worry about that shit, till you're in your thirties. You'll know when it's right, and you'll know when it's wrong."

"So do you think you'll ever do it?" I asked him next as I began to buff the last of his shoes.

"I don't know, eventually. We'll see. It's rough living with somebody now since I've lived by myself for ten years, and you know you get certain ways, which you just can't lose quickly. It doesn't happen like that, it cannot, it's impossible for people to just change like that." He climbed down from the stand, paid for his shine and left.

LEVERAGE

"HEY MAN, WHAT'S the difference between a glass and a bulletproof shine?" my next customer asked me with a British accent, pointing to the price sign.

"We basically add extra layers of polish to the shoes as we go up, so the shine lasts longer and protects the leather more," I replied.

"I'll take the bullet proof," he said.

"Step on up," I said.

He got seated, folded his jeans bottoms up and pulled the zipper of his boots up before leaning backwards in the chair and placing his arms on the arm rest.

"What time do you start?" he asked as I began cleaning his shoes.

"6 am."

"What time do you get here?"

"6 o'clock. I wake up at five and get here by six and leave at 1:30. It's not bad," I said to him as I shook my head from left to right. He agreed with me and said, "No that's not bad," then added, "These are my jogging shoes."

"I know. I see grass," I replied as we both began to laugh a little.

"You know, I wasn't supposed to wear these today, but I was rushing out and was like what the heck? Oh by the way, do you own this, or these are owned by a company?" he asked.

"It's owned by a company and I basically rent from them." I then went on to ask him where he was heading as I tucked his green shoe laces inside of his shoes to prevent the polish from getting onto them.

"Today, I'm going to Saratoga, thank goodness," he replied, with a certain expression of relief on his face.

"Oh, nice. Are you traveling alone?" I immediately asked next.

"Ah today, but my wife will join me soon"

Just was the opening I was looking for. "How long have you been married?"

"Twenty years."

"Twenty years, that's almost as old as I am," I said. I was surprised because this customer looked like he was only in his late thirties only.

"So what kind of advice can you give to me about marriage?"

"Don't get married," he replied blatantly, with no sign of joking. I repeated, "You said don't get married, and you've been married for twenty years, how unfair can you be to me? You've been married for twenty years and you're still in it," as we both began to smile.

"Well, well." He smiled then got silent.

"There must be some good to it," I said, since I wanted him to get into more details about why I shouldn't get married.

"You know what, I realized that when it was too late, then you're just going to have to roll with the bus, but it all depends on if you finds a good partner, and you know what, I married late so I knew what I was in for."

"Pardon?" I said as if I wasn't clear of what he was talking about.

"I said I knew what I was in for because I was already forty years old when I got married, for the first time. I was all in love, you know. I was all in love and then when I got married I said that this one was the right one."

"Were you wrong?" I asked as I looked up and made direct eye contact with him.

"No, I think the interesting thing is with women, I strongly get that they're becoming very bossy, because now they use the kids as a leverage, so when you get married and you don't have kids, it's the gold plan. Then as soon as you have kids, well now it's a different state because they get more bossy," he explained with a straight face.

I joked and said "The man becomes the wife?"

"Well, yes."

"I had a female customer one time and I asked her the same questions I'm asking you and she said "Whenever the guy gets married, he has a new boss and whenever the women gets married, she becomes the boss.""

"Oh yeah she's right, but let me tell you something, if I were to get a divorce right now, I would certainly have a girlfriend. I would not live with her, I would have my own place, she would have her own place, and whenever I felt like seeing her, we'd meet. It's like a date you know, because we can hang out, spend some time together, and then go back home. You do your thing, and you don't have someone telling you to do this, to do that, you didn't do this, or you didn't do that. After a couple of years, the sex is not so hot anymore and then it's phase two, when things get quiet," he said, gesturing his hands for emphasis. I immediately asked him, "So what do you do when that happens, when that boredom strikes?"

"Well, you should get another girlfriend," he joked.

I continued to brush the polish into his shoes for about thirty seconds then went on to my other question, which was, "What are some of the good stuff about marriage?"

"Ok, well if you want a family, because family life can be very rewarding, if it is what you want and make sure that's what you're really want," he stated then asked "Are you single? Are you in college?"

"Yeah, I'm single and I just graduated college."

"What's the next step?" he asked.

"I have two websites, so I'm going to be focusing on them. I have a photography website, and a small clothing line, where I design apparel."

"You want to go into that business?"

"Yeah, they're both relative careers and I enjoy doing them both."

"My wife is in the fashion business. She's very, very successful. She works for an English design company and she's the CEO, and she's very bossy," he said as he smiled before continuing his sentence, "When she gets home, I have to remind her that this is not her office, this is her home," he said, as I smile and began to buff his shoes.

185

"Oh that's a nice buff man, looks good. So now, what is this, is it the bulletproof?"

"Yes it is, this is the bulletproof. It's going to last the longest and protects the leather the most."

"Look at this; too bad I don't have the other pair of shoes. You can't get a nice shoeshine anymore, where do you go for a nice shoeshine?"

"You come to me for a nice shoe shine, that's where you go," I replied, as I nodded my head and smiled.

"Ok, thank you, good job," he said as he carefully stepped down from the stand.

"Thank you," I said to him as he paid me.

He then said, "Next time I'll take a trip just to get my shoes shined," before taking off.

58

ATTITUDE

"How about a shine, sir? I can clean those up for you. How about a quick shine? It only takes eight minutes." These are some of the lines that I would be saying to the people that pass my stand as I sit on it with nothing to do. I always thought that sending out an invitation to the customers was a good strategy to get them to pay for a shine because even if they say no, they're still going to be aware that there's a shoe shiner in the building and you never know, sometimes they change their mind, whether it's because of a delay, canceled flight or just realized that their flight is 5pm instead of 5am and decided to stay in the terminal, since the drove all the way from Connecticut or whatever. I've seen it numerous times, "How about a shine, guys?" I approached a couple that was passing the stand.

"Do I need a shine, hun?" my next customer asked the woman that he was with.

"Yeah, go ahead, I'll just go and get something for us to drink in the meantime," she said to him before placing her bag at the side of my stand and walking off.

"Which chair should I sit in?" he asked.

"Any one. It's your choice," I proclaimed, as he climbed up and took a seat. I went straight into asking him what shine he would prefer to have.

"Aren't they all the same?"

"No. As we go up from basic to bulletproof, the next lasts longer than the one below," I advised him.

"Then make it bulletproof. You need to kind of clean it up, because I walked through a lot of mud and got all kinds of shit on it. I have wanted a shine for a very long, long time," he added, as he picked up the newspapers and then immediately put them back down, as if it was not what he was expecting to see.

"So how are you doing so far, sir?" I asked.

"I'm doing great because I'm going to Florida, somewhere warm," he smiled and said, as I went on to ask him, "Is that's your wife you're traveling with?"

"Yeah, we're escaping New York. We're running away. We really got hit by the storm. Our house is all banged up and wiped out. We spent two weeks with no heat and no power, so we're going to go down to get some warm weather," he said, as he smiled.

"Oh that's nice. Sorry to hear about your home," I added, before moving on to ask him, "So how long have you guys been married for?"

"Uh, I don't know," he said, as he laughed aloud, then went on to say, "Almost thirty years, twenty-seven, twenty-eight or something like that," as if he was unsure, or just didn't remember.

I nodded my head and said, "Yeah, I think that marriage is a beautiful thing."

"It really is, at least for the second time. The first time I didn't get it right, but the second time I got it right," he said, while rubbing his wedding band.

He then look down at me working on his shoes and said, "Damn, you're doing a good job."

"Thank you. How long were you married for the first time?"

"Ah, eight years, something like that, "he replied, with no sign of interest to that question, but that didn't stop me from staying on track and asking him another question pertaining to his first marriage, since I figured I needed to hear more, so I said to him, "What was the downfall of that marriage? If you don't mind me asking."

"It was a bad match. We were attracted to each other, but we weren't supportive of each other. We were always fighting all the time. This marriage is much better," he added, then went on to say, "It all depends on the attitude that the person has."

"Their attitude?"

"If you've got the right attitude then you can make it work. If you've got the wrong attitude, it doesn't matter how badly you love the person, it's not going to work. Are you married?"

"No, I'm thinking about it, though."

"You got a girlfriend?" he asked next.

"No, I'm single right now."

"How old are you?" he asked next.

"I'm twenty-six years old, "I replied then quickly tried to change the focus from me with a question, so I asked him, "So what kind of advice can you give to me, like to know if the woman is the right one?"

"I don't know. I honestly think I got lucky," he said with a straight face.

"You got lucky?" I asked as I stopped brushing his shoes, and looked at him.

"Oh yeah," he said, then paused for a second, before going on to say, "The only advice I can give you is you've got to know what it really is, and what you really want and what she really wants. If you're really committed to making it work, then you'll make it work. If you think that you're going to get married and it's going to be really wonderful, then you're in for a shock, a big shock. If you think that all is going to happen magically, you're wrong. It's a lot of work. Days, weeks, months and years of work, and I got to tell you, to go through a divorce when you have kids is bad for the kids. We had a little boy, he's all grown up now, 30 something, so at the time he was like 5, 6 years old, and it was very, very hard on him. That's the only advice that I can give to you. You've got to make sure you know what she wants and what you wants. If you want kids, how many? What are your plans for raising them? You know, those kind of things," as he paused. "That was one thing that happened in my first marriage. We just rushed into it, got married, and then afterwards, we started to have all these arguments about what we should do. I wanted to go on and build my own company and all that stuff. She didn't wanted me to deal with that. You've got to get that all sorted out before getting married," as he took a deep breath.

"Does marriage ever get boring, though?" I asked him to keep him going before I was done shining his shoes, since I was applying the last layer of polish.

"Oh yeah, sure, and that's when you take her to Florida," he said, as we both laughed. "If you can afford it. If you can't afford it, take her somewhere, take her out to dinner. That's a big part of it, for men. You've got to pay attention, you've got to at least once in a while say, 'I want to surprise her, make her feel special.' If you don't do that, you don't have a chance, but it's different for everyone."

"Yeah it is."

"My wife will be happy if I say, 'This Saturday afternoon, I want to take you to a movie.' If that's one of the things she likes to do, just do it," he advised. "So where are you from originally?"

"I'm from a small country in South America called Guyana." I replied.

"Ok, I know where that is. So why are you here where's its cold when you could be there where it's nice and warm?" he asked, smiling to his own question.

"The opportunities. There are endless opportunities in America," I stated, as I buffed his shoes.

"Yeah, that's right. I'm an invader too. I'm from Canada. Where I come from is colder."

"You're good. What do you think of your shine?" I removed the foot rest from the stand to allow him to get down safely.

"They look fabulous," he responded. "My wife is going to love them."

COVENANT

"How about a shine?" I asked my next customer who was standing gazing at the price sign as if he was in love with the fonts, the design, or was just amazed with the prices.

"I never knew there were three levels of shines. What's the difference?"

"As we go up from basic to glass to bulletproof, we add extra layers of polish to the shoes that last longer and will protect the leather more," I gently explained to him.

"These prices are very high. I'll just take the glass shine," he requested, has he placed his coffee on the shine box, stepped up to the chair and took a seat.

"Raise them up, please," I advised him as I placed his feet on the foot rest to begin cleaning his shoes.

"How are you?" he asked, as I began cleaning his shoes.

"I'm great. So far, so good. What about yourself?" I flipped questioning immediately, since I always like to ask questions instead of answering them.

"Ah I'm good, it's just a little too early for me. I'm from Philly, so it was 4 o'clock in the morning there when I left," he stated, then went on to ask me another question as if he was really interested in whatever I had to say. "Are you a native New Yorker?"

"No, I'm actually from Guyana, and I just moved here four years ago."

"Ok."

I took that as a chance to generate my next question which definitely was going to be "Are you married?" So I asked him.

His quick response was, "Yeah, married with kids. My oldest is twenty-eight and he's engaged, but he's not getting married until next May," then went on to ask me the same question.

Are you married?" he asked.

"No, I'm not married, but it's a though that's in my mind, so I just like to get people's advice and opinions, like what to expect, what to look for, the downfalls, you know, whatever I could learn from."

"I love being married. I have a great wife. She's like everything I'm not personality and life views, strength and all those things too. She's one of those who completes me and makes me feel better about myself, so she's worth it," he explained.

I then went on to ask him if this was his first marriage.

"Yep, and the only one," he quickly responded, then went on to say, "A lot of people get divorced, I know a lot, but I don't think they understand marriage is a covenant and not a consumer thing," as I nodded my head and continued to work on his shoes. He then said, "Exactly, they think it's like if you don't do what I need you to do, I'll find another person, but what about the promise you made. For me it's different. I don't have any conditions on that; I said for a lifetime and I mean that and she does too. People mess up too, not everything's perfect, but I'm committed to my marriage, the institution of marriage, and my wife as well. She's a really special person."

"I still believe that marriage is a beautiful thing, but I just don't think that it has the same values today that it had, twenty, thirty years ago," I said.

"Me neither, but that doesn't mean that guys like you shouldn't step up. Seriously, it's just the culture that's going that way, but I don't think it's going to hurt anything that's happening in our world to have a commitment like that. If you can't commit to something like that, how can you commit to anything else? You can't trust people then. I don't know. It's a sad world, I know, but there's a lot more to it. I don't feel you should think about it that way. I tend to live my life that way. I think its right," he said.

"I understand what you're saying, it makes a lot of sense that if you can't be committed to a relationship, to a marriage, that you definitely can't be committed to a job. If you can't trust your wife, you definitely can't trust anybody else, it's being realistic."

He then went on to say, "I don't want to live life like that. I don't want to fail to believe that a person isn't going to do right things, to be faithful and all that. I mean, people let you down, but that shouldn't mess it up for you. You have a girlfriend?"

"No I'm single. You're good," I said to him as he was all set.

"Thank you," he said as he paid me and then walked off.

60

KIND

"CAN YOU DO this?" my next customer asked me as he raced towards my stand, as if he was late for a shine or late for his flight.

"Yeah, of course. I have navy blue also," I assured him.

"I'll take the basic one," he added, as he got seated in the chair and made himself comfortable.

I placed my dust mask onto my face, put my gloves on and began cleaning his shoes.

"How are you today?" he asked.

I smiled and said, "Good, and yourself?"

"Very well, no complaints man. I'm going down to Montego Bay Jamaica," he said, as he folded and raised both of his wrists up off of the arm rest, with a big, bright smile on his face, and then added "I love the sun."

"You're going to have that good fun in the sun. Are you traveling by yourself?"

"I'm going down there for my grandchildren. I'm going to see them; they're down there."

"So you have a young girlfriend down there or something?" I joked with him.

"Unfortunately, no," and the tone of his voice changed, got lower.

"So where's the wife?" I asked next, as he looked at me and said, "She died, a few years back."

I apologized to him for hearing about his loss and tried my best to be quiet afterwards, but he went on.

"That's all right. We were together for over fifty years. Now I'm a bachelor who's too old," he said.

"Over fifty years, damn. That's a long time. I'm sure those were the best times of your life."

He smiled and said, "Yes, that was a long time ago."

"So what kind of advice can you give to me on marriage, because it's a thought that's in my mind," I asked him as I began to stain his black shoe sole.

"Just always be kind to each other–that's the best advice I can give to you. How old are you," he then went on to ask.

"I'm twenty-five years old."

"And you're already thinking about marriage? Twenty-five is pretty young."

"Remember, I said I'm just thinking about it."

"Well I guess it doesn't hurt to think," he responded, as I agreed with him by saying, "Nope, it doesn't hurt to think."

"You can't tell how it's going to be, as I said. You just have to be kind to each other, because you never know. First of all, you're never going to understand a woman, it's totally impossible. A lot of times they're a lot smarter than you think they are, and that kind of upsets you a little bit," he said.

"Ok, you are all set," I said as I began to take my gloves off.

61

PERSONALITY

"OUR FLIGHT GOT delayed, so I've got time," my next customer said to me as he approached the stand. I recognized that he was a passenger that I had offered a shine earlier when he passed by the stand with a woman, but he said he had no time because his flight was boarding.

"Step on up, make yourself comfortable." I urged him to take a seat as I began to take out my supplies. He then got seated and I started to clean his shoes.

"You don't use alcohol, do you?" he asked, steering down at his shoe

"No, I mean, I might use it back home and in the bar and stuff, but not at work. I can't use it at work." I joked. I then went on to say, "No we don't use any kind of alcohol on the shoes."

He nodded and said, "Ok, that's good."

"Where you guys heading to?" I immediately asked next.

"We're headed to Houston Texas, to see our grandchildren for Thanksgiving. I mean it's early, but what the heck? I want to get outta this place," he said with a smile on his face.

"I know, right?"

"Yeah, all that heat down there, why not? So did sandy hurt you?"

"Yes she did. She acted like an angry ex-wife, that's how she acted, and I've never been married before," I joked as we both laughed aloud.

"I've got one of those," he joked, as we laughed some more. "You're not a man, until you've had one."

"Really?" I asked in shock as I looked up at him.

"Yup."

I then repeated, "You're not a man until you have an ex-wife? Ok, I'll remember that," as I continued to work on his shoes. "So you know the type of hurt I'm talking about?"

"Oh I do, yes I do!" he responded and gave me a strange look as he continuously nodded his head. "This is my second marriage, and she deserves it."

I smiled and said, "She's a very beautiful woman."

"Well I don't know about that, but she's good," he joked, as we both laughed aloud. He then went on to say, "She has a beautiful personality, and that's what's important."

"That's it?" I stood up and asked, since I wanted him to say more, and he did.

"There's this comedian, I forget what his name is . . . A captain actually told me about him, so I went online and checked out some of his work. He was like, 'When you get married, don't get married for looks, because in twenty years when Barbara's boobs start to hang down, you can fix it with surgery, if she has hearing problems, you can fix that. You can laser her eyes, get Botox for her face, but you can't fix stupid.' You cannot fix stupid. There's no class for stupid, so you have to be really careful. It doesn't matter how she looks, just make sure the person is intelligent."

I began to apply the last layer of polish to his shoes. I then looked up at him and said, "So what other advice can you give to me about marriage?"

He stared at me for about five seconds, then said, "You know what? There's a poet from London, and he wrote, 'To keep your marriage brimming with love in the loving cup, whenever she's right, admit, and whenever she's wrong, shut up.' That's good advice. That works for me. Never, ever be right," he added.

"Those are looking great, and I still have my white stitching." He stared down at his shoes with a smile on his face.

"Yes, that's because I used the neutral polish, so you don't have to be afraid of the color changing."

"Great, ok." He smiled and nodded as he began to climb down from the stand.

"Thank you," I said to him as he paid me, then said, "This has got to be a pretty damn good business here."

"Yeah, people like you make it that way," I replied.

"Ah yeah, ah yeah," he said.

"That's why I love my job, and thank you for the business," I said to him as he walked off.

62

HONESTY

"ARE YOU THE only one here?" my next customer asked me as I was shining another customer's boots.

"Yeah, today I am, but I only have about five minutes more remaining on this shine, so have a seat, I'll be right with you," I advised him, as he nodded his head and walked back to his gate which wasn't too far from where my stand was located.

I could still see him where he was sitting, as I continue to work on my customer's boots. I soon was finished with my previous customer, so I then placed my supplies back into the shine box and went over to the gate that the guy was sitting at, who had approached me for a shine earlier, and said to him, "You're up,"

He then got up and began to follow me back to the stand. "Which chair should I sit in?" he asked, as he stood in front of the stand.

"Any one, it doesn't matter."

He then got seated.

"What level of shine would you like to have? We have three different levels; the bullet proof, the glass and the basic, each offers more protection to the shoes and the shine lasts longer." I explained to him.

"I'll have the glass shine please. I don't need the bullet today," he joked with a smirk on his face.

He seemed like someone who wanted to talk.

"Are you traveling alone?" I asked.

"Yeah, I'm heading to Houston."

199

"So are you married?" I asked next.

"Yeah, thirty years now," he replied.

"So what kind of advice can you give to me about marriage?" was my next question as I fixed the laces of his shoes.

"Well, you always want to make sure she's got a smile on her face, and never keep an argument going. You also want to make sure that nothing is as big as the two of you, because that's when you start to complain about everything. You complain about money, you complain about who ate the last bagel and who left the toilet seat up, all that stupid stuff. If, on the other hand, you've got the other person's back, you're going to look past all that. The world is a big fight so you're going need each other to survive, so just make sure that your goals are the same and you have same values and morals." He then continued by saying, "If I was in a grocery store and someone gave me back a twenty dollar bill instead of a ten dollar bill, I'd give them the change back, and my partner would have done the same thing, so honesty also plays a big role. You also want to make sure that the marriage is important to the other person, just as it is important to you," he advised me as he continued to stare down at his shoes. "Is this terminal six?" he asked next.

"Yes, it is," I quickly responded.

"Where is the rental parking?" he asked next.

"Federal Circle; you will have to take the air train," I said to him.

He looked at me and said, "Oh good, and I could go over to terminal one that way, too?"

"Yes, you can," I replied, as I began applying the final layer of polish to his shoes.

"Did you make out ok in the storm?"

"Not really. Our basement got destroyed, but it could always be worse, so you still got to give thanks for life and what is left," I explained to him.

"I live in a town call Galveston Texas. Five years ago we had hurricane Irene, and it killed 140 people, and no one has never even heard of it," he said to me, as he shook his head from left to right.

"That's crazy, but how come it didn't make the news?" I asked.

"Well because it was right when the President won for the first time, and the economy had crashed, so they took it right out of the media," he stated, as he paused for a few seconds then went on to say, "And everybody still talks about Katrina, and that was a man-made disaster."

"Oh. And the crazy part about Sandy is that people weren't prepared for it."

"Yeah, how would you be, why would you be?" he replied, while making hand gestures.

"Last year, the media exaggerating about Irene and then it came and nothing happened, but a bunch of trees got blew down, so this time everybody felt like that was going to happen again," I explained to him.

"See that's what happens. Where I live, we get hurricanes all the time and most of them aren't bad, and five years ago we had one and everybody evacuated, and people died in the highway, trying to get out, it was insane, so at this point man, no one knows. And you know it's so vulnerable here with all the water that you never think about."

"You're good." I said to him as I removed the footrest for him to step down from the stand.

"This looks good. The only reason I came is because you came and got me. I had already forgotten about you. That's how you do business," he said as he paid and walked off.

"Thank you," I said to him.

63

TOLERANCE

"How ABOUT A shoeshine sir?" I approached my next customer, who immediately walked over to the stand and said, "How fast can you do it?"

"It all depends on which shine you want," I replied, then went on to explaining the shines and how long they would take.

"I'll have the bulletproof please. I want to impress my daughter," he said as he got seated. I then began to wrap the balm rag around my hand and started to work on his shoes.

"How's your morning going so far?" he asked as I was applying the leather balm to his shoes.

"So far, so good, and yours?"

"Well, I've been on a plane for four hours, but I guess you can say its ok," he replied, as he nodded his head.

"Are you traveling alone?"

"Yeah, my wife is at home. I'm going to see my daughter." he said.

"How long have you been married?" I asked.

"Thirty years, and this is the first time in thirty-three years we haven't been together for Thanksgiving," he stated.

I looked up to him and said, "That must be hard."

"Well, not so much," he replied as he began shaking his head from left to right.

I continued to work on his shoes for about two minutes, then went on to ask him another question which was, "Did you ever think for a second that your marriage was going to last this long?"

"No, I was thinking maybe two years at the longest," he replied with a straight face.

"If you don't mind me asking, what would you say made your marriage last this long?"

"Tolerance of each other," he stated, then went on to add, "Marriage is a compromise because you don't always get everything you want. Just wait and see."

"Ok."

He then placed his arms of the arm rest of the chair and said, "This chair is very comfortable, the view up here is great, and there are a lot of hot women walking by." He smiled broadly.

"Yes it is. That's why I chose the job facing the chairs," I joked, as we both began to laugh aloud.

"I could sit right here for the rest of the day," he said, as he continued to laugh, then asked, "What is that place over there?" while pointing to a small dining area in the terminal, not too far from my stand.

"That's just a small restaurant, where you can have a glass of wine, a beer, or even get something to eat, like a donut, a hot chocolate, something to start the day."

"You see everybody in the world here, don't you?" he asked with a smile on his face.

"Yeah, of course. This is a very diverse terminal, so you see a little bit of everything," I assured him, as he continued to stare around the terminal.

"A woman could be beautiful and not hot take care of herself, but when you see a woman who's not beautiful who takes great care of herself, it says a lot, and I bet you see that a lot, working here."

"Yep, and the best part about it, is whenever you think you saw the best looking woman, ten seconds afterwards you see one that's better looking than her," I assured him, as we both began to smile.

"Yes, I would get in trouble standing right here. A lot of trouble," he joked as we laughed some more. I had already placed the last layer of polish to his shoes, brushed it in, and was about to buff them, so I figured I should ask him one more question, so I did. "Is it true that marriage can get boring sometimes?"

"Ah, I'm not sure for some people, but it didn't for us, at least it didn't for me. We both work a lot. She's got her career. I've got mine, so that helps. You know, sometimes it's good to do different stuff, to allow yourselves to miss each other," he advised me.

"Do you think your daughter will be impressed?" I asked him, as I removed the footrest.

"She'll be like 'Dad, you shined your shoes!'" he joked and we both laughed. He then stepped down from the stand, paid, and took off.

64

EXPECTATIONS

"WHERE ARE YOU heading to?" I asked my next customer as I began to clean his shoes.

"Austin, Texas."

"Are you traveling alone?"

"No I'm with my wife; this is my sixth wife."

"Do you guys live in New York?" I asked him next, as I began staining his shoe sole.

"No, I work in New York, but we live in Texas."

"How long have you been married?"

"Forty-four years. Do you think it's going to last?" We laughed.

"No it definitely won't last," I joked.

"Well I think there's hope. Forty-four years is a very long time, but I'm still trying it out."

"Do you think it's going to last?" I asked next.

"I don't have a choice," he responded, as we both laughed some more. I then continued working on his shoes for a few seconds, then went on to ask him another question.

"So what kind of advice can you give to me, so that whenever I get married that my marriage will last for more than forty-four years?"

"She should be your best friend, and you also want to make sure you both knows what each other's expectations are at the beginning of the relationship," he advised me. He then asked me if I was married.

"No I'm not," I quickly replied.

"You got a girlfriend?" he asked next.

"No I'm single, but I definitely would like to get married one day," was what I said to him as I continued to work on his shoes.

"Ok, so whenever, you do get married, make sure she's your best friend and make sure you're her best friend, because it has to go both ways or it's not going to work."

"What are some of the issues that you guys had to deal with a lot, after being married for so long?"

"To tell you the truth, I was very lucky," he stated, then continued by saying, "I was twenty-four years old and that was the age to get married back then, not too, not too young." He began to cough a little. "Excuse me," he said, then continued, "So yeah my wife was always a special person and at that time she was all I ever wanted, and now, forty-four years later, she's still the woman I want.

"Is this your job, do you own the stand?" he asked next.

"No, I work for the company that owns the stand. They lease it from airline and we pay them a percentage of what we make," I explained to him.

He raised his right hand and pointed to a woman that was approaching the stand and said, "There she is," with a broad smile on his face.

"Oh, she's beautiful," I complimented him.

"Yes, she is," he agreed as he continued to smile. She came up to the stand and stood at the side, without saying one word, so I said to her, "Your husband was just telling me that he's about to renew his vows," as we all began to laugh aloud.

"That's a good one," he said as we all continued to laugh. He then looked at her then looked back at me and said, "You know you're going to get me in trouble right?" We all laughed.

"So where do you live?" he then asked.

"I live right here in Queens, but I'm originally from Guyana," I said to him, as I continued to work on his shoes.

"Do you have family in Guyana?"

"Yes, my entire family is in Guyana from my mother's side. I live here with my dad," I replied.

"You like it here?" he asked.

I looked up at him and said. "Yes, America is still the land of opportunities. I was given a chance to go back to school, just graduated in September. I got my Associates degree in Business Management, I own two websites, I'm a part-time photographer and I also do a little bit of designing, on apparels, so yeah, I do like it here." I assured him.

"Oh, that's good, you work hard, you cannot fail," he assured me.

"America loves people with potential, once you're willing to work, a lot of doors will open for you," I said to him, as he nodded his head, then asked me, "So where do you see yourself in ten years?"

"I see myself running a much more established clothing line and photography company, because those are my passions and there are related careers, and probably two, three books down the line," I said to him.

"What would you write about?" he asked.

"General stuff about life, like my years as a shoe shiner, my shoe shining experience, you know, stuff that I've learned here at this job, because every day I learn a lot, every day I get more knowledge, and I certainly think that people would be interested to read about it, especially since it's a very diverse terminal. I meet and talk to people from all over the world and learn a lot from them, you know, not just one group or one set of cultures, so it will be credible information."

"I wish you luck man, if you have a vision, you should grow into it."

"Yes you should," I agreed with him.

"So more polish really makes it last longer?" he asked next, as he stared down at his shoes.

"Yes it does, three layers is definitely better than one," I said to him, as I gave him the thumbs up, before removing the footrest and urging him to watch his steps as he stepped down.

"Can I get a five back?" he requested, as he placed a twenty dollar bill into my hand.

"Here, thank you," I said to him, as I give him back a five dollar bill.

"Good luck" he said as he walked off.

"Yeah thanks," I replied.

65

STABILITY

"CAN I HAVE a bulletproof shine please, and do we get a special discount?" my next customer asked as he approached the stand and placed his pulley luggage in front of the cabinet.

"Yeah, you guys gets a three dollar discount, so you would only have to pay nine dollars for the bulletproof shine," I explained to him, as he got seated and began to roll his pants bottom up.

"It's ok, leave that, I'll roll it up," I said to him, as he raised up and lean back in the chair.

"Those are nice color socks, where did you get them?" I asked him as I began cleaning his shoes.

"I bought them on the Internet," he quickly responded.

"Ok, I like them," I said to him, then added, "I have a few different colors.

"Yeah, I like the strip ones," he added, then began gazing around the terminal, before asking me, "Are you going to have turkey today?"

"At work, probably not, I don't think so," I replied to him, as I began to brush the balm off from his shoes.

"How many shoes do you do in an hour?" he asked next.

"In an hour, sometimes three to five." I stated.

"Oh really?" he asked.

"Yeah, but it's not that busy today," I said.

"How about yesterday?"

"Yesterday was expected to be busy, but it only was busy in the airport. A lot of people didn't wanted their shoes shine." I explained to him.

"Oh really, I guess everybody just wanted to get on their flights," he stated.

"Yeah, I guess," I replied.

He looked down at me and asked how old I was, so I said, "I'm twenty-six years old." a

"Don't get married that young!"

I then looked up at him with a smile on my face, thinking to myself that I'm right on track, because he mentioned marriage. "Why not man, I though marriage was supposed to be a good union."

"No, it is a good union, but one of two ends in divorce. That means half get divorced," he said, as he stared down at what I was doing with his shoes.

"But why is that?" I asked quickly.

"I don't think people are meant to be together that long," he joked. "It's true, let me ask you something, would you eat the same thing every day?"

"Of course not," I replied.

"Good, because that will get boring," he assured me.

"What if you try adding different spices to that same meal, and changed it up from time to time?" I asked next.

"That's what I'm saying. Life is about variety, but that's the thing about society. My point is, marriage is for the women, not the men."

"It's for the women?" I asked since I wanted him to explain what he meant exactly.

"Yeah, think about. They want the house, they got to have the kids, for real they have to have stability, they don't care about getting laid every night, they just want to have the kids, and you go make money and go fuck off," he said with a straight face. "But if it wasn't for them we wouldn't have a population.

"Yeah, that's true."

"Are you married?" he asked me next.

"No, I'm not married. I'm far from being married, but it's a thought that's in my mind."

"I don't even know the word marry, what is that, just to say that's my wife . . . that's nothing. Love goes away, everything does. It does not last, nothing lasts, and unfortunately, that is the truth."

"Yeah, unfortunately it is," I nodded and agreed with him.

"That's very smart. Let me ask you a question, do you have a tattoo?" he asked, with a disgusted look on his face.

"No man, I don't do tattoos." I responded, as I looked up at him, since I wanted to know how come he asked me about tattoos.

"Seriously, what are all these people with tattoos doing? In my day, no one ever had tattoos. If you had a tattoo you were in the hells angels, and now everyone has these tattoos today, and it's forever." He shook his head from left to right, as if he was disgusted from even talking about it. "Now they're making it more visible, it's on their faces, their necks and everywhere that people can see it. I really don't understand why."

I gave him the thumbs up and removed the footrest. He then stepped down from the stand and said, "These look great; this is for you," and placed a twenty dollar bill into my hand before walking off.

"Thank you, sir."

PROBLEMS

"It only takes eight minutes sir, step on up," I said to a man who was passing the stand, as I tried to sell him a shine.

"Eight minutes is not enough. I have two hours to kill in this place," he joked as we both began to laugh.

"Ok, I'll give you a two-hour shine then," was my response as we laughed some more.

"Nah, don't go past ten minutes, Stop at a bulletproof," he said, as I began cleaning his shoes.

I didn't hesitate to ask him my first question, since his first impression clearly said that he's willing to have a conversation, the way he approached me and how he was joking, it was clear, so I asked him, "How's your day going so far?"

"So far so good, it's a beautiful day to be alive" he replied.

"Where are you heading to?" I asked next.

"Florida. I'm heading back home, and I'm glad you spotted me. I've been meaning to get these shoes shined for a very long time, but I never got the chance, so make sure you do your best job," he said.

"Oh definitely man, that's what I intend to do," I said, as we both smiled.

"These are nice shoes, by the way."

"Yeah, I guess," was his quick response, as he continued to stare down at me shining his shoes. I had applied the first layer of polish to his shoes and was getting ready to brush it into the shoes.

"Are you traveling alone?

"Yes, you can't go wrong traveling alone," he nodded and replied.

"Are you married?" I asked next, as he began to gaze around the terminal.

"Yeah, thirteen years now," he replied, as he continued to gaze around the terminal.

"Is the divorce rate really high in Florida, and is it a big problem?" I stop working on his shoes and asked him.

He then looked down at me and said, "I think it's about the same as in New York, but that's not the question, what's important is how to solve the problem. Sometimes you do, sometimes you don't. If you have a good supporting staff, you try to work out your problems, and you don't get divorced. But every couple's got problems. It doesn't matter if you're Jewish, Christian or Muslim, black or brown or white or yellow. If you get married, you will have problems. That's why you, always, always compromise, and you must have tolerance."

"Hmm. What's the regular stuff that married couple fights the most about?"

"Money, always money. Money is the biggest problem. Kids can also create problems."

"But I thought kids were supposed to bring you closer," I said.

"It depends, like if the mother spoils the kids and the father doesn't spend enough time with the kids, that can cause problems, and even if the father and the mother is working and not spending time with the kids and they're watching too much TV, not doing good enough in school, they don't go to bed on time, they don't get up on time, it's crazy problems," he explained.

"Yeah, that would be crazy," I agreed with him.

"But if you have a marriage and you work out your problems, it will last. If you're faithful with your wife, you will learn how to compromise, and then you'll have patience. If you fight with you wife and you just don't have patience, guess what? You're not going to have patience with your kids, either. The problem is when you have kids. It's not their fault, you got to give them the benefit of the doubt, you want to be a miserable son of a bitch because you married the wrong person. That's your problem. Leave the kids out of it. Fight with your wife, but never in front of the kids.

"Ok," was my quick response.

"So you work twelve hours a day, and you know what you do? When you leave work, you go to a bar have a drink, fuck it. When you're married, there's no day off, you're never off, there's no twelve hours and then you can go somewhere else. You work all day for twelve hours, then you have to go home and deal with shit, like I wasn't dealing with enough shit for the past twelve hours at work."

I then said, "Yeah, with your boss, co-workers and customers right?"

"Yeah, but with marriage there are no breaks. With work there is: You have lunch hours, you go to work, you chill out, smoke a cigarette, take a break, relax. With marriage there's no break, there's no cigarette break.

"I think it's a beautiful thing to be married," I said to him as I brushed his shoes.

"Yeah it is, trust me, but it's also a lot of compromising. Most men always look for the best looking girls and the nicest ones, but the bottom line is, if you get married, they will be fighting, you will fight with each other. As long as you're married, you're going to fight, there's nothing that you can do about it," he assured me, with a straight face.

"Relationships are problems, right?" I said, with a smile on my face as he began to smile himself, then said. "Both ways, if you're looking to have a cheesy one then you're in trouble, you got to worry about what you do, If both of you have the same attitude, and that is, I'm giving in for her and she says I'm the giving for him, you'll never get divorce, if she says he's got to give in and if you say she's got to give in, goodbye."

"You're good," I said to him, as I removed the footrest.

"How can you say I'm good, and you don't even know me?" was his quick response as he stepped down from the chair, with a smirk on his face.

"Because you're alive and once you've got life, you're good." I responded.

"Yeah you're right. Waking up on the right side of the fence," he replied, then paid and took off.

"Thanks for the business sir."

67

BEAUTIFUL

"I DON'T LIKE the snow anymore, although when I was growing up, it was ok. I played a little hockey and stuff like that but I didn't enjoy it that much. So I was telling my friends, when I get out of school, I'm leaving, and they were like you're crazy man. You're not going anywhere. You're stuck with the rest of us." My next customer was explaining to me why he decided to move out of Maine, while I began to clean his shoes. "I had a job so I saved money for a whole year, and then the money I got when I graduated. The next morning I was out. It took about three weeks to get there. I visited a couple of friends, like who had moved and stuff, then went and got a job. I went to San Diego first and got a job in like three days, a tough job though. I was working in a factory making pallet. Then I started going to school, and got my degree. Then moved up north to Santa Cruz California, which is the new San Francisco, and started working and eventually ended up at GemCo, and I've been there my whole life. So now all my friends is like you really did it man" with a smile on his face.

"Yeah, once your mind can conceive it, it's possible," I said to him, nodding my head.

"Yeah, you can bullshit about it or you can escape it. I did not like the snow so I didn't want to stay there," he explained.

"Ok." We both got silent for about thirty seconds as I continued to work on his shoes and he gazed around the terminal.

He then looked down at me and said, "So I just was visiting my dad, and he's very, very ill, so I took some time off to stay with him. He's about ninety years old. He lived a big life, he told me he's ready to go. He's very ill though, some days he doesn't even know who you are, and then the next day he wakes up like, 'Hey how you doing?' So we got him out one day, my brother and I. My brother is his full caretaker and he's doing a wonderful job with him. He's in a wheelchair, so one day he was so good we loaded him into a wheelchair van and took him to a titty bar and had a nice night."

"Really?" as I looked up at him.

"Yeah, he got titties in his face and had a big smile on his face," he said as we both began to laugh. They were really good with him. We all had a really good time. They took really good care of him, but he only lasted maybe an hour, so we went to dinner, and then we took him back home."

"That's nice, at least he had fun," I said as I continued to work on his shoes.

"We didn't think that he would have wanted to go, but then we asked him, 'What do you think about us taking you to one of these places?' 'What place?' 'A place where women are going to shake their tittles in your face,'" he said as we began to laugh. "He had a good time, and we had fun too. I didn't mind it. My wife would probably shoot me if she found out, but it's alright to look and touch. She already told me, 'I don't care where you get your appetite, as long as you eat at home," he stated with a smile on his face. "I'll always remember that; we've been married forty-one years."

"Forty-one years?" I repeated.

"Yeah." Was his quick response, as I went on to ask my first question, even though, we'd been talking for a few minutes. "What is it like, being married for forty-one years?"

"Well it's been good. We've had very few rough times, because we're always very natural with each other. I could count the amount of fights that we've had in forty years," he explained to me, as he gazed around the terminal.

"Ok, so how do you deal with the fights?" I asked next.

"Everyone's different. It depends, when we were young we had most of them. Our first maybe five years together was pretty, pretty crazy you know, both independent young people that wanted their own way, but we both learned to give and take a little bit and before you knew it, ten years in, before you blink your eyes again another ten. Now our daughter is twenty-six years old," he explained, then got silent.

"Wow, life really goes by fast, huh?" I said, then went on to ask, "Is your wife traveling with you today?"

"No, I'm alone, she's home. She's working," he replied.

"So what kind of advice can you give me about choosing the right woman to marry?" was my next question, as I applied the last layer of polish to his shoes and began brushing it in.

"Well, let me tell you, when I met her, I was at a party at my Aunt's' house. It was a big party, and she needed a bartender. She had a nice big house, big patio, big bar, everything, so I said no problem. She's maybe ten, fifteen years older than me, so most of her guests were going to be older than me. So about halfway through the evening, she walks through the door, she's a couple years older than me. When she walked in the door, I almost fell on the floor," he said with a straight face as I began to laugh." He then continued, "Totally beautiful, and some guy walked in with her, and I thought, 'Oh boy, that figures,' then as the night went on, I talked to her once, then twice, then I finally said to her, 'Where's your boyfriend?' and she goes 'What are you talking about. I didn't came with anyone. He just happened to get out of his car at the same time as me. I don't even know his name.' So we spent the rest of the evening talking about everything. I told her I wanted to take her out tomorrow she said ok and to pick her up. Of course, I was supposed to pick her up at noon. I couldn't wait; I got there about 10:30 in the morning," he said as we both began to laugh aloud, he then continued, "And when she came to the door, she still had curlers in her hair and everything and she said, 'Guy I told you twelve o'clock,' and I said I couldn't wait, so she goes alright come on in, so I went in to wait, and we have been together ever since,"

"Wow," I responded.

"You can't plan it, it has to be natural, and it did for me, and it just kept growing, and now it's been forty years and I don't even think about it until someone makes me remember." He said smiling, as I smiled and replied, "That makes sense."

"They're doing it already, they're boarding. Time really flies fast when you're having fun," he said as I nodded and agreed with him.

PREFERENCE

"You got time for one more or you want to take a break?" my next customer asked me as he approached the stand and noticed that I had just finished shining a previous customer's shoes.

"Hey welcome back, man. How've you been? Step on up. I don't need a break." This guy always gets his shoes shined with us when he travels.

"How's your morning going, man?" he asked as he got seated and placed his foot on the footrest.

"Good, and yourself?" I replied.

"Good, so far. Just got to make it to Vegas and it's going to be even better," he stated.

I nodded and said, "Work, I hope."

"No, a little play."

Remember what happens in Vegas, stays in Vegas . . . except herpes."

"Exactly, that's what I'm saying."

"Classic line. Best movie ever," I stated with a smile on my face.

He agreed by saying, "Sure was."

"How long are you going to be out in Vegas for?" I asked next.

"Till Tuesday night, so we'll see what happens . . . whether I come back broke or not," he said as we laughed some more. I then fixed his feet properly on the footrest and went on to ask another question. "Are you traveling alone?"

"No. My brother is meeting me out there, so it should be fun," he said and smiled broadly.

"Are you married?"

"Yes, I'm married with a kid, yes, sir," he responded, with a smirk on his face.

"And what does your wife have to say about this trip?" I stood up and as asked him next.

"She's good with it. She knows me too well, and we've been together for a long time, so we're all good."

"Ok, so how long have you been married?" I questioned him.

"Eleven years," he replied

"I think marriage is a beautiful thing," I said to him.

He stared at me and replied, "Sometimes it can be, but there's other times when you're going to be like, 'I'd rather have a root canal before getting married again.'"

"Haha, well eleven years is a very long time, so marriage must be good to you," I said to him next.

"I guess, but it's going to cost me a lot more to get out of it," he laughed.

"So is it true that women change after you say 'I do'?" I asked him.

"I don't know, depends on how you look at it. I'm sure they do. We all change, but women . . . you can't predict them."

"That's true." I nodded and agreed with him, as I continued to work on his shoes. I then asked him one last question before finishing up his shine, since I was already brushing the final layer of polish into his shoes, "So what kind of advice can you give to me about choosing the right woman, what do you look for?"

"Oh, I don't know, that's a personal preference, but you know what, the only advice I can give to you is make sure you are happy, that's all that matters. Life's too short. You should talk to her, do whatever it is, because at the end of the day, if you're not happy, it's not worth doing, and that's with anything in life. If you're not happy, there's no reason to live."

"That's true," I agreed with him, then said, "You're good," as I removed the footrest for him to step down.

"Well, these are looking nice, good luck with everything man, be well."

"Thanks man, enjoy."

69

DO-MORE

"HOW ABOUT A shine sir? Let me show you something," was how I got my next customer, who was walking past the stand and decided to turn back to see what I was going to show him. I then reached into the shine box as he got over to the stand and took out the cognac cream polish, showed it to him and said, "I have the perfect color for those shoes that your wearing," which happened to be a cognac, boots that was made out Ostrich skin.

He then smiled and said, "Ok, what heck? Let me have the basic shine," before he got seated.

"Just put it right there," I urged him to put his bag pack on the shine box, as I began wrapping the balm cloth around my hand.

"Ok," was his quick response as I began cleaning his boots with the leather balm.

"How are you today sir?" I asked him.

"Pretty good, what about you?"

"I'm great, no complains here, nobody listens." I said smiling.

"People listens, they do, but no one cares," he said.

"So where are you heading?"

"I'm going to Buffalo, no snow, that's good," he said.

"Ok, no snow is always good," I said as I began to apply polish to his shoes.

"That's where you're originally from?" I asked next.

"No. I'm just visiting. Is the airport busy?"

"Not really, it's been mad slow lately."

"Ok, that's probably a tough time for you, huh?" he asked.

I then looked up at him and said, "A very tough time." We both began to smile, and at that point I noticed that he was wearing what seemed to be a wedding band, so I didn't waste any time with my next question.

"How long have you been married?" I asked next.

"Twenty-seven years, no it's thirty-two," he said, correcting himself.

"Thirty-two years?" I repeated.

"Yeah, I forgot five," he said as we began to laugh aloud, then added, "Yeah, the kids are thirty-two, thirty and twenty-seven.

"I'm actually thinking about marriage; I think it's a beautiful thing," I said to him.

"It is you know, usually most times, but you just have to work hard to make it work out, but other than that, make sure you find the woman that you can settle with, and you got to give more into the relationship, than you get."

He advised me, as I nodded and said "Ok." He then went on to say, "And if you think it's 50/50, it doesn't work, so you always got to think that you got to do more, because that's what the other partner thinks, too."

"Yeah that's true. I know for sure that the 50/50 thing doesn't work at all." I said, as I agreed with him.

"No, it doesn't ever work and don't let the little things bother you," he advised me.

"Ok," I quickly responded, as I continued with his shoes.

"Yeah, because a lot of people get tied up with the little things and forget about the stuff that really matters."

"Do you think marriage still has the same value today that it had twenty, thirty years ago?" I asked next.

"Somewhat," he said, then added, "It's all about trust. I have three children and none of them are married yet. "Well, people get married older these days. In my time, it used to be eighteen, nineteen, twenty, twenty-three. Today, it's twenty-eight, thirty, thirty-four, thirty-five. People are older so they tend to value it more."

"Ok, you're all set," I said to him as I gave him the thumbs up.

"Looking good," he said as he stepped down from the stand to pay. "Excellent, I love them."

"Thanks sir, for the business and the advice," I said to him.

"No problem. Good luck to you," he said as he walked off.

70

FORMULA

"WHICH OF THE shines would you like to have today? We have three levels, we have the basic, the glass and the bulletproof, each offers more protection to the shoes and the shine last longer," I explained to my next customer, who was sitting in the chair. He then requested to have the bulletproof shine. So I immediately began to take the supplies out of the shine box, and that was when I noticed that he was wearing a wedding band. I wasn't sure even though it was on his ring finger, because I've never seen and silver or platinum wedding ring. So I asked him, "Is that's a silver wedding band?"

"This?" He pointed to the ring while raising up his left hand.

"Yeah." I nodded and responded.

"I think its silver; I've had it so long that I don't even remember. My wife would kill me, if she knew I just said that."

"How long have you been married?" I immediately asked next.

"Ah, like eight, nine years now," he replied as if he was unsure, then went on to asked me, "How long have you been shining shoes?"

"Almost two years now," I responded, as I brushed his shoes.

"Is it a good job?" he asked next.

"Yes it is, it's a great job," I said with a smile on my face.

"Yes, I bet it is," he replied, as he continued to stare down at me working on his shoes.

"Yes, I love my job. You just got to find something that makes you happy, and you're going like it." I stated.

"Yes, I agree. How many booths do you guys have?"

"Well we have two booths in this terminal, which is our only New York location as of now, but we have a couple of stores in San Francisco, and that's where the company was started," I explained to him, then changed the topic by asking him, "So what kind of advice can you give to me on marriage?"

That's when he smiled and said, "You know the cliché happy wife, happy life? It's true. It's not always easy to do, but it's a guaranteed formula for success within marriage."

"You've got to do whatever to make it work right?" I asked him.

"Yeah, you know how it is, do whatever to make it work. I do it and it's good for the two kids also."

"You have two kids?" I asked him next.

"Yeah, and that's the winning formula." He then asked my age.

I told him that I was twenty-six years old and his response was just, "Ok." So I went on to ask him another question.

"Is this is your first marriage?"

"Yeah, it is," he replied and again, went on to ask me another question about my job, "How many people do you do a day, on average?"

"It depends, on the time of year, like in the wintertime, it goes up, to fifteen, twenty shines a day," I explained to him.

"Good that people are still wearing shoes." he said.

"Yeah of course, because a lot of women wear their boots and get them shined and in the summertime it's all flip-flops and sneakers."

"Yeah, I know. When I'm going to business meetings I always get my shoes shined. A good shine is good for the feet. It's like a good haircut," he stated.

"There good."

"Good, thank you very much," he responded as he stepped down from the stand.

"Thank you, and please watch your step," I urged him, as he stepped down from the stand.

"Here man. It's yours," he said as he placed a twenty dollar bill into my hand.

"Ok, thank you. Have a great day."

71

STAGE

"ARE YOU OPEN or are you taking a break?" my next customer asked, as he approached the stand, while I was sitting in the chair.

"I'm open. I don't have time for break," I replied, as I stood beside him.

"A break is not a bad thing," he said, as he climbed the stand and got seated.

"Where are you heading today?" I immediately asked him, as I fixed his feet on the footrest.

"Jacksonville."

"Which of the shines would you like to have on these shoes today?" I asked next, as I began to take out the supplies out of my shine box.

"What's bulletproof?" he asked as he stared at the sign.

"That's the one with the most layers of polish, and the one that will last the longest, and the one that I strongly, strongly recommend," I explained to him, with a smile on my face.

"Alright, alright, give me that one," he said, as he began to smile also.

"Do you live in Jacksonville?" I asked next, but instead of answering my question he said, "So it's going to cost me fifteen box to get my shoes shined?" while he continued to gaze at the sign.

"Not fifteen bucks, twenty-five dollars," I joked, as we both began to laugh.

He then went on to say, "No, we live here."

"So how long have you been married?" I asked next, as I began to clean the soles of his shoes.

"This coming December it's going to be twenty, no, thirty-six years," he said with a smirk on his face, as he gazed to the food court.

"So tell me, what do you do to make your marriage last for thirty-six years?" I asked, as I looked up at him.

"Fight a lot," he joked, as we both began to laugh aloud. "We have three boys, you don't know how that goes."

"Marriage is not something that I want to do now, but it's definitely a thought that's in my head," I said to him.

"Think really hard," he advised me, then got silent for a few minutes, then continued by saying, "Make it fun while you're in your twenties, but you get somewhere else in your fifty's and it's hard to make something work like that, when you're that old.

"Ok, so what is the most common issue that you guys fight about? Since you said you guys fight a lot," I asked him next.

"You always fights about money, but that's when you always have to think about the kids. You should always think about the kids. The thing is, once you have a kids, usually people don't get a divorce, just for the kids' sake. It happens half of the time, because it affects them one way or the other, and that's not fair for the kids."

"You're absolutely right," I agreed with him, then went on to ask "Do you think that your wife changed?"

"Oh yeah we both have, but I think the hardest she is, is with the kids," he stated, then added, "And then when the kids leave home, it's just your wife and you again. Then she looks at you and says 'Who are you?' Now that's the other thing, that's the biggest problem, that stage. It's very bad, and that's when you find out if you really love each other."

I nodded and said to him, "You're good."

"All right, magic. These shoes look pretty damn good to me," he said as he stepped down from the stand and paid for his shine.

"Yes they do," I responded, as I began to take the gloves and my dust mask off.

"In the old days, the guys that did this never wore that mask to save their lungs, but you would've thought that they would've thought about that," he said then walked off.

72

SEX

"Can I have a shine, please?" a passenger said to me as he approached the stand, while I was restocking the backup supplies box in the cabinet.

"Sure, have a seat." I urged him to sit and he got seated.

"These are some comfortable chairs you got here."

"Yes, they are." I agreed, as I nodded and placed the footrest up for him to put his feet on. "How are you today?"

"Good, fine, and you?"

"Going good so far, which of the shines did you decide that you were going to have?" I asked next, as I began to take out the supplies out of my shine box

"Ah, I don't know, give me the middle one," he requested, as he stared at the sign, confused.

"Down the middle, we go," I said, as I began cleaning his shoes.

He then looked at me and said, "You know what, just make it the bulletproof, but what does that mean?"

"We add extra layers of polish, so it will last longer, so instead of one layer of polish, you get two extra layers." I explained to him, as I continued to work on his shoes.

"So, it's veterans and women owned, which one are you?" he joked, as we both began to laugh aloud.

"That was a good one. You're funny. Which one do you think I am?" I replied, as we laughed some more.

He then said, "Neither," as he continued to laugh.

I then asked him "Is that your wife?" as I pointed to the woman that he was walking with, who went and got seated in the food court, as he got his shoes shine.

"No she's my girlfriend." he responded, with a smile on his face.

"How long have you guys been dating?" I looked up at him and asked.

"Twenty-five years. I'm a little slow like that, I'm afraid to pop the question."

"Oh yeah? 'Cause when you pop the question, everything goes wrong, right?"

"I hear after you get married, there's no more sex, so I decided not to marry her," he joked as we both laughed some more, then went on to ask, "What do you think?"

"I think you should pop the question," I said.

"You think so?" he quickly asked.

"Yeah, you should pop it right here, right now. Get the loud speakers, and pop it over the intercom," I advised him, as we smiled with each other.

"Ah, I don't know man, we'll be together for one week, and it will be hard from this day onward," he joked, then added, "Plus I'm shy like that," as we laughed some more. I continued to clean his shoes, as we both got silent for a few seconds. He then looked down at me and asked if I was married.

"Nope, I'm not married, but it's a thought that's in my head. With all the stories I hear every day about marriage, I be thinking a lot."

"So have you decided if you're going to pop the question?"

"Of course. I think marriage is a beautiful thing," I said to him as he smiled.

"Really, it's obvious you haven't been married. Ok again, are you the Veteran or the Woman? As we laughed, "Nah, I'm joking," he stated as he continued to smile.

I then went on to tell him, "I hear a lot of negative stuff about marriages every day, but the majority is all good stuff, about 70 percent of the stuff I hear about marriage is good," I assured him.

"Really?" he responded, as if he was shock at what I had just told him.

"Well, it depends on who you're talking to." I nodded and said, "Yeah, but twenty-five years though, what do you do to keep it together for that long?"

"We were separated for twenty-four out of it, so," he joked.

"For real what's the secret?" I repeated, with a smirk on my face.

He looked at me and said, "Let me tell you the secret, it's simple. A lot of money and a lot of sex, and that's it."

"A lot of money and a lot of sex?" I repeated.

"Yeah that's it. Seriously, most marriages break up because of arguments of money or, not a good sex life, so that's it, money and sex," he stated, then went on to say. "Those are looking nice," as I buffed his shoes.

"You're good," as I give him the thumbs up.

He then stepped down from the stand and placed a twenty dollar bill into my hand and said, "Can I have a five back, damn, those chairs are so comfortable, I might just stay a little bit longer," as we both smiled.

"Thank you," I said to him, as he walked off.

73

PARTNERSHIP

"HOW ABOUT A shine, sir?" I asked my next customer, who was walking past the stand very slowly.

"Can you do anything with these shoes?" he stopped and asked, as he stare down at his shoes, then looked at me.

"Yeah, of course, have a seat," I said to him, as he nodded his head and said "Why not?" Then added, "This feels like you're stepping into heaven," as he climbed up the stand.

"Have you been to heaven before?" I joked, as we both began to laugh.

"Which of the shines would you like to have today sir?

"Oh these don't deserve anything but the regular basic," he said while looking at the sign, then added, "and you could darken them, I don't mind.

"Ok," I began to work on his shoes, as he sat and gazed around the terminal, then looked down and asked me "How's your morning going so far?"

"So far, it's good," I quickly responded. Are you traveling alone?"

"Yup, going down to sunny Florida," he replied with a broad smile on his face.

"Ok, you live they're or you're just visiting?" I asked next, as I began to brush his shoes.

"Ah, I live there; but I work here for two weeks, so it's two weeks here and two weeks there." He explained, then added, "I spent a month and a half in New Mexico, then two weeks

229

here, now I'm going home for two weeks, and then I'm going to California for six weeks."

"Now what does the family thinks about that, how do they feel about that, especially the wifey?" I asked.

"Ah, my wife doesn't like to travel, but she could go with me . . . all my kids are grown," he replied, as he stared down at me.

"How long have you been married?" I asked next.

"Fifty years," was his quick response.

"Fifty years, damn, that's a long time." I said, as I was kind of surprised, because he didn't look as if he was fifty years old. I then stood up and said to him, "That's older than my parents are."

He nodded his head and replied, "I could tell."

"So what's the secret to make a marriage last that long, what do you do?" I went on to ask him next.

"It has to be a two-way partnership, you have your ups and down, and you got to remember when you're down, to think of all the up times and get over it," he advised.

"That makes a lot of sense."

"You only stay mad for a little while. Women have the pussy, and they control life," he said as we both laughed aloud, as he went on to add, "You can go out and get something different, but it's no different, like what you had in the beginning. All that loving and touching and feelings, and then it goes away, so you got to bring it back.

"Ok, so you're saying that you could fall out of love or like lose love for each other after a while?" I asked him since I wasn't sure of what he meant.

"You feel like you are, because everything becomes a routine," he explained to me, as I nodded my head.

"I could only imagine how much stuff you did hundreds of times before, within that fifty years,"

"Oh yeah," he nodded and replied, then went on to say, "Still you're tempted to go astray, I mean young women today are gorgeous. They didn't dress the way they do today when I was growing up, and that's when you look at your wife, and you look at them, then you look back at your wife, the mother of your children and the sacrifices she went through, What do you do, you go with the younger women?" he said, as we both began to laugh aloud.

I went on to add, "Some people do," while nodding my head.

"Exactly and what do they do, four months later, they're looking for somebody else. The girl that was so sweet, turns out to be a b#@ch, so now you don't know what you can get away with, you don't know what you can do, but with your wife, you already know what you can get away with, and what to expect," he advised me.

"Yes," I responded, with a smile on my face, as I began to buff his shoes, since I was almost finished with his shine.

"There's no business travelers here, just kids, it's a vacation central in this terminal. If you go to terminal two or eight, you would definitely do better," he advised me, as I nodded and asked him, "What do you think?" while pointing down to his shoes.

"Basic, eh? It looks more like a bulletproof, brand new," he said, as he paid then took off.

74

APPRECIATE

"HOW ABOUT A shoe shine, sir?" I asked my next customer, who came walking towards the stands.

He then looked up at me and said, "Can you make these look brand new?"

"Yeah, that's what I do," I assured him, as he smiled and got seated, then requested to have the basic shine, as I smiled and said, "Sure, basic it is." I then began wrapping the balm rag around my hand, after I had taken the supplies out of the box.

"So how's your morning going so far?" I asked him, as I began to apply the leather balm to his shoes.

His quick response was, "Good." So I decided to ask him another question, which was, "Where are you heading to?"

"I'm heading too Bermuda," he said with a smile on his face, then added, "The people on the island are going to be like, 'Where did you get those shoes from?' and I'll be like the guy from JFK terminal 6 hooked me up.

"You live there? I asked next.

"No, but I have a few girlfriends out there," he joked as we both began to laugh aloud.

He then went on to say, "Nah, I'm only messing with you. I'm going out there for business," as I smiled and went on to my other question, which was, "Are you traveling alone?"

"Yeah," he responded, as I began to polish his shoes. I then went on to say, "So none of the girlfriends are traveling with you this morning?"

He smiled and said, "Well the only girlfriend I'm even interested to travel with is my wife of fifty years?"

"Fifty?" I repeated.

"Fifty!" he replied.

"Five zero or one five?" I asked, as I began to smile.

"Five zero," he responded.

"That's nice, that she's still your girlfriend and not just your wife," I said to him, then went on to say, "Fifty years huh, I actually just met a couple that is married for fifty years now."

"Ok." He replied as he quickly looked at his watch.

"Yeah, that's crazy, but what do you do for fifty years to keep the marriage going?" I asked next.

"Well, each partner has to have their own life," he said.

"Their own life, outside of the marriage?" I quickly asked.

"No, no, well part of the marriage I mean, you have to have your own people that you can communicate with on a regular basis. My wife stays there for the winter, and I say to everybody when I arrive, she gives me a big kiss, and when I leave to come home, she gives me a big kiss. We've got our own friends and everything and we've got a hold on life and it works out very well. If you're always together, then that can get messy."

"So it's not good being together all the time?"

"They say that being away makes the heart go fonder. You appreciate the other party more when they're not around you all the time, and we also have three children and eight grandchildren, so life is pretty good." He stated, with a smile on his face.

"Life is good, huh?"

"Yep, it's good," he responded.

"You're good sir," I said, as I give him the thumbs up and removed the footrest. He then stepped down, paid for his shine, then said "Thank you," before walking away.

"Thanks for the business."

75

HEADACHES

"WHAT'S THE PRICE for a shine?" my next customer asked me as he approached the stand and placed his iPad on the chair.

"We have three different prices, eight, ten and twelve," I responded.

"Ok, let me see if I have enough money," he said, as he reached into his pocket and pulled out his wallet, then asked, "Do you guys take credit cards?"

"No, but there's an ATM right there," I replied, as I pointed to the ATM machine that was located not too far from the stand.

"Ok, I'll take a shine," he said, as he looked at the ATM with a smile on his face and got seated. I then began to take the supplies out of the shine box and as I was about to start cleaning his shoes, he asked me, "How is it going?"

"It's going good, how about yourself?"

"Not bad, can't complain," he said, as I went on to explaining the types of shoe shines that we have to offer to him.

"We have three levels of shines sir, we have the bullet proof which is our best shine, we have the glass and we have the basic, each offers more protection to the shoes and a longer lasting shine, which one would you like to have?"

"Bulletproof," he said, as he stared at the sign.

"Bulletproof it is, good choice," I said to him, as I continued working on his shoes.

"These shoes are the best shoes," he then said to me, as he pointed down to his feet.

"Why is that?"

"Because it's the only pair I can wear, and they fit the best," he assured me, with a smile on his face.

"Oh, that's good," I replied, as I brushed off the leather balm from his shoes.

"They last long, too. I really should have worn my brown ones. The brown ones need it more than these. They're kind of worse, but it's all right, next time," he said.

I didn't give him a chance to say another word, since he clearly was in a talking mood, so I went on to ask him, "Where are you heading today?"

"Dominican Republic, for vacation," he said as he smiled, then added, "Punta Canta."

"Are you traveling alone?"

He looked at me, smiled and said, "No I wish, nah I'm playing." As we both began to laugh aloud, he then went on to add, "No, I have my family with me, my wife and kids. It's all good."

"All good," I repeated. "How long have you been married?"

"Too long," he joked, as we both laughed some more. He went on to say, "A lot of years and a lot of headaches."

"Good years and good headaches I hope," I said to him.

"Well, mostly yeah," he responded, as he nodded his head. We both got silent for a few seconds, as I continued to work on his shoes.

"Look at the ass on that one, oh shit, nice cute little ass," he stated, as he stared down the terminal at a female passenger who was passing by.

"Hmm, hmm, I see that all day, every day," I told him.

"I fucking love it; I'm jealous man, can I have your job?"

"That's why I chose the job with my face facing the chairs, because the terminal is a very diverse terminal, so you get to see them all, in every color and in every size."

"And the dogs, too?" he asked, as a passenger passed by, holding a little dog in her hands. But this time, he didn't have a smile on his face, instead he seemed disgusted, by the way he look at the dog.

"Yeah, I see those too." I said, as I nodded my head and continued to work on his shoes.

"Where do they put those dogs, do they put them on the plane or something?" he asked, with that same disgusted look on his face.

"Yeah, they keep them at the bottom of the plane, I think. I'm not sure." I said to him.

He then looked down at me and replied, "If I ever had a dog next to me on a plane, I would die."

"Ok," I said, with a smirk on my face, as I began to brush the second layer of polish into his shoes.

"No, no, no, I'm allergic," he said, as he shook his head from left to right.

"You're allergic?" I said, as I stood up and looked at him.

"Yeah, like you want to kill me, you get a cat or a dog." he stated as I began to smiled, then added, "Does your wife know that?"

"Yeah, no, nah, she knows," he joked.

"Oh damn," I said, as I continued smiling, as he went on to say, "That's how she could kill me; she could put a little dog hair in my food." We both began to laugh aloud.

"Wowed," I then said.

"Yeah, that will be the end of me, see you later, good night," he said as he laughed some more.

I then added. "That's crazy; you got to be a good boy all the time."

"Ah man, that's the thing, I'm not," he assured me, with a smile on his face. I then smiled back at him, then went on to ask, "What would you say is the best part of marriage, at least for you?"

"Ah, I'll be honest with you. If you're not going to try to have kids, I don't believe in marriage." He said to me, as he stuttered his first words, then added, "That's just my opinion."

"So you're saying, it's only for the kids?" I asked him, since I wanted him to elaborate more on what he had said.

"He went on to say, "For the kids, I think it's for the kids and the wife, because they want to settle down and have kids. I've lost three girlfriends. Diversify. We were talking about diversification earlier. Look at all the different people coming through here. Life is too short man, you got to take whatever you can get."

"Yeah that's true," I agreed with him.

"Yeah, but it's all for the kids, you know the old joke, right?"

"Which one?" I asked, as I stop brushing his shoes and looked up at him.

"Why is the bride smiling when she walks down the aisle on the wedding day?" he asked, with a smirk on his face,

"Why?" I asked.

"Because she knows she gave her last blow job." he joked, as we both began to laugh aloud. He then went on to add. "Watch what happens if you ever get married. Everything stops."

"That really happens, isn't that a joke?" I asked him, with a smirk on my face.

"No shit. That's why you got to get it somewhere else."

"That's crazy," I said to him, as I began to buff his shoes.

"Tell me about it, it nuts." He responded, then went on to ask me if I was the owner of the shoe shining company.

"No, I work for the company," I said to him.

"How do they pay you, do they give you a percentage of each?" he asked next, as he stared at the sign.

"Yeah, they do." I assured him.

"Oh yeah?" He asked, as he nodded his head.

"Yeah, it's not bad," I replied him.

"No, that's great," he said.

I went on to add, "I love my job, "I get to meet a lot of interesting people on a daily basis, I don't have any manager on my back 24/7 telling me what to do and I learn a lot every day."

"Yeah, you hear a lot of funny jokes," he smiled and added.

"Yes, I definitely do. What do you think?" as I pointed to his shoes.

"I love them," he assured me, then began to step down from the stand.

"Thank you," I said to him, as he paid and took off.

76

BELIEVE

"Where are you heading to?" I asked my next customer, who was already sitting in the chair, waiting for a shine, since I had taken a bathroom break.

"I'm going to the Dominican Republic," he said.

"Oh really, my last customer was heading to DR also." I said to him, as I began cleaning his shoes, then went on to ask him. "Do you live there?"

"No I live over here, but I'm originally from DR, so I visit a lot." He began to gaze around the terminal.

"Are you traveling alone?" I asked next.

"Yeah, today I am, but my wife is coming this Friday to meet me," he replied, as he continued to gaze around the terminal.

"Oh, ok. How long have you been married?" I asked him, as I began to apply polish to his shoes.

"Twenty-seven years," he said to me as he stared down at his shoes while I polished them.

"That's older than me. That's older than I am," I said to him, as I smiled and nodded my head.

He then went on to add, "I've been married before, for six years. My first wife passed away and then I got married again."

"Oh? Well, what kind of advice can you give to me about marriage?" I then asked as I looked up at him.

"Ah, I don't have a problem with my wife," he stated, with a straight face.

I repeated, "You don't have a problem with your wife?"

"No, we've been married for twenty-seven years and we have never had a problem. No arguments, either."

"No arguments?" I repeated.

"No, no arguments. We have four kids, but they're grown already," he said.

"How did you manage prevent arguments, though?"

"How? By talking to her," he said.

"By talking to her?" I repeated.

"Yeah, make sure she believes in you and you believe in her."

"Ok, communicate?" I asked.

"Yeah communication. Understand her, talk to her, go to church—I don't mean every day, but like at least once a week—and talk all of the time, communicate all of the time. That keeps it going."

"How do you know when it's the right person, like what do you look for in a woman?" I asked next.

"Don't look for anything, just take her to meet your mother." He then went silent.

"Take her to meet your mother?" I asked, as I looked up at him, since I wasn't sure of what he meant.

"Yeah, just take her to meet your mother," he said again, then went on to add, "Mothers always knows what's best for their kids, especially their sons. Remember, your mom is a woman, so she will know exactly if your wife is up to know good just by having one conversation with her."

"Wow, I never really thought about that," I said to him. I thought it was a strange theory. I then began to buff his shoes.

"How old are you?" he asked next.

"I'm twenty-six years old," I said to him.

"Do you have any kids?"

"No kids, not as yet," I replied, as I shook my head from left to right. He then nodded and went on to ask me if I was from Jamaica.

"No. I'm from Guyana."

He nodded his head once more.

"You're good," I said to him, as I give him the thumbs up, signaling his shine was complete.

"Nice and shiny," he said, as he stared down at his shoes, then stepped down from the stand.

"Yes, they are," I agreed with him, as I took off the gloves from my hands.

"Thank you, have a good day," he said, as he paid and took off.

"Yeah, you too man. Enjoy, thank you."

COMPASSIONATE

"WE HAVE THREE levels of shines. We have the bulletproof, the glass and the basic. Each shine offers more protection to the shoes and a longer lasting shine," I explained to my next customer, who came up to the stand and requested to have a shine, before taking a seat.

He then stared at the sign and said, "Let's go for the full thing."

"Good choice," I said. "Where are you heading to?"

"We're off to St Marten. We were just in for the weekend," he said, as he stared down at his shoes.

"You said 'we,'?"

"Yeah, me and my wife. She's floating around here somewhere," he replied.

I smiled and immediately went on to my next question. "How long have you guys been married?"

"Ah, we got married in 2002, so a little longer than ten, eleven years?

"Ok," was my quick response, as I continued to work on his shoes.

"We come down here once in a while, for a long weekend, to see what's going on, and there's always something going on here in New York," he stated, with a broad smile on his face.

"Yeah, that's true," I agreed with him, as I began to brush off the second layer of polish from his shoes. "Do you think that marriage has the same values today, that it had twenty, thirty years ago?

"Yes, I do, I certainly do," he responded, as he nodded his head.

"You do?" I looked up at him.

"I really do. It's still definitely a commitment. It's not just, 'Let's see how it goes for six months, then I'm going to move on' kind of thing, so I guess I'm kind of old school about that. What do you think?"

"I think somewhat, because a lot of people are still getting married every day."

"Yeah."

"How do you know if it's the right time and the right person? What should you look for?"

"Hmm . . . that's a tough one," he said, then paused for a second or two. "When I talked to Sherra about getting married, I had like two or three things . . . she called it the interrogation. I think the first thing was that I wanted her to be a Christian, the second thing was, I was looking for somebody with a strong will, and she has both."

"Ok," I said, as he continued by saying, "And the third thing, I was looking for somebody who's compassionate, and she is. Things are going great, so, I won't say to look for anything, I would say, say a lots of prayers. For me, it felt like a force coming. You just know."

"Is this your first marriage?" I asked next, as I began to clean the soles of his shoes.

"No, it's actually my second marriage," he replied, then added, "My first wife unfortunately died, and I had a strange feeling after that. I felt like the odds were against me and I'd be looking for somebody, the numbers were working against me, or I was going to get it wrong or whatever. You go through a lot of stuff in your head when you're trying to figure out whether you want to go down that route again or not."

"Yeah."

"But the way I looked at marriage, it goes two for two, and that's pretty good."

"Yes, it is," I agreed with him, as I continued to work on his shoes.

"Is there somebody in the wing?"

"No, not right now. I'm single, but I just like to hear everybody's opinions on marriage, especially those who are actually married or have been married before, 'cause it's definitely something that I want to do one day."

"Ok, don't worry. It will happen so fast you won't believe it."

"But then, you know, I hear a lot of stories every day about marriages. This is one of the main topics that I talk to my customers about, and there are so many stories."

"Is it about 50/50?" he asked.

"No, 60/40." I countered.

"Really?"

I looked up at him and said," Yeah."

He smiled and said, "Be careful, you're going to end up in the New York Times, in a little article."

"But the majority of the stories are good stories. I think at the end of the day, it's all about the individuals and what they stand for. Once you want it to work, it will definitely work."

"Yeah, it's all about you, in the end," he added. "So where do you live in town?"

"I live right here in Rosedale," I replied.

"Oh? Then is it easy to get here?"

"Yeah, very easy," I said as I continued to work on his shoes.

"I wish I could hear some of the conversations that you get. I bet you hear everything."

"Every single thing, I've heard it all," I smiled and assured him.

"I could only imagine," he smiled and responded.

"You're good," I said to him as I removed the footrest.

"Good to go?" he smiled and asked.

"Yeah, what do you think?" I said, as he began to step down from the stand.

"They look great," he assured me, as he paid me.

I agreed with him by saying, "Yes they do."

"Hey, are you going to be here for a second?" he then asked, as my response was.

"Yeah."

"If you're not busy, I'll bring Sherra over, and you could ask her some questions and see what she says."

"Ok, that will be great."

He left, but never came back with his wife.

78

COMPLICATED

"You already got them scuffed up?" I asked my customer, since I had just finished shining his shoes not more than twenty minutes ago, as he just laughed.

"Looks like the same shoes, are they?" I asked, since they looked identical.

"No, no, no, it's the same company, but different shoes."

"Ok." Then went on to ask him "How long have you had this pair?"

"Already five years," he replied.

"They're still in good condition. Did you ever have to re-sole them?"

"Yes, but only once," he stated.

"Well that's the only thing you're probably going to have to do with good leather shoes, get them resoled like every now and then, but the leather will last for a lifetime," I said.

"Good to know." After some silence, he said, "This work was very popular, couple of years ago."

"Yeah, and we're bringing it back to life; we're rejuvenating the essence of a good shoe shine."

"Oh that's nice. Do you know how to make shoes?" he asked, as he stared down at me working on his shoes.

"No, not yet."

"You only work here?"

"No, we have two stands in this terminal; we have one in front of the smoothie store, and this one. We rotate from time to time."

"But only here in the airport, right, or in the city also?"

"No, we only have stands in this airport in New York, but we have a few other stands out in San Francisco."

"You guys do special events, too?" he asked, looking at the sign.

"Yeah, my co-workers just actually did one yesterday, at the Jacob Javits Center."

"Jacob Javits. I was there last November.

"I was there last, September, for my graduation actually."

"Where did you graduate from?" he asked.

"From LaGuardia Community College. I got my Business Management Degree over there."

"So you want to continue with business?"

"Yes, of course," I replied, then went on to add. "I have two websites. I'm an aspiring photographer and I also do a little bit of designing, so that's what I'm going to be doing in the future."

"Designing?"

"Yeah. I have two websites and now that I'm finished with school I'm going to take a year and try to pay some attention to them and see what can happen, and if nothing happens within a year, I'm going to go back and get my bachelor's."

"How old are you?" he asked.

"Twenty-six."

He smiled and asked me if I was married.

"No, I'm not married."

"So you want to get married?" he asked next.

I stood there and thought to myself, Is he writing a book also? Why all the questions? But I just smiled and said, "Yeah, I would love to get married one day. I think it's a beautiful thing."

"You think that? I'm already married twenty-two years now."

"So what kind of advice can you give to me about marriage?"

"Get married while you're young, because everything gets more complicated when you're getting older."

"Ok," I said as I continued to work on his shoes.

"When I was young, I had my first child at twenty-one years old and everything was so easy for me; now I have my second child at thirty-eight, and everything is difficult. I cannot sleep at night, I have to wake up to go to the doctor. It's more complicated.

You don't take it so seriously when you're young, everything goes smoother," he smiled and said.

"So are you going to give me the money to get married?" I asked him, with a smile on my face, as we both began to laugh, then added, "I want a big fancy wedding," as we laughed some more.

He then looked at me and said, "The wedding is not so important."

"What is important, the ring?" I quickly asked.

"No. A nice apartment, a good job, and a good relationship between you and your wife."

I then went on to ask him if he was going to give me the good job.

"Sure, why not?" as he began to laugh aloud. He then went on to ask me, "What kind of job do you want?"

"Whatever job you got that's good and pays well," I replied, as I smiled and began to add the last layer of polish to his shoes.

"Where do you live?" Was his next question.

"I live right here in Queens, five minutes from the airport," I said to him.

"Do you know a little marketing?" he asked.

"Yeah, I did a few marketing courses in college which were fun," I said.

"Yeah, so tell me, what can you sell?"

"Whatever can be sold. I just sold you two bulletproof shine, didn't I?" I replied as we both began to laugh.

"Yes you did, you certainly did. I like you." He laughed some more, then said, "I have a company. A Dental agency, you know, we sell all stuff for your teeth, your mouth. You want to sell teeth?"

"Yeah of course, people need teeth."

"Absolutely."

"Is it a good business to you?" I asked him next.

"Yeah, it's a great business," he enthused. "I have a good amount of employees, but the thing is, you have to do all the marketing. You have to go out to the doctors' offices and sell them our products. I have a dental lab."

"Ok," I responded as I began to buff his shoes.

He then said to me, "Give me your number, and what's your name?"

"Sure, and my name is Lancelot."

"Lancelot, woo," he smiled and said, as if he was surprised of what my name was. "Your name has a long history. Do you know that?"

"Yes, I do." I said.

"Lancelot, how did your parents came up with that name?"

I laughed and said, "It's also my dad's name. You're good."

"They look good," he said as he stepped down from the stand and paid me. "I'll give you a call when I get back on Thursday."

"Ok, thanks for the business."

79

100% SURE

"HOW ABOUT ME clean those boots up for you ma'am?" I asked a female passenger that was passing the stand for the second time that Monday morning.

"No, I'm good. I actually like them like this," she responded, as she continued to walk.

"I'll take a shine," my next customer said, as he approached the stand, then added, "I have two pairs. Can you do them both?"

"Of course man. Step on up," I said to him, as I also advised him to watch his steps while climbing the stand.

He got seated and requested to have our best shine, which was the bulletproof shine, as I placed my gloves and my dust mask on and began working on his shoes.

"Where are you heading today?" I asked him, as I began to brush of the leather balm from his shoes.

"Bahamas, how about that?" he responded, with a broad smile on his face.

"Nice, how long are you going to be out there for?" I asked next.

"From there, I'm going to New Zealand and China and then to the Middle East, so I'll be gone for a couple weeks," he stated.

"Vacation?" I asked next, as I looked up at him.

"Well a little fun for the first few days, and then all business," he smiled and said.

"Anywhere else is better than New York right now," I joked.

"Yeah it's pretty chilly and awful this morning."

"Yeah, mother nature just turned up the AC without any warning," I joked once more as we both began to smile. I then continued to work on his shoes for a few more seconds before asking him another question, "So, are you traveling alone?"

"Yeah," was his quick response as he nodded his head, before adding, "I'll meet some people in New Zealand and then China and then I'll meet some other people in the Middle East. A lot of people are traveling today. That's a lot business. Are you busy?" he asked, as he gazed around the terminal.

"Yeah, the terminal has been busy, because a lot of people are going on vacation."

He went on to ask if I was ok through Hurricane Sandy.

"No, we lost our entire basement," I replied then asked him, "What about you? Were you affected in any way?"

"Yeah, we lost everything. I have a house on Long Island, and twenty-two trees came down, twenty-two big, big oak trees, and my heart's broken for all the people in the Rockaway's and in Lower Manhattan, cause they really, really had it bad."

"I live right there in Rosedale and we have a little lake behind us so our entire area lost their basements. The water didn't like come in from outside the window or so, it backed up from through the sewerage, so it wasn't just like water, it was that nasty stinky sewer water in our basement and the scent was there for over two weeks."

"Eww, damn," he responded with a disgusted look on his face, then went on to say, "That sucks."

"Yes it does, but when you have your life you have hope still. It could have always been worse. There were people who lost their lives, so we're grateful for what we have left." I said to him, as I continued to work on his shoes.

Another guy came up to the stand and said to my customer, "I'm heading to the gate. I'll see you when you get down there," and took off.

My customer's response was, "Ok," while he nodded his head. He then went on to say, "So his sister is getting married in the Bahamas and that's where I'm going first."

"Oh nice, so are you married?" I asked next.

"Yeah I am, I also have two little boys nine and seven."

"How long have you been married?"

"Thirteen years," he said, as he smiled then added, "I got a good one," he beamed.

"So how do you find the good ones, what do you look for?" I stood up and asked him next.

"It's so rare because I had a bad one to start with first. So I was married with no kids, but for two years only, and you have to be very careful. She's was a nice girl, the first one, but it's very hard to find a partner."

"A partner? It's easy to find a girl, but it's hard to find a partner, that's what you're saying?" I asked, as I began to apply the last layer of polish to his shoes.

He then looked down at me and said, "It's easy to find a girl, and this girl, the first girl—my wife is very pretty, don't get me wrong—but the first girl was a beautiful girl, a model and all that. She went from the most beautiful girl to the ugliest girl, because if you're not happy, it doesn't matter what they look like, if you see what I'm saying."

"Yeah I get it," I replied, as I nodded my head.

"Happiness is a lot different because my current wife is more relaxed and happy. She gets up happy, she doesn't break my balls at all, she works hard with the kids and takes life in easy stride; I love being married to that woman," he said, as he smiled broadly.

"That's nice," I said to him, as I myself began to smile.

He then asked me, if I was married.

"No, but I'm thinking about marriage, because I think marriage is a beautiful thing."

"It is a beautiful thing, let me just tell you one thing: Unless you are dying to run up the aisle, don't do it—meaning if you have doubts or feelings of 'maybe,' don't do it—unless you are 100% sure. Not a little Sure, 100% sure," he stressed on his last words. "You've got to feel it throughout your entire body, if you're saying, 'Well, on the one hand, she's nice and pretty, and on the other hand, I don't like this and that about her,' Ah! Don't! Don't do it! It has to be 100%, and you'll just know, and if you don't just know, that means no."

I began to laugh aloud, then said "That makes a lot of sense."

"It's funny, it's a very sensitive thing. There's no maybe about marriages, if you see what I'm saying," he said next.

I nodded, then said, "Remember you're in a marriage, so I have no other choice but to listen to you and try to learn."

As he nodded then said, "Yeah man, but I 100% agree with you, with the right woman, there's nothing like it, because it really does make you happy, and you feel like you have support in life and you feel like there's somebody you share things with, and you feel like you could build something with somebody, talk about things with, and laugh about stuff and that's what you can't replace by being single."

"Yeah," I said, as I agreed with him.

He then went on to say, "It doesn't always work, but there's nothing worse than being in a bad marriage. It is better to be single your whole life than to be in a bad marriage."

"Ok, you're good to go," I said to him, as I removed the footrest for him to step down from the stand.

"That's awesome, thank you," he smiled and said, as he stood in front of me, then placed a twenty dollar bill into my hands and said, "That's for you."

"Thank you," I said.

"I appreciate it," he said as he walked off.

PARAMETERS

MY NEXT CUSTOMER approached the stand and said, "I'll take a shine, are you open?"

I was in the cabinet straightening out the deposit. "Yes I am." I quickly responded and immediately when over to him, "Take seat," I urged him to sit, as I place my gloves and my dust mask on.

"Where are you heading?" I asked him, as he placed his feet up on the footrest and I began cleaning his shoes.

"Fort Myers," he responded, while staring at his shoes, then went on to ask me, "So how's business?"

"It's slow right now, but some business is better than no business," I responded to him, as I continued to work on his shoes. He then smiled and said, "At least your customers pay you before they leave. I have to be begging like a dog for my money."

I laughed and asked him what kind of work he does.

"I do construction, and nobody wants to pay their bill. I wish I could just charge them on a credit card or something," he stated.

"So do you live in Fort Meyers?" I immediately asked next.

"No, I've got a condo down there and my wife's there also, but I've got to work."

"Oh? Let me ask you, which one of the wives is down there, number one, number two or number three?" I joked, as we both began to laugh aloud.

"There's only one, one is enough."

"Only one, that's good," I looked up at him while brushing his shoes.

"I had too many, many fun times," he answered. "You could go broke, with all those woman."

"So when you're single, you spend more?"

He shook his head from left to right and said, "No you spend a lot less. Family takes money; now I'm broke."

"There must be some good to marriage, though."

"I know you're not married," he quickly responded, as we both laughed.

"No I'm not, but it's a thought that's in my mind."

"Ah, you just got to do it the right way because you don't want to grow old alone. First you have to find the right one, cause as you grow older, it gets harder and harder," he advised me, as he paused for a bit. "Everybody out there is a wack job."

"A wack job, yeah that's so true; you think you got the right one and it's the total opposite," I said, as I agreed with him. He then nodded his head and said, "Yeah." I then went on to ask another question, which was, "So how long have you been married for?"

"Forty years," he smiled and said.

"That's a long time," I said to him. I nodded my head, then went on to ask, "So what kind of advice can you give to me about marriage? I mean, you've been in it for forty years, so you must know everything about marriage."

"Set up the parameters before you get married, especially for money; you need to know how and what you're going to spend money on while married."

"Ok," I quickly responded, as I began to add the last layer of polish to his shoes.

"Wives are like Washington: they don't do budgets, they just spend. So make sure you have good rules before you tie the knot."

"Good rules?" I repeated, as I looked up at him.

"Yeah, because once they say 'I do,' everything changes. They 'yes' you to death before you marry them and then when you get married all that changes."

"They 'yes' you to death?" I repeated, as I began to laugh aloud. He then went on to ask me my age.

"I'm twenty-six years old."

He then stared me in the eye and said, "You've got a few more years to go."

"A few more years, huh?"

"Yeah, but if you find the right one, that's great."

"But how do you know? You just said that they change. How can you really tell if she's the right one? I guess it's a chance you just have to take?" I asked as I began to buff his shoes.

"Your stomach has to tell you, you know. Your gut."

"You're all set sir, what do you think?" I asked him, as I removed the footrest.

He stepped down and reached into his jacket pocket and took out his wallet and placed a twenty dollar bill into my hand and said, "Can you break that? Just give me a $5. Work for you?"

"Yeah, thanks for the business."

81

UPSIDES

"CAN YOU DO sneakers?" my next customer asked me as he approached the stand.

"Yeah, I can. They're leather, right?" I asked, as he placed his backpack on the stand and then said, "You guys don't take credit cards, right?"

"No, we don't, but there's an ATM right there at gate number seven." I responded as I pointed to the gate.

He then picked up his bag and said, "I'll be right back," before walking off to the direction of the ATM.

"Oh that was fast. Have a seat and make yourself comfortable," I said to him as he returned to the stand. He then got seated and I placed my gloves and my face mask.

"It's good that you wear that mask."

"Yes, it is," I responded, with a smirk on my face, then went on to say to him, "I'll give you our bulletproof shine, ok?"

"Oh that's what they need," he replied. I began to stain the soles of his sneakers first, since it was very discolor and noticeable, then went on cleaning the rest of his sneakers with the leather balm.

"Damn, this weather. But you guys have been cold just as we are," he stated, as I was about to apply the first layer of polish to his sneakers. Then he asked, "So, how's the Job?"

"Great, man. Not that busy, but you've got to accept what you get, because it could always be worse right?" I replied.

"Yeah, well that's a good way to look at it, because everybody always wants more, more, more but it could be a lot worse," he smiled and agreed, then added, "In other countries, they don't even have jobs. They don't have a lot."

"Exactly." I agreed as I continued to clean his shoe.

He then smiled and said, "That's a good attitude to have."

"So what are you doing on this side?" I quickly asked.

"We're in the beauty supplies business in Buffalo so we had to go to LA for a hair convention." Then he said, "You could get a very good view from here, huh?" gazing around the terminal.

"Yeah, and you could also get distracted very easily," I replied, as we both smiled. I then went on to add, "And you know what the craziest thing is, you see her?" I pointed to a sexy female passenger that was passing by the stand.

"Yeah."

"In five or ten minutes, maybe less than that, you're going to see another woman that looks way better than her, in every form."

He began to crack up and said, "Paradise, man," and I began to laugh with him.

He then said, "My son is going to come up next; you might not want to let him know that, because he might want to stay here."

I laughed. "Are you married?"

"I am."

"How long have you been married?" I asked next

"Oh, I don't know, thirty years I think. I got married when I was twenty; it was a good time."

"So what kind of advice can you give to me about marriage, because it's a thought that's in my head."

"If you can get through the first ten or twelve years, you might have a chance to make it last."

"If you could get by the first ten or twelve years, just in a relationship or married?"

"Married—big, big difference. "But, if you could get the attitude like you said about the job and everything, because there are more upsides than downsides, well that's all you ever want to remember."

"Ok," I quickly replied as I continued to brush his shoes. He then continued by saying, "Now for me, I have two sons, I have a thirty-year-old and I have one that's going to be twenty years. My wife and I were married for about eight years, then got separated and divorced for two years. Then we got married again, ten years later after our first marriage. Then, I got another kid, so I got lucky."

"So you guys married and got divorced, then married again. That's nice. That shows what's for you in life is definitely for you." I said to him, with a smile on my face.

"Yeah, you never know, because everybody is so different, and it also depends on what family they're involved with and all of that is crazy, so unless you're going to do some magic and make the right woman appear, it's going to be hard, they all are so different and have some elements of crazy."

"So is it true that women changes one way or the other after the get married?"

"I think they do after a while, I really do. First of all, you've got to remember that they're women to begin with," he joked as we both began to laugh. He then continued by adding, "They are just different than we are, you know?"

"Yeah, you're set. What do you think?" I asked him as I removed the footrest from the stand.

"Looks great. Give me a fifty and keep the rest; I'll pay for my son." He stepped down from the stand.

"Ok, you said give you back a fifty?" I asked, since I thought that he may have made a mistake.

"Yeah, give me a fifty back. I'll pay for my son, and I'll give you a tip." He placed a hundred dollar bill into my hands.

"Ok. Thank you sir," I said, as I gave him the fifty dollars in change.

"Thank you. You're a good salesman," he complimented as he walked off.

"You're welcome."

82

BIG REWARD

"I'VE BEEN TRYING to get these boots polished for two months," were my next customers words as she approached the stand."

"Well you're in the right place. Take a seat," I smiled and urged her to sit, as I began taking out the supplies out of the shine box. She got seated and placed her feet up on the footrest, then looked at the sign and requested to have the bulletproof shine.

"Ok, so where are you heading to today?" I quickly asked, as I began to clean her shoes.

"Ah, to the Javits Center," she said before saying, "Well actually tomorrow is the Javits. Today we're going Time's Square and walking around the city."

"Where did you come from?" I asked next

"Maine," she replied, with a smile on her face. I then continued to work on her boots for a few seconds, then noticed that she was wearing a wedding band, which triggered my next question.

"Is that a wedding band?"

"Yes."

"That's cute," I complemented her, then went on to say to her, "Let me ask you a question, which of the wedding rings are more important to the woman, the engagement ring or the actual wedding band?"

"Depends on the girl," she quickly responded without any hesitation, then added, "The band should be the most important ring, but a lot of girls especially younger women, would prefer the bling that comes with the engagement ring."

"Which was more important to you?" I asked her immediately.

"Well getting engaged in my time, this little ring was a big deal. It was nothing less than I expected."

I then asked her how long has she been married.

"Thirty-five years."

"What do you do for thirty-five years to make it last that long, because if you look at a lot of marriages these days, most don't last that long."

"Yeah, you know what? Learn to become committed. It has a big reward," she said with conviction, then stared at the sign and asked, "So what does bulletproof do?"

"We add extra layers of polish to the boots so they last longer than the other shines and more polish is definitely good for the leather." I explained to her, as I began to add the last layer of polish to her boots.

"So, do you have a girlfriend?" she asked, as I looked up at her and responded, "Not right now. I'm single, having just came out of a four-year relationship."

"That's sad, you know. Young people have been together for so long then they get married and then they break up right away. My son has two friends. One was a girl who was with her boyfriend for eight years; they got divorced two months after they got married. The other one was married for six years. They just got divorced—and they were together for fourteen years before they got married." She explained as she shook her head from left to right with a look of disdain on her face.

"What would you say happened?" I stood up and asked her, as I began to buff her boots.

"I don't know. I think when you don't have children, it's easier to say 'Well you know what? I don't want to deal with this anymore,' and just leave," she stated.

"That's crazy, because you go through so much preparing for the wedding, the ceremony, other people's time, your time, and then just throw it all away? That's crazy.'

She nodded. "A lot of marriages break up in thirty years, because the kids are gone. Then you say, 'The kids are gone. I don't want this anymore,' so you get a divorce. I think it's easier, though, to pray to God for the right woman to come your way."

I then began to laugh and added, "Of course. You need to pray for that, and that she doesn't change, right?"

"Absolutely. So where are you from originally?" she asked.

"I'm from Guyana." I replied.

She looked down at her boots and said, "Those are looking very nice," with a broad smile on face, then added, "They keep getting darker and darker."

"Yeah. That's why whenever you get them done, ask them to use the neutral polish so the color won't change." I advised her.

"Ok, there you go, thank you." She stepped down from the stand, paid and took off.

"Thank you, and thanks for the advice."

PREGNANT

"Which of the shines are you going to do?" I asked my next customer, who was already sitting in the chair as I began taking out my supplies out of the shine box.

"I'll do the glass shine," he said, as I nodded and began to clean his shoes.

"So where are you heading to today?" I immediately asked.

"My nephew is getting married in Texas. It's a western wedding, so that's where I'm heading. Is there somewhere here that you change money for foreign money?"

"Yeah, there's a currency exchange right over there. Just keep going straight and you'll see the sign," I said to him, as I pointed down the terminal.

"Are the rates pretty good?"

"Yeah."

"Cool, I'll just get enough for the cab ride," he said as we both got silent for a few seconds before he asked me, "Where are you from?"

"I'm originally from Guyana, but I live here in Queens. What about you?"

"South Carolina," he responded, as he began to stare around the terminal, then said, "So is French Guiana down by Trinidad?"

"Yeah, but I'm from the one that was once called British Guiana."

"British?"

"Yeah, we were called British Guiana, when we were a British colony, but it's just Guyana now, because we're an independent country. There's still a French Guiana," I explained to him.

He then nodded his head then asked, "You have pretty women there, too?" with a smile on his face.

"Yeah, yeah of course. It's a very diverse country."

"Everywhere has them. There are pretty women everywhere."

"Yeah that's true."

"Except for here. They are all evil women that just want to know how much money you have." He said with a straight face.

"Are you married?" I asked.

"No, divorced. I was married for twelve years."

"And then you just gave up?" I asked.

"No. She wanted the money. I had a little bit of money and that's what she wanted—the money, the land, and the stuff. She was a good actress."

"An actress?" I repeated, since I wanted him to elaborate.

"Yeah. She had the plan in her head from day one, while I was working my ass off."

"So did she succeed?" I asked next.

"She got it. I have three daughters," he said. "I had a farm with horses on it and I wasn't going to take that from them."

"So would you ever get married again?" I immediately asked.

"Yeah." was his quick response.

"But what would you do differently this time?"

"I'd make damn sure that if I have any doubts about the woman, I'll leave her alone, 'cause I did have doubts about this woman in the back of my head, even though we got along well. We got together when I was young, I was single, and she was a couple of years older than me. She wanted the kids, that's all she wanted. So she got pregnant and I married her, but I wouldn't have married her had she not been pregnant, and she knew that."

"So that was your first marriage?" I asked, as I began to brush of the last layer of polish from his shoes.

"Yes, it was. I wanted to be married to her for the rest of my life, but she divorced me, so now I'm trying women from all over the world."

We shared a laugh and he then went on to say, "If I was going home, I would've put the bulletproof shine on them. I'll have to get that on the way back."

"What do you think?" I asked him as I removed the footrest and began to take off my gloves.

"Thank you, man," he smiled and said, before walking off.

84

INSTITUTION

"HEY ARE YOU shining shoes?" my next customer asked me as I was opening up the stand one Saturday morning.

"Yes I am. Just give me five minutes to set up," I requested.

"Ok, I'm here, just let me know when you're ready."

I continued to set up the stand to begin working. Although I was fifteen minutes late and that was my first customer, I wasn't too happy that I had already had a customer, because I hadn't taken my morning stroll around the airport to get my treats. But I figured after I was done with him, I still could.

"Ok you can have a seat," I said to him when I was done setting up the stand. He then got seated and requested the bulletproof shine. I began cleaning his shoes.

He then looked at me with a smirk on his face and said, "If you want to hurt my eyes, probably the best shine would do that." As we both began to laugh aloud. I then smiled and said, "And it's going to last too, don't you want eye problems?"

"I don't want to have eye problems; I want to see where I'm walking." He smiled and said, as I continue to clean his shoes.

"Where are you heading to?" I asked next.

"Tampa, Florida, for a quick meeting this afternoon. Then I come back tonight," he responded, then added, "If the weather permits, though."

"Ok, that's not bad," I said to him.

"But the weather is bad tonight."

"Ok, so how's your day going so far?" Was my next question, as he looked down at me, smiled and said, "So far, so good, how about yours?"

"So far so good, no complaints, because nobody listens right?" I responded with a smirk on my face.

"That's so true, not even your wife or kids listens." Then began to laugh aloud.

I then smiled to myself, because I felt like it was the right time to get on track to my preferred topics, so I asked him how long he had been married. He then shook his head from left to right and said, "Too long. Thirty-five years." He asked if I was married.

"No, I'm not, but it's a thought that's in my mind. So what kind of advice can you give to me about marriage?" I asked, as I stared him in the face while brushing his shoes.

"Oh, I can't come up with anything for you," he quickly responded, then got silent.

I continued to look at him and said, "You can't come up with anything?"

He smiled then went on to say, "Marriage is a great institution, and if you like living in an institution, go get married." We both cracked up.

He then stopped laughing and said, "All I know is, if I would have murdered her on our wedding night, I would have been out on parole by now, but instead, I'm still serving the same life sentence." He was smiling.

I laughed and said, "You're good."

"Thank you. Good luck with everything, 'cause once you get married, you're going to need it."

I then smiled and said, "Thank you, enjoy, and thanks for the business."

85

ACCOMPLISH

"HOW ABOUT A shine sir? I have the perfect brown polish for those shoes," I said to my next customer as I tried to sell him a shoe shine.

He then stopped and said, "Ok, let's do it; I'll take a glass shine."

As I began taking out the supplies, he climbed the stand and took a seat, then said, "This is the most comfortable shoe shining chair I've ever felt," with a smirk on his face.

"Yep." I then began to clean his shoes with the leather balm, and without any hesitation, I asked him if he was married.

"Do I look like I'm married?"

"Of course, you're neatly dressed at five in the morning," as we both began to laugh aloud.

He then went on to ask me if I was married.

"No, I'm not married."

"That's good. Don't rush. Make sure you accomplish everything that you want to have in life before. If you like traveling, go travel. Do whatever you like to do now, because once you get married, there's no more I and you, it's we, it's us, it's you and me" he advised me, then went on to say, "I've been married for two years."

"Oh? That's still a fresh marriage." I replied.

"I know, too bad it can't stay like this," he said, with a low tone.

"So how's the marriage life treating you so far?" I asked next.

"Very good," he responded as he nodded his head, then went on to add, "We're having our first baby, so everything is fresh."

266

"Do you think everything can stay like that forever?"

He quickly said, "No." as he shook his head from left to right. We both began to smile.

"Are you already seeing signs?"

"No, but you know, you have to recognize that nothing lasts forever, right?" he replied with a straight face, as I agreed with him, then went on to ask him another question.

"So what's the best part of your marriage, other than the fact that you're about to get a kid?"

"The best part for me is we're good friends, so we can talk about anything," he stated as he nodded his head.

I then smiled at him and added, "Yeah, you have to be good friends, because then you communicate more, you learn how to tolerate each other more and all that, so yeah it's good that you guys are friends."

"And that's what a lot of relationships don't have, but that's what every relationship needs, because everything else goes away."

I nodded my head and said, "That's true."

"So where are you from originally?" he went on to ask.

"I'm from Georgetown, Guyana," I said as I began to apply the last layer of polish to his shoes.

"And when did you move here?"

"Five years ago." As I began to buff his shoes, I looked up at him and asked, "So did your wife pick this suit out for you?"

"No, she was asleep when I left," he stated as we both began to laugh, while looking at each other.

"The scenery is good in this terminal, and I like the lights," he said next.

I agreed with him and added, "Yes it is. It really doesn't feel like you're in an actual airport, and it's a friendly environment."

"Yeah, it's very lively," he responded, before me telling him that I was finished shining his shoes.

"Thank you, and give me back a five."

86

LISTENS

"Hey man, remember me? I told you that I was going to come back, so I brought another pair for you to work your magic on," my next customer said to me as he approached the stand.

"Ah yeah, how can I forget you?" I replied, as I urged him to take a seat. This customer was a returning customer that I had did a job for a few weeks back. He promised he would come back for a shine once he traveled through the terminal again.

As he got seated, I began taking out my supplies. He then asked me how was I doing, and I responded, "I'm doing well, what about yourself?"

"No complaints," he said, as he shook his head from left to right.

"Nobody listens, right?" I said next.

"Not my wife at least; she never listens" He then look at the sign and said, "Give me the top shine. I'll take the bulletproof," as I began to clean his shoes. I applied the balm to his shoes and brushed that off and was about to apply the first layer of polish to his shoes.

Then I looked up at him and asked him, how long he had been married.

"Ah, twelve years."

"Is this your first marriage?"

"Yeah, and I'm not doing anymore."

"You won't do it again?" I asked him as I stood up and looked at him.

"Once is good enough for me," he said with a straight face, then paused for a few seconds and continued by saying," I would never get married for a second time."

"Why not?" I asked him, a bit shocked, as if he was telling me something wrong.

"Ah man, have you ever been married?"

"No," I smiled and replied.

"Alright, but if you ever get married, believe me, you would never want to get married again."

I began to laugh.

He then continued by saying, "I love my wife and all, don't get me wrong, but once you're married and you do it right, you're never going to do it again."

"So are you doing it right?" I smiled and asked him next.

"Yeah, I have no other choice," he answered as I continued to work on his shoes. He then looked at me and asked, "Where are you from?"

"I'm originally from Guyana."

"Oh yeah?" he said quickly as if he was shocked to hear that I was from Guyana, then went on to ask, "They make a lot of rum down there huh?"

I nodded and said "Yeah," as I continued to work on his shoes.

He then said, "I know a couple of people from Guyana that work at Nigel's Supermarket. We do a lot of business with them."

"Really? I worked at Nigel's Supermarket when I was living in Guyana, I said to him, as he nodded and smiled.

"So let me ask you something, do you have a lot of fights within your marriage?"

He shook his head from left to right and said, "No."

I then asked him how he prevented the fights.

"We respect each other. You've got to respect the woman before you married her, and it's vice versa. Because once you don't respect the woman, the home is not going to be a happy place. It doesn't matter where you are in that house, if the woman is unhappy, you're not going to like it, because she's going to make sure that no one in the house is happy. Never forget that—it's really important."

I nodded my head and said, "You're good," as I was finished with his shoes. I then removed the footrest to allow him to climb down from the stand.

"Alright, looks good," he complimented me after climbing down from the stand.

"Yes, thanks for the business, I said to him as he paid and took off.

87

FIX-IT

"HOW ABOUT A quick shine sir? It only takes eight to ten minutes," was what I said to my next customer as I tried to sell him a shoe shine.

He then stopped and said, "Ok, I got ten minutes," as the woman that he was walking with said, "I'll go use the restroom, while you do that."

"Ok Hun," he said as she walked off. He then placed his pulley at the side of the stand. I urged him to take a seat and make sure to watch his steps.

"You need an elevator for this stand," he joked, as he climbed the stand.

I then responded, "I know, right?" as we both began to laugh.

He then got seated and asked about the differences between the shines, which I explained to him, and he requested to have the bulletproof shine.

"So where are you guys heading to?" I immediately asked as I began to clean his shoes.

"Florida, for vacation," he smiled and said, as he reached into his jacket pocket and took out his ringing cellphone and answered it. He spent at least three minutes on his cellphone, while I continued to work on his shoes.

"Sorry about that," he said, as he removed his cellphone from his ear.

I looked up at him and said, "No problem," as I continued to work on his shoes, and he began to gaze around the terminal.

"So is that beautiful woman your wife?" I then asked.

He nodded his head and said, "Yes," then joked about only being married for a couple of days, as we both laughed aloud. "We've been married for thirty-eight years."

His wife came back from the restroom and stood beside the stand and began to observe what I was doing, without saying a word.

"Make sure you see what he's doing so you can do this at home for me," he said to his wife.

As we all began to laugh, she smiled and said, "That's what I'm doing."

I then went on to ask another question, but instead of asking the husband the question, I asked his wife, "Is he a good husband?"

Without hesitation, she smiled and said, "It lasted right?" We all laughed some more.

I then looked up at him and said, "She said it lasted, so I'm guessing you're doing something right."

"I must be doing something right," he smiled and said.

I added, "You're making her happy—that's what's you're doing. One of my previous customers said 'happy wife, happy life.'"

They both began nodding their heads.

"Is that true, 'happy wife, happy life'?" I asked the wife as she stood there.

"It should be like that," she smiled, then went on the other side of the stand and took a seat.

"So what's the best part about marriage for you?" I asked, as I began to brush his shoes.

"There's no such thing. Every single thing is good. It's just what you expect, your expectations. You think about what you have in mind when you're getting married, because you're looking for company, and if you look for other things, it's bad."

I then looked over at his wife and asked her, "Did he change, after you said 'I do'?"

She smiled and said, "No."

The husband then went on to say, "Once the kids are born; you really see the changes," as he began to laugh.

"How many kids do you guys have?" I then asked.

"Two."

"So, are you married?" he asked, as he stared at his shoes.

"No, I'm actually thinking about it," I said to him.

"How old are you?" he asked next.

"I'm twenty-six."

He then looked at me with a smirk on his face and said, "Oh, and you're thinking about marriage? You're thinking too much."

"I'm thinking too much?" I stood up and repeated.

"Yeah," with a straight face as we both began to laugh aloud. He then continued by saying, "I was twenty-two years old when we got married, but back then, that was the age to get married. Right after college, you get married and all that, and if it doesn't work out later on, you hold on and try to fix it, instead of throwing it away. But now, when you look at the divorce rate, it's like, 'I do,' is just a phrase.

"They don't really mean it when they say 'I do' these days." I smiled and said.

"That's why you got to make sure that you find the right one."

"Yeah, and if I don't find her I'm going to try to create her on the computer," I joked as we both began to laugh aloud.

"I think those are the best ones, you can always delete her, whenever you don't want her anymore."

"But I don't think that a lot of people value marriage today as much as they did back then," I said to him as I began to apply the final layer of polish to his shoes.

"I think a lot of people do. You would be surprised that there are a lot of people out there that do. They call them the silent majority."

"The silent majority?" I repeated.

"Yeah, they don't go around making trouble, you don't see them in the newspaper, in jail, killing each other, so nobody knows about us, and we like it that way, but unfortunately we should be more," he calmly explained, as we both got silent and I began to buff his shoes.

He then looked down on his shoes and said, "Those are looking nice," with a broad smile on his face, as I smiled and told him that I was finished with his shine, before removing the foot rest. As he began to step down from the stand, he looked over to his wife and said, "He's cute, and he has no problems," as his wife smiled and nodded her head.

"Yeah, no problems, no stress, no worries," I smiled and said to him.

He smiled back and said, "Not yet," as we both began to laugh again. He then paid as his wife got up, and they went off.

"Thanks for the business," I said, as I waved them goodbye.

GOOD-LIFE

"I'M NEXT OK?" a passenger came up to the stand and said to me, as I was finishing up another customer's shoes.

"Yeah, no problem, you can have a seat," was my quick response, as he got seated and I continued to work on my customer's shoes. I then got done with my previous customer and went over to start working on his shoes.

"Thanks for your patience," I greeted him.

"No problem."

I then went on to ask him which of the shines would he prefer to have and his response was, "Let's go with the glass shine."

"Glass it is," I said as I began to wrap the balm rag around my hand. As I began to clean his shoes, I notice that all of his attention was on what I was doing, so I took advantage of that and asked him my first and trademarked question, that I would asked most of my customers, and that was, "Where are you traveling to?"

"Back to Maine, thank God. I've been up here since Sunday," he said with an exhausted look on his face.

"The weather is about the same, right?" I asked him next.

He took his eyes off of his shoes, looked at me and said, "No, it's worse. I'm going home and I parked outside and it snowed . . . so I'm not looking forward to it. I definitely got to clean up my car when I get back. He sighed.

"Do you live out there alone, no kids?"

"Well, I have two daughters and one five-month-old boy, so you know they're not cleaning that, never in history," he smiled.

"So how long have you been married?" I noticed that he was wearing a wedding band on his ring finger.

"Twenty years," he replied.

I smiled and stated, "That's a long time. I'm barely older than that."

"Well, you don't want to know how that feels . . . when you're the old guy that used to be the young guy," he joked, as we both began to laugh aloud.

I then went on to say, "But you're still looking young. I would have never guessed that you were already married for twenty years."

"My nephew lives in the city, so I took him out last night, and it felt weird hanging out with him and his friends. We departed about 11o'clock. I don't know what he did, but I went home and slept," he said.

We both chuckled.

"So what do you do to make it last for twenty years?" I went on to ask him.

"We've been together for twenty-five years, so it's much easier now, but you just have to work at it, you know, try to stay committed to it, and we did that. Now we have a good life. We have good kids, not perfect kids, but good kids . . . there's no such thing as perfect kids," he explained. "So I stay in shape these days, and any guy that comes to the door knows that.

I laughed. "So what other advice can you give to me about marriage?" I asked.

"You have to find somebody that you can't live without—not for a month, a week or even a single day. Once you can spend a day without hearing from that person and it doesn't make you feel like your world is ending, then you know you should not get married," he advised me. "A lot of people spend months apart from each other and it still works, don't get me wrong, but for me it won't."

"Gotcha." I began to buff his shoes.

"Are you busy on the weekends?" he asked.

"In the winter time, sometimes, but in the summer, not at all."

"The thing in our area that affects the shoes is the salt. There's so much salt on the road and on the sidewalk to melt the ice and when that shit gets on your shoes, it messes them up. They say you can use vinegar and try to like buff it out, but the salt still ruins the leather."

"There's something by the name of de Salter—I don't know if you have ever heard of it—that you could purchase from a lot of stores, like in shoe stores. It takes out the salt completely from the shoes. That's what we use here," I said as I reached into the shine box and took out a bottle and showed it to him.

89

SACRIFICE

"IS THERE A coffee shop in this terminal?" my next customer asked me as he approached the stand, before requesting to have a shine.

"Yeah, straight ahead," I said to him, as I pointed down the terminal.

"Ok, I'll get the coffee after I get the shine," he said, as he removed his backpack from his shoulders, then asked, "Which one should I sit in?"

"Oh, any one, it doesn't matter, it's your choice," I responded as I began taking out the supplies from the shine box.

He then got seated, placed his feet on the footrest and said, "I feel like a king siting in this chair. Maybe I should take it home and sit in it," as we both began to laugh aloud. He then looked at the sign a requested to have the basic shine, so I began to clean his shoes, as he gazed around the terminal.

I didn't waste any time with the questions, I just went straight for the kill and asked him if he was married.

"Yeah, for thirty-three years," he replied, with a smile on his face.

"So how do you make it last, what do you do?" I asked next as I stared at him.

"You both have to want the same thing in life," he said, as he continued to gaze around the terminal.

"Same things, like similar interests?" I asked since I wanted him to go more into details about what he meant.

"Not interests, similar goals, and you have to want to work together for them."

I smiled and said, "Ok."

He then went on to add, "We always wanted to have a lot of money, we always wanted to have nice kids, and we were always willing to work for it. When we got married before moving to the America, we had nothing, but if you both want the same things that you find tough to accomplish, you sacrifice, and you work together."

"Yeah, and once you work hard for it, you tend to value it more," I added.

"My wife's parents were very rich, so she never had to work as hard as I had to, then I came along, a working class kid, to which her family was totally against, but we loved each other and that was the only thing that mattered to either of us, so we got married and moved to the States. We got a little house together, which wasn't much, but it was what we both wanted and we stayed in it together, side by side, working hard day and night, and now we can look back at those days and appreciate what we have now more, because it didn't come easy. It took a lot of hard work and dedication from the both of us."

"You're good, what do you think?" I asked him since I was finished with his shine.

"Jeez, nice job," he replied, with a smile on his face as he stared down at his shoes. He then stepped down and placed a twenty dollar bill into my hand and said, "Give me back a five please."

I reached into my pocket and give him a five dollar bill back, then said, "Thanks for the business."

"Anytime. So the coffee place is down that side?"

"Yeah," I said, as he took off.

90

SUCCESSFUL

"NICE SHOES MAN, how about I clean them up for you?" I said to a passenger that was walking past the stand.

He replied, "Thanks, but I don't have time," as he walked off.

I then took a seat on the stand and heard a voice say, "I'll take a shine."

I got up and said, "Sure, have a seat."

He then took off his jacket, placed it on the other chair and got seated.

"This is a very popular brand, and a good brand, too," I complimented him on his shoes, as he placed his feet on the footrest.

"That's true, and you're going make them look better."

"Yes, I'm going to give you our best shine, the bulletproof shine."

He then smiled and said, "I'm cool with the glass," as I began to clean his shoes.

"So where are you heading today?" I immediately asked him.

"Sarasota Florida," then switched it up and asked me, "So how long have you been here today?"

"I started 6am and I'm leaving at 1:30pm," I replied, as I continued working on his shoes.

"When you get off today, what are you doing? Anything good?"

"Not really, it's mad cold outside," I smiled and said to him.

He smiled back and responded, "Oh yeah," then went on to ask if I was going to attend any Super Bowl parties.

280

I said to him, "Probably not, because I have to be back here at 6am tomorrow."

He nodded and said, "Ok."

"What about you, do you live out there in Florida?"

"No, I live in Chicago."

"So what are you doing in New York? I looked up and asked, as I began to brush his shoes.

"I had to come down and see some people. Now I'm headed to Sarasota, to stay down there for a couple of days, then right back to Chicago." He then began to gaze around the terminal, as I went on to ask him if he was traveling alone.

"Yep, nobody to worry about but me. I like it that way."

"So I'm guessing that you're not married?" I said to him.

"I like it that way, too." he smiled.

"So you'll never get married?" I asked next, as I looked up at him.

His response again was, "I like it that way, too," as I began to laugh, while his face was straight, as if he was very serious about his answers.

I then asked him if he had any kids.

"Not that I know of," then went on to ask me if I was a father already.

"No, I'm still a baby. Look at me," I joked.

He smiled and said, "Me too."

"Yes, we are. But marriage is definitely a thought that's in my mind."

"Good for you, and that thought," as we both began to laugh aloud. I then began to clip off the loose stitching from his shoes, as he gazed at what I was doing.

"So would you ever get married?" I asked.

He looked at me and said, "No fucking way. It won't work with my work. I'm gone too much."

"Oh ok, understandable."

"And I'm not with that committed shit, that isn't for me. I don't want to be a part of all that love shit, I love you, and I love you more. You know why?"

I stopped working on his shoes and looked up at him and said, "Why?"

"Simple. I want to be successful, and being in a devoted relationship won't work when I'm trying to travel around the world to sell my products."

"That's true," I agreed with a smile.

"Marriage is good for some, but it's not for me."

"Yeah, well at least you're happy the way you are, and that single life is working for you," I said.

"Yep, if it's not working with one, you can always go find another. Nice and easy."

We both got silent, until I was finished with his shine. "You're good."

"Ok, good job," he complimented me, as he reached over to the other chair to get his jacket, then paid and took off.

"Thanks for the advice and the business, sir."

91

RELIGION

My next customer approached the stand and began to gaze at the sign for a few seconds, as I went on to say, "Would you like to have a shoe shine, sir?"

"Yeah, I'll take one," was his response as he came closer to the stand and took a seat. I then began to take out the supplies from the shine box as he placed his feet on the footrest.

"How've you been man?" he asked, as I began cleaning his shoes.

"I've been well, what about you?"

"Ah, I've been hanging in there."

"Would you like me to give you our best shine, the bulletproof shine?" I asked next as I looked up at him.

He then said, "What do you suggest?"

"The bulletproof, of course," was my quick response, as I continued to clean his shoes.

"Ok, and that will last the longest?" he asked.

"Yes, and even look better."

"Bring it on."

I applied the first layer of polish to his shoes, and as I was about to brush it in, I looked up at him and asked where he was traveling to.

"I'm heading back home to Rochester to see my grandfather. He has Alzheimer's, so we're going to put him in a nursing home."

"Sorry to hear," I said.

He shook his head and added, "It's one of those things; you just lose your mind," in a low tone.

"I'm sure he's had a good life, though," I smiled and said to him.

"Oh yeah, very good. I'm hearing a little bit of a Jamaican accent. Are you from Jamaica?"

"No I'm from Guyana. I'm Guyanese," I responded, as I continued to work on his shoes.

"Guyanese?" he repeated.

"Yeah, the culture is very similar, but I'm from Guyana."

"I went to Jamaica for my honeymoon. That's what a lot of people do. My wife call's it fun in the sun." He then began to laugh.

I began to laugh along with him and as soon as he was finished, I immediately asked him, "So how long have you been married?"

He then smiled and said, "Almost twelve years now, a few months before 9/11."

"Ok, so how's the married life treating you?" I asked next, as I began to brush his shoes.

"Pretty good. There are ups and downs, you know, but I have a beautiful son and he means the world to me. I can't complain."

"What kind of advice would you give to someone like me, who's actually thinking about getting married in the future?"

"Expect a home, you know, something that can really grow, something that you don't have to think about," he answered."

"Ok."

He then went on to add, "If it's the right person, you don't have expect or worry about getting a divorce, or anything like that. You should build something so strong that you would never believe in walking out on each other, and that would be the best part of being married. My wife and I are the same religion also, and that makes our marriage a lot easier, you know what I'm saying?"

"Yeah, similar values."

"Right, right, right."

We both got silent for a few seconds as I continued to work on his shoes.

He then looked at me and said, "You know, with marriage if you think you've got an easy way out, then you might take it, because it's rough. There are going to be a lot of rough days, especially when the first baby comes and the woman's hormones are all out of whack. That's when they need the right support, emotional support, and that's when you become the punching bag."

"They use you as a punching bag?" I asked him, with a smile on my face.

He smiled back and said, "Oh yeah, and that's when you've got to take the punches like a man, you know. Once you play it out, you learn there's some goodness from it and everything else, because you both benefit from it in the long run, know what I mean?"

"Yeah, I do," I responded as I began to buff his shoes.

"So whom are you rooting for?" he asked next, as I smiled and said, "The 49ers, of course. Our company is originally from San Francisco, so I'm going to be biased on this one."

"What about you?"

"I didn't even know who was playing until yesterday. I'm not really a Football fan."

"You're not a football fan?" I asked, as I continued to buff his shoes.

He then said, "I used to be, but then the kid came and I just got more involved with him."

I then put my two thumbs up at him and said, "Ok you're good."

He looked down at his shoes and said, "All set?"

"Yeah," was my quick response, as he climbed down from the stand.

92

HARD AND PAINFUL

"HOW MUCH WOULD it be to do these?" My next customer asked as he approached the stand, while pointing down at his cordovan boots.

"We have three different prices. Eight, ten and twelve: the basic, the glass, the bulletproof."

He requested to have the bulletproof shine before sitting.

So how's your day going so far?" he asked next, as I placed the footrest up on the stand.

"Very good, sir. Raise it up, make yourself comfortable," I urged him to place his feet on the footrest, to begin cleaning his shoes.

He placed his left foot up followed by his right, then said, "It's like a car wash."

I smiled and replied, "Yes, it is."

"As I began to brush his shoes, he looked down at me and asked what my name was.

"My name is Lancelot."

"Oh, I'm Mike. Whose idea was that, to give you that name?"

"It was my grandma's idea. She named my dad Lancelot, and my mom took the name and gave it to me," I responded, as I continued to work on his shoes.

He then smiled and said, "You know with a name like Lancelot, you have to be creative, right?"

I smiled and nodded my head. I then noticed that he was wearing two wedding bands on his ring finger, so I asked him about them.

"Yeah, I'm married and have five women," and we shared a laugh.

I then went on to say, "You have five women? It's possible in this world we live in."

He said, "This is actually my wedding band," pointing to the ring that was at the bottom of his finger. He pointed to the top ring and said, "This one was actually my aunt's ring and she gave it to me, because I liked it a lot. My wife loves it, though. She's afraid I'll get too drunk one night and take one off, but then there will still be another one on." We both began to laugh aloud.

"She's a very smart woman," I smiled and said next.

"She is."

I continued to work on his shoes as he stared at what I was doing

"Are you married?"

"No I'm not. I'm actually thinking about marriage, though. It's a thought that's definitely in my mind. How long have you been married?"

"Twenty-five years."

"Wow, that's one year younger than I am."

He then smiled and said, "That's a good age."

"To get married?" I looked up at him and asked.

He shook his head and quickly said, "No," and smiled. "Well, I got married at twenty-five, but that was a different time compared to now. I was a little too young I think but I didn't want to lose her, and I'm glad I didn't."

I then smiled and said, "Good for you."

"Yeah, good for me. But it's got to be right, because it's going to be hard and painful."

"So what kind of advice can you give to me about marriage?" I asked him next, as he looked at me for about five seconds.

"Well just a lot of sacrifices, and a lot of stuff is just constant compromising."

"Constant compromising?" I repeated, for him to elaborate more on.

"Yeah, that's what you got to get used to. It's not about you—it's we. It's always about two people, and that's kind of hard for some people to adjust too, but we have kids and it's nice to come home and know that you have a strong family that has your back. So . . . where do you live?"

"I live right there in Rosedale, but I'm originally from Guyana," I said to him, as I began to apply more polish to his shoes.

"Really, when did you move here?"

"2008."

"So do you like it or not?"

"Yeah, of course. America is still the land of opportunities. You can still be all you want to be here, but you just have to be willing to work hard," I responded.

"Yeah, it is," he agreed.

"You get a chance to go back to school, to follow your dreams, you know? That's priceless."

"So did you do it, are you going back to school?" he looked down at me and asked.

I nodded my head. "Yeah, I just actually graduated last September. I got my Associates Degree in Business Management from LaGuardia Community College."

"That's great," he said with a smile on his face.

I gave him the thumbs up, signaling that his shine was completed, then began to move the footrest as he removed his feet from it.

"Oh, thank you," he smiled and said, as he stepped down from the stand. I smiled and replied, "Your welcome."

"They look brand new—this is certainly the best they've ever looked." He paid and took off.

93

TEAM

"HEY DO YOU take credit cards?" my next customer asked as he came over to the stand with a laptop in his hands.

"No, we don't," I replied, then said, "There are ATMs all over the terminal, though."

His quick response was, "Yeah, where's the closest one?"

I pointed him to the eastern direction of the terminal.

"I'll be back," he said before heading towards the direction of the ATM. I sat on the stand for about five minutes and thought to myself that he must have changed his mind, since it normally doesn't take customers that long to return from the ATM machine on the eastern side of the terminal. I then began reading the newspaper for about two minutes and then looked up and noticed that he was coming back to the stand, so I quickly got up, placed my gloves and my dust mask on, and began to take my supplies out of the shine box.

He then went and got seated as he returned and requested to have the basic shine.

"You said the basic?" I quickly asked, to make sure, since his shoes were really scuffed up badly and I seriously didn't think that a basic shine was the right choice for them.

"That's all I've got money for. I wish my wife would give me more money."

"You said you wish your wife would give you more money?" I repeated.

"Yeah."

"You got a wealthy wife?" I asked, as I began to brush off the leather balm from his shoes.

"No, no, no," he shook his head from left to right.

I went on to say, "I was about to say that you're a hard worker, because you would have had to been working hard for that money." To get the ball rolling and get on the track of my prefer topics, I asked him, "How long have you been married?"

"Ah, eighteen years."

"That's a very long time."

"Yeah it sure is."

"So what can you tell me, what should somebody like me expect before getting married?" I asked him as I began to apply the polish to his shoes.

He then looked down at me and said, "Depends on you and depends on her."

"Ok, so you're saying all married couples don't face the same problems?" I asked.

He said, "They do, but at the end of the day, it still depends on the individuals that are involved. It's like in sports. Do you like sports? What kind of sports do you like?"

"I like soccer," I said.

"Ok, there are a lot of teams out there, but there are not many that play like Barcelona," he said.

"Ok."

He then asked, "Why do Barcelona play well?"

"Because they play together," I said, as I stood up and looked at him.

"Cause the play together," he repeated. "And Barcelona plays well together because they've played for a long time. Messy was playing with Barcelona since he was twelve years old, and Messy went to Barcelona because, at that time, they were the only team that was willing to pay for his growth hormone therapy. Messy was very tiny. But he was exceptionally talented, and Argentina didn't have the resources to afford the medical treatment that he needed, like the doctors and the medicine that he needed to grow. So Barcelona said, if he played for them, they'd make sure he got the best doctors and treatment possible. That's why his parents put him there. But then Barcelona showed him that they cared about him;

they showed him that they were willing to commit. And then they had all sort of guys in their academy that started playing together at a very, very young age, so they eventually got to know each other and learned how to work as a team, and they learned that you could be a great player, and there are lots of great players, but if you don't play with your team, it won't make you any better."

"Yeah, that's true," I agreed with him, as I continued to work on his shoes.

"So somebody else could be better, but the message is, you've got to play with your team and that is what will make everyone better."

"Ok, you're good."

"You're finished already?"

I nodded and said, "Yeah."

He stepped down from the stand.

"That was quick," while he paid for his shine and took off.

"Thank you," I said to him as he walked off.

94

HONEYMOON

"HOW ABOUT A shoe shine ma'am?" I asked my next customer as she passed that stand.

She stopped and said, "You know what? I'll take you up on that." She then came over to the stand and got seated.

"This is the first time, I've ever done this. I never had my shoes shined before," she said as she placed her feet on the footrest.

"Which of the shines would you like to have?" I then asked her.

She look at the sign and said, "I'll have the basic."

I then began cleaning the soles of her shoes, and asked her where she was traveling to.

"Turks and Caicos," she replied giddily.

"Turks and Caicos, oh nice. Vacation, I hope?"

"Oh yeah. Leaving you guys in the snow."

"So are you traveling alone?" I asked next as I fixed her right foot properly on the footrest.

"No, my miserable husband is somewhere around here," she smiled and said.

"How long have you guys been married?"

"Eight years," she responded as she began to laugh aloud. "Damn, time flies so fast. It seems as if it was just last year that he proposed to me."

"Eight good years, though?" I nodded and asked her next.

She responded by saying, "Yeah, best years of my life," with a broad smile on her face.

"That's great," as she stared down at me working on her shoes. "So what would you say is the key to making your marriage last that long?"

She looked at me and said, "I don't know. Just don't sweat the small stuff. Leave the small stuff alone, because a lot of small stuff is going to happen, and instead of harping on it, just go and enjoy life and live. Forget about those things. Look at it as a honeymoon every day."

"Honeymoon every day. I like that," I repeated. "So tell me, which of the rings is more important to the woman, the actual wedding band or the engagement ring?" I asked her next, as I began to buff her shoes.

"Oh, I don't know, that's not important to me. You know a lot of the younger women are all about the bling, they want the ones with the most diamonds, but I never cared about that, all I was happy about is that the sucker proposed and we got married," as we both began to laugh aloud.

Then a man approached the stand, who happened to be her husband. She pointed to him and said, "There's the sucker," as we all began to laugh aloud. She then turned to him and said, "What's the secret to a long-lasting marriage?"

He smiled and said, "Marrying you."

"Wow, that's nice, that's the best answer I've heard ever," I said to him, with a smile on my face, as I was finished with her shine.

"Here, take my hands and watch your step," I advised her, as she began to climb down from the stand.

"Oh, thank you, you're such a gentleman," she replied, as she paid and wished me good luck, before taking off.

95

SERIOUS-STEP

"How's YOUR MORNING going so far ma'am? I asked my next customer, as she settled in the chair.

"Not bad, yours?" She asked.

"So far so good," I assured her, then went on to say, "Just make yourself as comfortable as possible," as I lifted her left foot and placed it on the footrest, followed by her right.

"Oh, thank you," she smiled.

"No problem."

She then went on to say, "I love this terminal; this may be the best terminal in New York."

I smiled and said, "It is. So where are you heading today?" I went on to ask her, as I applied polish to her shoes.

"Oh, St. Marten," she quickly answered.

"Nice to be escaping this weather, huh?"

"Yeah. I have a place down there, but I live in New York, so I go back and forth," she said.

"Cool. Are you traveling alone?" I asked next.

"Yeah," she said while nodding her head.

"I noticed you're wearing a wedding band, that's why I asked."

"Yeah, yeah my husband is down there already," she said to me, while I continued to work on her shoes.

She then began to gaze around the terminal for a few seconds, then placed her focus on me and her shoes again, so I decided to ask another question.

"So how long have you guys been married?"

"Twenty-nine and half years," she responded as she began to laugh, then went on to add, "Isn't that love?"

I smiled and said, "Definitely," then went on to ask her another question, to avoid killing the momentum. "So for people who are now thinking about marriage, what kind of advice would you give to us, what should be our expectations, before getting married?"

She asked me if I was thinking about getting married.

"Yeah I am. It's a thought that's in my mind/"

"Good for you," before adding, "But you have to find someone that you can compromise with. It's all about compromising. You have to make a lot of compromises," she said seriously.

"Ok."

"And you also don't want to be with someone who likes it their way or the highway, you know what I mean? That sucks. Most people are like that actually, so marriage is about wanting to do things for that other person that you don't always want to do, and accepting that it's not always going to be about you."

"Yeah," I responded.

"So, do you have someone who you're going to propose to?"

"No, I'm just thinking about it."

"Ok, just remember that it's a big and a serious step. I have a very good marriage; I think that's why I've been married for so long. A lot of people say that the other person takes them for granted, and you can't let that happen."

"Ok," I responded, as I gave her the thumbs up, signaling that I was finished with her shine.

"Damn, these look better. My goodness, I love them; they really needed it," she said, as she stepped down from the stand with a broad smile on her face, paid and took off.

96

COURTING

"Hey, can you clean these?" my next customer asked as she approached me at the stand and pointed down to her brown, discolored boots.

"Of course, and make them look brand new also," I assured her, as she smiled and got seated.

"I'm so happy to see a shoeshine place; I desperately need my boots shined," she said to me, as I smiled and assured her that she was in the right place for a shine, then went on to asked her. "So which of the shines would you like to have today?"

"Ah, I guess the bulletproof," she requested, as she stuttered her first words.

"Good choice," I nodded. I then asked her where she was traveling to.

"Florida."

I immediately went on to asked if she lives in Florida and she said, "No I live here; I just have to go there for work, but it'll be nice."

"Nice weather, right?" I said.

"Yeah, it hasn't been that cold here as yet so you know, it's not like I'm dying to get to warm weather," she smiled and said.

"I don't think that it's going to get like that. Last year it wasn't that bad," I said to her as I began to apply the polish to her boots, as she smiled and said, "I feel the same way."

"So are you traveling alone?" I asked next.

"Yeah, which is nice because, you know, if I travel with my kids I never get to sit and rest," she said, as she smiled.

"So are you married?" I looked up at her and asked next as I brushed her shoes.

"I am, and I have three boys," she responded with a smirk on her face.

I asked her how long she'd been married.

"I have been married for eleven years."

"That's a long time," I nodded and said to her, as I continued to work on her shoes, then said to her, "I think that marriage is a beautiful thing, but most guys always say that women change after they say 'I do.' Is that true?"

"Well, I think guys change too. I mean, after you get married they're not bringing you flowers every week anymore. The courting stops, so everyone changes. Oh no, they're calling my name over the intercom; my flight is boarding."

I then buffed off her shoes immediately, as she paid me, stepped down from the stand and took off to her gate.

97

CONSTANT-WORK

"HEY CAN YOU do a quick one on these? I only have seven minutes," my next customer asked, as he approached the stand.

"Yeah, of course. Take a seat," I responded, as he got seated.

"We have three levels of shines and each level offers more protection to the shoes and a longer lasting shine. Which one would you like to have?"

"I'll go with the basic," he said, as he stared at the sign.

"Basic it is then," I smiled and said, then immediately asked him, "So where are you heading to today?"

"Vermont, back home," he replied.

"Ok," then went on to say to him, "I noticed you're wearing a wedding band. How long have you been married?"

"Three years now," he smiled and responded as I began to brush his shoes.

"Is this your first marriage?" I asked next.

"Definitely not the first," as I myself began to smile, because of his facial expression when he answered me.

"So what kind of advice can you give to me about marriage?" I asked him next.

"It's constant work. You've got to give and take," he said, as he nodded his head, then went on to add, "You've got to always work at it, although it can be a beautiful thing, you just got to, and when times get tough, you remember what it's all about and you pull through the tough times."

"Ok," I said, as I stopped brushing his shoes and looked up at him.

"He then added, "Marriage is like any other thing in life: Whenever you have to struggle to get something or even work a little harder than you had expected to, you value your accomplishments more, and marriage is just like that. Whenever you pull through the tough times and overcome your problems, you learn to value not only what you have, but you learn to value each other more," he advised me.

I then began to buff his shoes, and I as I was about to ask him one final question, his cell phone rang.

"Excuse me, I have to take this, you mind?"

I shook my head from left to right and said, "No, not at all."

98

FAITH

"HEY, IS THERE an ATM close by? I want to get some cash for shine," a passenger approached the stand and asked me.

"Yeah," then pointed him into the direction of the closest ATM.

After he left to go to the ATM another customer came and requested to have a basic shine, so I began shining his shoes. As I was about to start buffing my customer's shoes, the previous passenger came back to the stand and stood at the sign.

"You can have a seat," I urged him, as he placed his pulley luggage in front of the cabinet and got seated.

Within less than two minutes, I was done with my previous customer and went over to start working on his shoes.

"What's that for?" He pointed at my face mask.

"Oh, this is for the fiber and lint that comes out of the cloth, because I'm allergic. Whenever I'm buffing the shoes, the fiber that comes out of cloth goes into my nose and makes me sneeze a lot," I explained to him, as he smiled and said, "Oh."

"Do you want to see?" I joked and placed my right hand on my dust mask, as if I was about to take it off.

He quickly said "Oh no, hell no," and we both began to laugh aloud. He then went on to say, "I thought there was some weird flu going around."

"No, not that I know of, but I've been wearing this since I started the job, like from the second week I found out that I was allergic to the fiber." I explained. "So where are you heading to?" I asked next as I began to brush his shoes.

"Florida, my wife and I just moved down there," he stated, as I smiled and went on to ask him another question without any hesitation.

"How long have you been married?" I asked next, as he looked at me and said.

"It's been fifteen years now, and I have two little kids."

I then looked up at him and said, "A lot of people say that kids are the best part of being married, is that true?"

"Yeah I guess, but my wife is my best friend. We get along so well, so that's the best thing for me." "It's pretty cool, but yeah the kids do make it better."

"Were you guys best friends before you got married or afterwards?" I asked him next.

He smiled and said, "Before. We knew each other, then we started dating for a little bit, then went our separate ways and then reconnected."

"Oh, nice," I smiled.

"So it's good."

"So how do you know for certain if it's the right time to pop the question?" I asked him, as I continued to work on his shoes.

"Well we were living together for a while, then I moved from Seattle to New York and I asked her to come out here, so she kind of knew that I wouldn't ask her to move here with me and cross the country unless we were ready to get married, but I knew she was the one. When I moved out here, I began to miss her so much as the days went by, so she was on the next plane out here," he said, as we both began to smile.

I then said to him, "Me and my girlfriend of four years just split."

"Oh yeah?" he quickly responded, as if he was shock, as we both began to laugh a little.

I then went on to say, "Yep, but you just gave me a little bit of hope there."

"Yeah, we did that too. Like, we broke up for a while and for some reason we were still friends. We talked and stuff and then dated a few people here and there, but it's faith. Then we came back to each other."

"Faith, right?"

"Yeah," he smiled and replied as I began buffing his shoes.

"So where are you from originally?" he asked next.

"I'm from Guyana."

"Oh, where's that?" he asked with an unusual look on his face.

"That's in South America," then gave him the thumbs up, signaling that his shine was completed.

"All right, thank you," he smiled and said as he stepped down from the stand.

"Thank you, man," I replied, as he paid and took off.

RELATIONSHIPS

"GOODBYE," MY PREVIOUS customer said to me, as he paid and took off.

"Enjoy, man. Thanks for the business," I smiled and responded, then immediately went over to my next customer who was already siting in the chair waiting for his shoes to be shined.

"Thanks for your patience, man," I said to him, as I began wrapping the balm rag around my hand.

"Oh, no problem," he smiled and said, then requested to have a bulletproof shine.

"Bulletproof it is." I began to clean his tan loafers.

"Are you traveling alone?" I asked.

"No, my wife is sitting over there," as he pointed to the sitting area. "We've been sitting here for two hours already."

"Did you guys have a delay?" I looked up at him and asked.

"Yeah. We flew in from South Africa and the first flight out to Maine will be leaving at 5 o'clock."

"Oh damn, sorry to hear," I said to him, with a sympathetic look on my face, since it was only 11am.

"It's alright. We're only five days late," he joked, then went on to say, "We couldn't have get into New York for five days because of the storm."

I nodded and said, "Tell me about it," then went on to ask him if he was originally from South Africa.

"Yeah, originally, but we now live in Maine."

"So how long have you guys been married?"

"More years than you have been alive. Forty-years."

"Wow, that's a long time. Almost double my age," I smiled and responded.

He raised his left hand up and showed it to me then said, "How about that? No wedding band."

"How come? I was just about to ask you about that." I stood up and said to him, as I stopped brushing his shoes.

"In South Africa, we never had any," he responded.

This was the first time I've ever heard something like that. "You guys don't wear wedding bands in South Africa?"

"Some of the young guys do, but in general, not really," he said.

"So what do you do to symbolize that you're married?"

"We never, I don't know, it just wasn't a common thing to do." He shook his head. "If I had lived here at the time, I probably would have worn one."

I nodded my head and said, "Ok." I then continued to work on his shoes, as he gazed around the terminal. "So let me ask you a question. Do you think marriage has the same values today that it had forty years ago when you guys got married?"

"I don't. I don't think so," he shook his head and responded. "Why, are you having marriage problems?"

"No I'm not. I'm not even married," I smiled and responded.

He smiled back and said, "I'm just teasing you," as we both began to laugh aloud.

I then went on to say, "I just like to get everybody's opinion on the topic, because I would like to get married one day."

He then looked at me with an unusual smile on his face and said, "Don't do it unless you mean it, because today too many people get married and they don't mean it. Then they fight it out for a year and a half before getting a divorce and throwing everything down the drain."

"Ok." I then went on to asked him a final question since I was already buffing his shoes. "What would you say is the key factor to make a marriage work and last for years?"

"Hmm . . . you've just got to give and take. You don't ever want it to be one-sided because that can mess any kind of a relationship up," he offered.

"Thanks. You're good to go. Watch your steps," I said as I finished.

REGRET

MY NEXT CUSTOMER was one of my favorite returning customers, because I would never have to ask him any questions for him to start talking and he would always have a funny story to tell me every time he visited New York. I would never get tired of hearing him speak, and I seriously didn't know if it was because of his Australian accent or the fact that I would be laughing throughout entire time while shining his boots. Cowboy boots, that's what he called them. I welcomed him that morning and as he got seated, he didn't wasted anytime to begin talking.

"How you been, man?" he asked.

"I've been great, what about yourself?"

"Here, living this life," he responded with a smirk on his face, as we both began to laugh aloud then got silent for a few seconds.

"So there's this movie, right, with this guy who loves this beautiful girl. She's drop dead gorgeous. I mean, you can't help it. She wears no makeup, she's simple, she's a good girl, and she loves this guy more than anything in the world," he said. "And the guy goes to work and tells his co-worker, 'I'm getting married,' and his co-worker said, 'Are you outta your mind?' as he reached into his pocket and took out his wallet to show him a picture of a woman, then said, 'Look at this woman. I was in love twelve years ago; now I work for her. I got nothing. She took everything.' and the guy is like, 'Dude it's different with her.' His co-worker shook his head and said, 'No it's not. They're all the same,'" he said, as he kept smiling. "Meanwhile, when the guy who's getting married is at work, his fiancée is hanging out with his mother, because the guy is at work all day and she's working with his mom to get ready for the wedding. So guess what happens?"

"What happens?" I asked eagerly, expecting to hear something funny. He then looked at me with a straight face and said, "The guy went home from work early one day, and caught his fiancée in bed with his mother. She hooked up with the mother."

I burst out laughing, completely stunned.

He then went on to say, "That shit was crazy. How do you make a movie about that? That should be a triple-X-rated movie." He then went on to say, "I've got another one."

"Oh yeah?"

"A buddy of mine that works for my firm in Australia. One day we were talking and he showed me a picture his wife, I'm like 'Holy fuck dude, why'd she marry you? Look at you.' She was fucking beautiful, naked pictures of her . . . I mean this girl was fucking hot, right? So I'm like whoa, what's the problem, I'm like, 'Dude, you're married to that and you're complaining?' He says, 'Yeah but she's gained weight now. See that shit? That picture is not her anymore. That was when he met her. Now she looks like a fat pig. That's what they all do. They look great at first and once they've got you, all of that stops.'

"Honestly let me tell yell something. I'm sixty-one years old, and I've never regretted breaking up with a girl. Looking back, holy cow, I'm glad I'm single," he said as we both began to laugh some more. He continued by saying, "All of my friends are either happily divorced or miserably married, every single one of them. They all tell me the same thing. Every married guy I talk to tells me the exact same thing," he smiled and then continue by saying, "'I would kill you if you do anything to hurt my kids, but my wife, how much could I pay you to take her away?' Every single one of them tells me that."

I laughed. "That's crazy."

"That's why I keep it simple: nothing too serious and nothing that you can't walk out on in five minutes once you feel threatened."

Before he said another word, which he was about to do, I asked him if he was ever married and his entire facial expression changed, so I stood up and said, "Have you?"

"Nope," he shook his head and said. He got silent for a moment and then said, "When I was seventeen years old, I made a promise to myself that I would never get married and never take any woman seriously."

"Why, what happened?" I quickly asked him, as I continued to brush his shoes.

He looked at me and said, "I grew up with a single parent and just know this: It wasn't my dad who walked out on us."

I was standing there, cleaning his shoes, speechless and not knowing what else to say or what else to ask. I looked at him and said, "You're good," as I gave him the thumbs up and removed the footrest.

CONCLUSION/THOUGHTS

DID THESE CONVERSATIONS help me and did I get the answers that I was looking for? Yes, and the talks certainly helped–both the negative and positive ones–because now I realize where I went wrong in my past relationships and how I could work on correcting those mistakes for the sake of my future relationships.

Were all of these answers believable? No, they weren't, but I'm only focusing on what I could get some good out of, even if the stories weren't real or truthful. It is up to us as humans to take the good with the bad. In life, there will be good and there will be bad, so it will be up to you to transition your bad into good. Meaning, turning your negatives into positives, making your wrongs into rights, like I did after my break-up.

You've just got to let go sometimes and explore, because the people that are supposed to stay in your life for a lifetime will definitely be right by your side and will never forsake you in anyway, like my ex-girlfriend did to me. Was she the perfect girlfriend? No, she wasn't, but the mistakes she made while we were together didn't cause me to judge her, because honestly, those things never did add up to all the good that she did and what we went through for those four years, which I'm grateful for.

There were a lot of signs that I should have definitely paid more attention to. I would never take back the fact that the last five years were the best years of my life, because they really were. I migrated to America, started a new life, met the woman that I thought was my lifelong partner, got my GED, and started college.

While in college, I started Porkknockers Clothing and ShowItOff Photography, became a professional shoe shiner, and graduated LaGuardia Community College with an Associate's Degree in Business Management. I was able to go back to Guyana on a 3 week vacation, which I enjoyed with my mother, family, and friends. I then wrote a book, and I'm still going strong.

Were the last 5 years of my life all jolly and fun? Hell no. I came across a lot of distractions, heartbreaks, ups and downs, jobs losses, disloyal friends, deceitful family members, people that gave up on me, times I wanted to give up on myself, but a wise man once said, "Once you're destined to be successful and are on that road to success, whether it's the success of a marriage, your school, you as an individual, etc., you will come across stop signs, speed bumps, traffic lights, 20mph signs, detour signs, exit signs, and sometimes you might even get a flat tire on a lonely highway at three in the morning, but what should you do, give up? No, just put on your spare and continue to move on, because 'Success is a Journey and not a Destination.'"

THREE RANDOM CONVERSATIONS

JOB

MY NEXT CUSTOMER accepted my offer for a quick shine as she was passing by the stand.

"Ok, I'll take a shine," she said as she walked towards the stand. As she was about to sit, she said, "This is my first time having a shoeshine, but they need it; they're so nasty. We both smiled.

I then began applying the leather balm to her boots, and as I began brushing it off, I asked her where her destination was.

"Back to Canada. I'm going back home. How long have you worked here?"

"Almost two years now," I replied as I continued to brush her boots.

"So how is it?" she asked next.

"It's the best job in the terminal."

She then looked at me and said, "Seriously, why?"

"Because I get to meet a lot of interesting people, and I learn something new every day. And I don't have any manager on my back all day, telling me what to do. I'm my own manager; I manage myself."

"Yeah, and you don't have to stand in one place either, right?" she added.

"Yep. What do you do?" I then asked her.

"I'm a professor, and I teach dance at a University. It's a really great job, but I used to work in electronic stores and in retail in

311

New York City, and I hated that. I hate retail," she stressed, then added, "I was working in retail for a number of years, and wasn't going anywhere in life. Don't get me wrong, working in retail is not bad at all, but it just wasn't for me. It was just a job, it wasn't something that I was passionate about. I had already gone to school to become a professional dancer, which never happened, so I did the next best thing: I began to teach dance."

"How long have you been teaching?" I asked her.

"Actually, I've been teaching for almost ten years now, but not in the same place. I've moved around a lot. It's hard to find a job you like," said explained.

"But you're a good professor, though?"

"I hope so," she replied, smiling.

"Because there are some mean professors," I said to her as I continued to work on her boots.

With an unusual look on her face, she nodded her head and then said, "Are you in college?"

"I just actually graduated last September."

"Where did you go?"

"I went to LaGuardia Community College, right here in Queens," I said.

"Oh you did? I have a friend that used to teach dance at LaGuardia. Did you take any dance courses?" she asked, smiling.

I then began to laugh and said, "No, I was a Business Management Major, so there wasn't any need to take dance." We shared a laugh.

"So what do you want to do? I'm sure you don't want to shine shoes for the rest of your life," she said as she began to rearrange herself in the chair, to be more comfortable.

"I'm into photography and designing, so that's what I'm already doing other than shining shoes. I have two websites up and running," I said to her.

"That's awesome, so what kind of photography is it? Is it like fashion photography?" she asked.

"Fashion photography, parties, weddings, anything that has to do with photography I'm doing it. I don't really focus on any specific areas. Wherever the business is at, I'm at." I explained to her.

"No way, really? What's your website?" she asked with that same unusual look on her face as earlier.

"I'll give you one of my cards," I said and began to apply another layer of polish to her boots.

"Cool, that's awesome. So how was LaGuardia?" was her next question for me.

"It was nice. I really had fun times there. LaGuardia is like this terminal; it's a very diverse school, so I really never got bored. There are people from all over the world that attends LaGuardia," I assured her.

"Yeah, that's amazing. My college is really just like white, and nothing else, but that's because of where's it at, so yeah that can get pretty boring, seeing the same kind of people all day, every day, with one kind of culture." She paused for about fifteen seconds while I continued to work on her boots, then went on to ask me if I was born and raised in New York.

"No, I'm actually from Guyana, but I've been living in the U.S. for five years now."

"One of my friends is from Guyana, but he's Indian," she stated.

"Yeah, there's a large population of Indians in Guyana, so a lot of people don't know that there are actually black people in Guyana," I said to her, as we both began to laugh aloud. I then continued by saying, "A lot of people think that it's only Indians who live there, but honestly, we have people from all around the world."

"So how long have you been doing your websites?" she asked next.

"I started the photography site in November of 2011, and the clothing line two years before that.

"So what is the name of the clothing line?" she asked.

"It's called Porkknockers Clothing," I said to her.

"Pork Knocky?"

"No Porkknockers. There's a story behind the meaning. It's the name for prospectors of gold and diamonds, people that used to dig for those natural resources back in the day in Guyana." I explained. I stopped cleaning her boots, took out a card from my wallet and gave it to her. "This is the card. On the black side is the

313

photography information for Showitoff.us, and on the white side is the clothing line info for Porkknockers Clothing.

"Porkknockers, huh. That sounds cool. I'm going to check it out," she assured me, then went on, "So how did you get into this kind of stuff?"

"It was always something that I wanted to do, something that was always inside of me, but where I'm from, that was a 'no-no'. So after I came to America, I just saved my money and started them one by one.

"Good for you," she said, smiling.

"Yeah. There's a video on the front page of me explaining the concept of the clothing line," I said.

"I see," she said as I gave her the thumbs up, signaling that I was done with her boots. She then stepped down and advised me to continue to follow my dreams and to keep my positive attitude, because it says a lot about me, then paid and walked off.

"Thanks for the business, ma'am."

OTHER POSSIBILITIES

"HOW ABOUT A shine, sir? I asked my next customer, who was walking past the stand.

"Ok," he said and came over to the stand and got seated. As he got seated, I immediately took out my supplies and began cleaning his penny loafers.

"How are you today?" I immediately asked, as I applied the leather balm to his shoes.

"I'm alright," he quickly responded as I went on to compliment him on his shoes.

"Thanks" he replied, looking down at me.

"I hear a little bit of an accent, where are you from, Linden, Berbice, Georgetown?" he asked, and I was kind of shock since I've never had a customer that know that much about Guyana.

I then thought to myself that he must be Guyanese also, so I asked him, "Are you from Guyana?"

"No, I'm from Aruba, but I've been around."

"Oh, you've been around huh?" I said.

He laughed and said, "All around the world."

I continued to work on his shoes, and as I was about to add another layer of polish, he looked at me and asked, "When was the last time that you visited Guyana?"

"I just actually came back to America, at the beginning of January, I was home for a three weeks' vacation," I replied.

"Nice. Did you bring back some gold with you?" He asked.

"Yes, of course. That's a must."

315

"That's a must?" he repeated.

"The value for Guyana gold doesn't ever depreciate; it only goes up. So yeah, that's a must."

"So get all you can get man," he advised me, as I nodded. He then went on to say, "This seems like a good gig."

"Yeah it is. I mean I don't make all the money in the world, but–"

"There's nothing like the tips?" he interrupted.

"Yeah, the tips are good, but it's also something that I love to do. I get to meet a lot of interesting people all day, and the amount of knowledge I get here on a daily basis is priceless. Trust me, we meet everybody right here. Everybody comes to get their shoes shined here." I explained to him. "Are you traveling alone?" I asked next.

"Yeah, today I am. Today is a special day for me," he said and began to smile. "My daughter is in the hospital and she's about to have a baby."

"Oh, wow. Congrats man. Is this your first grandchild?" I asked.

"Yeah, that's why I'm going to Aruba."

"So how many kids do you have?"

"Just one. She's twenty-six years old," he stated then asked, "What about you?"

"No. I'm still a baby. Look at me," I joked, as we both began to laugh aloud. He then went on to asked how old I was and I said, "I'm twenty-six years old."

"At twenty-six years old, I was already married," he said smiling, then added, "You're not no baby."

"So what kind of advice can you give to me about marriage?" I asked him.

"Live your life while you can, because it goes by quickly." He then repeated, "Yeah, just live your life while you can."

"Ok. I just came out of a four-year relationship, and it's crazy how everything does come to an end," I said to him, as I began to stain his shoes' soles.

"I could tell you stories, man," he replied with a smirk on his face.

"I'm listening," I said. "Tell me whatever you think could be of some help to me, because I need it."

He looked down at me smiled and said, "First thing you should know is that you weren't born with somebody. You grow with them, and sometimes that comes with a fork in the road, where you have to make a decision."

"Sometimes it comes with a fork in the road, you said?" I repeated since I wanted him to be more specific.

"Yeah, there's always a fork in the road, you know, because you don't have the same values or want the same things in life. After a while, it's like you're going in two different directions. If you realize that's happening, you make a decision. You make your own conscious decision and sometimes you've got to shed. You've got to shed to open up the other possibilities. It's like if you have a cup and the cup is full, there's no room for anything else, right?" he asked.

"Nope."

"So sometimes you just got to walk around with an empty cup, allow yourself to be open. You get me?"

"Yup," I replied, as I continued to work on his shoes.

You've got to be open to the substance that you really desire. Anything else, don't open up yourself up to. Life is short, bro."

"Yep, very short," I agreed.

"When I was twenty-five . . . that feels like only yesterday. I'm telling you. "You've just got to make the best of it. Just remember, you could be having your worst day, but somebody else in the world is having their best day. You understand what I'm saying?" he stared at me and asked.

"Yep."

"So always have hope. Always have hope."

SORRY

"Let me move all of my junk. Is it in your way?" My next customer asked me as she pointed to her backpack that she had placed in front of the stand, and got seated after requesting to have a shine.

"No, it's not in my way, you can leave it right there. So which of the shines would you like to have?" I then asked her as I began wrapping the balm rag around my hand.

"The basic is fine," she said, as she smiled and nodded her head, so I quickly began to clean her boot.

"How's the work?" she then asked.

"It's good, it's very good, I love my job," I said, looking up at her.

"Where are you heading to? I asked her next.

"Syracuse," was her quick response.

"You live there?" I asked next.

"No, I'm from California. Are you from here?" she asked.

"No, not originally, I'm Guyanese. I'm from Guyana," I said to her, as I continued to work on her shoes.

"Guyana, no kidding," she said, as the tone in her voice changed.

I looked up at her and said, "Yeah, Guyana."

I notice her facial expression changed also, as she asked, "It's like the Caribbean, South America right?"

"It is, yeah," I responded, as I stop from working on her shoes, stood up, and looked her in the face, wondering where this conversation was going to end up.

"I come from California, where we know where Guyana is," she said to me.

I thought to myself that's nice, so I said, "Well, that's good."

"No its not," she responded, as she shook her head from left to right.

"Why not?" I asked, still looking at her in the face, still curious to hear what she was going to say.

"We sent evil people to your country thirty years ago," she said, as I stood there and said, "Oh." Since I didn't want to say anything that was going to offend her although, it was she who brought up the topic.

"Made a big mess," she went on to say, shaking her head from left to right.

"Yeah. Jonestown, huh?" I replied as I continued to work on her shoes.

"I'm from that neighborhood, northern California," she said.

"Ok, that's somewhere in San Francisco right?" I asked.

"Oakland San Francisco, Marin County, nutcase. Sorry about that, what an ugly mess." She said, as we both began to laugh a little. She then went on to say, "We prefer to be a little crazy and keep it local you know."

"Do people still talk about it in California?" I asked her.

"Yeah, they just had the 25th Anniversary, and it was a big deal, cause a lot of people died, including a Senator."

"Yeah, a Congressman," I added.

"People who are in power now went down for the complaints that they had received, so they were a bit traumatized by the craziness, but Guyana is beautiful," she stated, as I agreed with her by nodding my head. She then went on to add, "I bet it's like the Jungle."

"Somewhat," I replied, as I began to brush the polish into her shoes.

"And you came here to make your fortune?" she asked.

"Definitely, and that's what I'm going to do" I assured her.

"Ok, how are you going to do that?" she asked with an amused look on her face.

"I'm going to work hard."

"I know, it's really hard. I teach college in California" she stated, as I continue working on her shoes.

"But what was the whole purpose of him going to Guyana in the first place, did anybody ever find out why?" I asked her.

She then leaned forward in the chair and said, "There was an idea that he was going to make a different kind of life available for the people who he was with, a spiritual life, but it was a cult right? So people couldn't leave, and strange stuff was going on, so a delegate was sent down, and when the delegate went down, the whole thing exploded. So he killed everybody, to avoid anything from leaking out," she stated.

"Did they know that they were drinking poison? I asked her next.

"No, as far as I know, nobody survived to tell, to say whether, 'Oh we've all decided to kill ourselves together,' or you know, 'If it was a trick, that he decided to kill us because he couldn't fulfill the promises he had made, bringing us to this kind of life.'

"It was a weird time in California, it was a time of moving away from the commercialism of America and finding intellectual and spiritual freedom. They were looking for a way to be in a world that wasn't the same, because all these people came from all over the country to go to California to be hippies, to play music, to be happy, 'cause everybody has been working so hard from 1930 straight to 1950, and then it became obligatory. It was the only path; you either did that, or you were a loser, that kind of thing. People started to feel strange, so off they went to San Francisco to listen to music and have a lot of sex. They started these communities out there and some of them succeeded and some of them failed, and a lot of people just ended up making millions of dollars off tennis shoes, clothes or something else. They ended up going into business and got everything cheaper, and then there were a bunch of people who kind of fell out the system and they didn't know where to go and they became vulnerable to these groups that were, dangerous, unsustainable, and when somebody becomes unsustainable and people are xander, you know what xander is?" she asked.

"No."

"Xander is someone who thinks he's someone pretty special, and it's like psychological designation, like depression. The opposite of depression is actually xander.

"Ok," I replied.

"When, you're depressed, you're like, down, really shut down. Manic is like lahlahhhhh, dahdahdahhhhhhhhh," she said while placing her hands up in the air and shaking them pretty fast. "You're hyper, like big time, but crazy big-time. You're not sustainable. So then they crash, they become useless, and they can't restore," she explained, as she looked down to her shoes and said, "These look fantastic."

"Thank you."

"The Faith in me shall set me free Reflections" —Jah Cure